St Antony's Series
General Editor: **Jan Zielonka** (2004–), Fellow of St Antony's College, Oxford

Recent titles include:

Li-Chen Sim
THE RISE AND FALL OF PRIVATIZATION IN THE RUSSIAN OIL INDUSTRY

Stefania Bernini
FAMILY LIFE AND INDIVIDUAL WELFARE IN POSTWAR EUROPE
Britain and Italy Compared

Tomila V. Lankina, Anneke Hudalla and Helmut Wollman
LOCAL GOVERNANCE IN CENTRAL AND EASTERN EUROPE
Comparing Performance in the Czech Republic, Hungary, Poland and Russia

Cathy Gormley-Heenan
POLITICAL LEADERSHIP AND THE NORTHERN IRELAND PEACE PROCESS
Role, Capacity and Effect

Lori Plotkin Boghardt
KUWAIT AMID WAR, PEACE AND REVOLUTION

Paul Chaisty
LEGISLATIVE POLITICS AND ECONOMIC POWER IN RUSSIA

Valpy FitzGerald, Frances Stewart and Rajesh Venugopal (editors)
GLOBALIZATION, VIOLENT CONFLICT AND SELF-DETERMINATION

Miwao Matsumoto
TECHNOLOGY GATEKEEPERS FOR WAR AND PEACE
The British Ship Revolution and Japanese Industrialization

Håkan Thörn
ANTI-APARTHEID AND THE EMERGENCE OF A GLOBAL CIVIL SOCIETY

Lotte Hughes
MOVING THE MAASAI
A Colonial Misadventure

Fiona Macaulay
GENDER POLITICS IN BRAZIL AND CHILE
The Role of Parties in National and Local Policymaking

Stephen Whitefield (editor)
POLITICAL CULTURE AND POST-COMMUNISM

José Esteban Castro
WATER, POWER AND CITIZENSHIP
Social Struggle in the Basin of Mexico

Valpy FitzGerald and Rosemary Thorp (editors)
ECONOMIC DOCTRINES IN LATIN AMERICA
Origins, Embedding and Evolution

Victoria D. Alexander and Marilyn Rueschemeyer
ART AND THE STATE
The Visual Arts in Comparative Perspective

Ailish Johnson
EUROPEAN WELFARE STATES AND SUPRANATIONAL GOVERNANCE OF SOCIAL POLICY

Archie Brown (editor)
THE DEMISE OF MARXISM-LENINISM IN RUSSIA

Thomas Boghardt
SPIES OF THE KAISER
German Covert Operations in Great Britain during the First World War Era

Ulf Schmidt
JUSTICE AT NUREMBERG
Leo Alexander and the Nazi Doctors' Trial

Steve Tsang (editor)
PEACE AND SECURITY ACROSS THE TAIWAN STRAIT

C. W. Braddick
JAPAN AND THE SINO-SOVIET ALLIANCE, 1950–1964
In the Shadow of the Monolith

Isao Miyaoka
LEGITIMACY IN INTERNATIONAL SOCIETY
Japan's Reaction to Global Wildlife Preservation

Neil J. Melvin
SOVIET POWER AND THE COUNTRYSIDE
Policy Innovation and Institutional Decay

Julie M. Newton
RUSSIA, FRANCE AND THE IDEA OF EUROPE

Juhana Aunesluoma
BRITAIN, SWEDEN AND THE COLD WAR, 1945–54
Understanding Neutrality

Helen Belopolsky
RUSSIA AND THE CHALLENGERS
Russian Alignment with China, Iran and Iraq in the Unipolar Era

Christian Thorun
EXPLAINING CHANGE IN RUSSIAN FOREIGN POLICY
The Role of Ideas in post-Soviet Russia's Conduct Towards the West

St Antony's Series
Series Standing Order ISBN 978- 0–333–71109–5 (hardcover) 978-0-333-80341-7 (paperback)
(*outside North America only*)

You can receive future titles in this series as they are published by placing a standing order. Please contact your bookseller or, in case of difficulty, write to us at the address below with your name and address, the title of the series and the ISBNs quoted above.

Customer Services Department, Macmillan Distribution Ltd, Houndmills, Basingstoke, Hampshire RG21 6XS, England

Explaining Change in Russian Foreign Policy

The Role of Ideas in Post-Soviet Russia's Conduct towards the West

Christian Thorun

In Association with St Antony's College

© Christian Thorun 2009

All rights reserved. No reproduction, copy or transmission of this publication may be made without written permission.

No portion of this publication may be reproduced, copied or transmitted save with written permission or in accordance with the provisions of the Copyright, Designs and Patents Act 1988, or under the terms of any licence permitting limited copying issued by the Copyright Licensing Agency, Saffron House, 6-10 Kirby Street, London EC1N 8TS.

The author has asserted his rights to be identified as the author of this work in accordance with the Copyright, Designs and Patents Act 1988.

First published 2009 by
PALGRAVE MACMILLAN

Palgrave Macmillan in the UK is an imprint of Macmillan Publishers Limited, registered in England, company number 785998, of Houndmills, Basingstoke, Hampshire RG21 6XS.

Palgrave Macmillan in the US is a division of St Martin's Press LLC, 175 Fifth Avenue, New York, N.Y. 10010

Palgrave Macmillan is the global academic imprint of the above companies and has companies and representatives throughout the world

Palgrave® and Macmillan® are registered trademarks in the United States, the United Kingdom and Europe and other countries.

ISBN-13: 978-0-230-55372-9   hardback
ISBN-10: 0-230-55372-9   hardback

This book is printed on paper suitable for recycling and made from fully managed and sustained forest sources. Logging, pulping and manufacturing processes are expected to conform to the environmental regulations of the country of origin.

A catalogue record for this book is available from the British Library.

Library of Congress Cataloging-in-Publication Data

  Thorun, Christian, 1976–
    Explaining change in Russian foreign policy : the role of ideas in
    post-Soviet Russia's conduct towards the West / Christian Thorun.
      p. cm. — (St Antony's series)
    Includes bibliographical references and index.
    ISBN 978-0-230-55372-9
    1. Russia (Federation)—Foreign relations. 2. Post-communism—
    Russia (Federation)   I. Title.

JZ1616.T46 2009
327.470182'1—dc22   2008030653

10 9 8 7 6 5 4 3 2 1
18 17 16 15 14 13 12 11 10 09

Printed and bound in Great Britain by
CPI Antony Rowe, Chippenham and Eastbourne

For Franziska Lena

Contents

List of Tables and Figures ix

Acknowledgements x

List of Abbreviations xi

1. Introduction 1
   State of the debate 2
   Approach and hypotheses 6
   Explanatory and theoretical implications 12
   Definitions and limitations of coverage 13
   Chapter outline 14

Part I Theoretical Framework and Analysis of Discourse

2. Framework for Analysis 17
   Realism and foreign policy analysis: Strengths and weaknesses 17
   Social Constructivism: Endogenous interests and ideas on strategy 22
   Methodology, methodological challenges, and ways to address them 24

3. Evolution of the Russian Leadership's Foreign Policy Thinking 28
   Discourse on the nature of international relations 29
   Discourse on Russia's identity, international status and role, and its primary interests 32
   Discourse on strategy 39
   Conclusion 46

Part II Case Study Analyses

4. Russia's Approaches towards NATO 53
   External constraints and Russia's approach: Russia's decisions to join the PfP programme and sign the NATO–Russia Founding Act 56

The indeterminancy of the Realist power-maximization hypothesis and the impact of collective ideas	59
Conclusion	78
5. Russia's Responses to the Balkan Crises (1992–1999)	81
The indeterminacy of the Realist power-maximization hypothesis	84
Collective ideas and Russia's responses to the Balkan crises	86
External constraints and Russia's foreign policy	104
Conclusion	109
6. Russia's Response to the 11 September 2001 Terrorist Attacks	111
External constraints and Russia's response	113
The indeterminacy of the Realist power-maximization hypothesis	120
Collective ideas and Russia's swift and far-reaching reaction	129
Conclusion	132

Part III Implications

7. Conclusion	137
Summary of findings	137
Implications	141
Notes and References	152
Selected Readings	191
Index	198

List of Tables and Figures

Tables

3.1	Summary of the changing ideas about the nature of international relations and about Russia's identity, international status role, and primary interests	49
3.2	Summary of the changing ideas on strategy	50

Figures

2.1	Realism and foreign policy outputs	20
2.2	Collective ideas and foreign policy outputs	24
3.1	Changes in the Russian leadership's perception of the nature of international relations	32
3.2	Changes in the sources of Russia's great power status and in the definition of primary interests	39
3.3	Changes in the Russian leadership's thinking on strategy	46
7.1	Collective ideas as the dependent variable	151

Acknowledgements

Although I am responsible for the arguments put forward here and for all mistakes, this study would not have been possible without the input, support, and encouragement of a number of people and institutions. The study is based on my DPhil thesis, which I submitted at the University of Oxford in 2006. I am deeply grateful for the inspiration, input, and constructive advice of my DPhil supervisor, Alex Pravda. In numerous and endless sessions we have discussed parts of the DPhil thesis. He never tired of working to sharpen my argument and to challenge my analyses. Without him the DPhil thesis and, consequently, this study also could not have been written.

I am also very grateful for the valuable comments from my two DPhil thesis examiners, Margot Light and Adam Roberts. Their critical comments helped me improve my arguments. Over the course of writing, Yuen Foong Khong and Henry Shue gave me valuable inputs on early drafts. I am deeply grateful to several friends at Oxford University. Stina Torjesen, a constant critic of my work, read and commented on it, and always encouraged me to go the extra mile. For fruitful discussions about politics, international relations, and Russia and its foreign policy, I am greatly indebted to Michael Bhatia, Callee and Hunt Boulware, Emma Campbell, Tobias Dougherty, Christopher Edwards, Nicole Evans, Arunabha Gosh, Nicholas Miller, Brigitte Mooljee, Rahul Rao, and Liat Ross.

I am also greatly indebted to the Friedrich-Ebert-Stiftung and the Rhodes Trust, which enabled me to work on the DPhil thesis and this study without financial pressure. Research grants from the Maurice Latey Fund and the Friedrich-Ebert-Stiftung allowed me to conduct interviews in Moscow and Washington, D.C.

Finally, I thank close friends in Russia and my family. Nina Kolosova and Sergei Vonskj introduced me to Russia, taught me Russian, and made me feel like their son. My parents have always trusted me and supported me in whatever I have planned to do. My sister, Claudia Thorun, was always there when my enthusiasm waned and encouraged me to keep going. The most sustained debt is to my wife, Michaela Klement who endured both the moments when I was frustrated about the work and the times when I was so involved in the process of researching and writing that I was hardly able to focus on issues other than this study.

List of Abbreviations

ABM	Anti-Ballistic Missile
ACTWARN	Activation Warning
APEC	Asia-Pacific Economic Cooperation
ASEAN	Association of South East Asian Nations
CDPSP	Current Digest of the Post-Soviet Press
CEE	Central and Eastern Europe
CFDP	Council on Foreign and Defence Policy (SVOP)
CFE	Conventional Armed Forces in Europe
CIS	Commonwealth of Independent States
CPRF	Communist Party of the Russian Federation
CSCE	Conference on Security and Cooperation in Europe
CST	Collective Security Treaty
EAPC	Euro–Atlantic Partnership Council
ESDP	European Security and Defence Policy
EU	European Union
FRY	Federal Republic of Yugoslavia
GRU	Military Intelligence Service
GUUAM	Treaty embracing Georgia, Ukraine, Uzbekistan, Azerbaijan, and Moldova
IFOR	Implementation Force
IMF	International Monetary Fund
IMU	Islamic Movement of Uzbekistan
KFOR	Kosovo Force
KLA	Kosovo Liberation Army
LDPR	Liberal Democratic Party of Russia
NAC	North Atlantic Council
NACC	North Atlantic Cooperation Council
NATO	North Atlantic Treaty Organization
NMD	National Missile Defence
NPT	Non-Proliferation Treaty
NRC	NATO–Russia Council
OSCE	Organization on Security and Cooperation in Europe
PJC	Permanent Joint Council
RSFSR	Russian Soviet Federative Socialist Republic
SCO	Shanghai Cooperation Organization
SFOR	Stabilization Force

START	Strategic Arms Reduction Talks
SVR	Sluzhba Vneshney Razvedki (Foreign Intelligence Service)
UN	United Nations
UNMOVIC	United Nations Monitoring, Verification, and Inspection Commission
UNPROFOR	United Nations Protection Force
USSR	Union of Soviet Socialist Republics
WTO	World Trade Organization

1
Introduction

During the first decade and a half after the dissolution of the Soviet Union, Russia's foreign policy towards the West[1] underwent significant changes, creating four distinct periods. At first, from 1992 to 1993/94, Russia aligned itself strongly with the West in general and the United States in particular. Moscow indicated that it wanted to join NATO in the long term, did not object to NATO membership of Central and Eastern European countries, and cooperated closely with the West to find a solution to the conflict in Bosnia.

From 1993/94 to 2000, Russia's foreign policy became increasingly assertive and ambiguous. On the one hand, Moscow continued to cooperate with the West and agreed to join NATO's Partnership for Peace programme, signed the NATO–Russia Founding Act, and supported the final conflict resolutions during the conflicts in both Bosnia and Kosovo. On the other hand, Moscow at times carefully balanced against the West. For example, during the Balkan conflicts, Russia asserted its veto power in the United Nations (UN) Security Council, lent diplomatic support to forces that the West depicted as responsible for the escalation of the crises, and sometimes used aggressive rhetoric. This mix of overall cooperation and cautious balancing created the impression of an incoherent and irrational foreign policy.

While still far from cooperative, Russian foreign policy from 2000 to 2004 displayed a higher level of cooperation with the West, an increased degree of coherence, and a substantial effort to present Russia as a reliable and respectable partner on the international stage. This approach was best reflected in Moscow's reaction to the 11 September 2001 terrorist attacks against the United States. In contrast to the Kremlin's negative stance on military interventions in the mid and late 1990s, Moscow contributed to the war against the Taliban and al-Qaeda in Afghanistan substantively,

1

and acquiesced to the deployment of Western forces to Central Asia benevolently. Moscow's approach to the Iraq War in 2002/03 also reflected this set of objectives. Russia's criticism of the military invasion was muted; Moscow was careful not to be perceived as the spearhead of opposition to intervention, and in the spring and summer of 2003, it even tried to act as an integrator between France, Germany, and the United States.

Finally, the period from 2004 to 2007 was characterized by a growing number of disagreements between Russia and the West, a more assertive Russian foreign policy, and diverging views on matters of European and international security. Examples for this deterioration in East–West relations were Russia's critical stance on a further enlargement of NATO to also encompass the Ukraine and Georgia and its criticism about the planned deployment of a missile defence system in Europe.

These changes in Russian foreign policy towards the West are the focus of this study. In it I seek to shed light on two key questions. First, how can we best explain these changes? And second, what do these changes tell us about the Russian leadership's ability in the task of adapting the country's foreign policy to drastic shifts in the international distribution of power, which were a result of the end of the Cold War; a new discourse about Russia's identity, international status, and role; and a different Russian foreign policymaking context? Was the post-Soviet Russian leadership able to adapt the country's foreign policy more or less coherently and smoothly to post-Cold War conditions?

In answering these questions, I assess the impact of external constraints, ideational factors, and domestic politics on Russian foreign policy outputs and examine how the impact of these factors has varied over time and across policy areas. In a broader sense, this study aims to identify the limitations of existing approaches and, by combining different independent variables, to increase their explanatory scope and power. In particular, I strive to contribute to the body of literature that shows how material and ideational factors interact.

In the following Introduction, I will contextualize the focus of this study, outline its arguments and implications, and discuss limitations.

State of the debate

Broadly speaking, analyses of Russian foreign policy towards the West can be grouped into three more or less distinct clusters. Proponents of the first approach argue that Russian foreign policy can be divided into two phases. While they characterize the first phase of Russian foreign policy from the end of 1991 to 1993/94 as idealistic and strongly influenced by Gorbachev's? New Thinking, they argue that after 1993/94 Russian foreign policymakers increasingly put idealism aside, adapted Russia's ambitions to the country's relative power position more or less consistently, and settled on realpolitik.[3] For many of these scholars, the replacement of the first Russian Foreign Minister Andrei Kozyrev with Yevgenii Primakov in January 1996 represented a clear departure from the 'naïve' Liberal Institutionalism and 'sell-out' of Russian interests that characterized the early period of Russian foreign policy.[4] Some Western scholars in this group have compared Primakov with French President Charles de Gaulle,[5] and some Russian scholars have compared him with Russian tsarist Foreign Minister Aleksandr Gorchakov.[6] Both leaders, it is argued, skilfully rehabilitated their countries' status as great powers after devastating wars.

In the language of International Relations[7] theory, one might qualify this first approach to Russian foreign policy post 1993/94 as a Realist one. But what does it mean to say that Russia's foreign policy was based on realpolitik? What constituted the aim of this policy? And how was this aim thought to be achieved? Realists argue that for the first decade after the end of the Cold War, Russia's national interest lay in cooperation with the Western states, since they were the sources of investment capital, trade, technology, and entrepreneurial expertise.[8] The single most important reason for this dependence on the West was Russia's weak relative power position. In 1999 Kubicek argued that 'Russia is largely a paper tiger. It may be able to talk like a great power, but its capabilities are limited'.[9]

With regard to the strategies to maximize Russia's national interest, Realists formulate ambiguous expectations. On the one hand, they argue that due to Russia's weak relative power position during the 1990s, it was rational for Russia to bandwagon with the West. On the other hand, these analysts caution that overly close cooperation between Russia and the West was counterproductive. If the West took Russia's cooperation for granted, they argue, it would not provide Moscow with sufficient compensation.[10] Thus, Realists conclude that while bandwagoning with the West was the best overall strategy during the first decade after the end of the Cold War, balancing against the West was 'a tactic to improve the terms under which Russia [was] integrated into the West'.[11]

The increasing assertiveness of Moscow's approach post 2003/04 also does not come as a surprise for Realists. They see it as a logical consequence of Russia's improving relative power position. High commodity prices and the West's dependence on Russian oil and gas increased Moscow's independence and leverage.

In short, Realist scholars depict Russia after 1993/94 as an essentially rational actor that behaved strategically to maximize its relative power position. They therefore explain changes in Russian foreign policy after the initial period of idealism primarily in terms of changes in material incentives, to which the Russian leadership reacted more or less rationally. This view has an important implication for Russian foreign policy analysis. Kubicek concludes that 'concerns about relative power and international constraints and opportunities do better to explain actual changes in Russian policy'[12] than any other factor.

Although the Realist approach is a very common one in the study of Russian foreign policy, it has three serious weaknesses. First, since both balancing and bandwagoning behaviours fit the Realist hypothesis during the first decade of post-Soviet Russian foreign policy and since Realist scholars do not specify to what degree balancing was tactically prudent, the Realist hypothesis is difficult to falsify and therefore has limited analytical utility. Second, one might ask whether the Realist model offers an adequate account of Russian foreign policy. If Russia is seen as a more or less rational power-maximizer, how do Realists explain phenomena such as foreign policy reactivism and foreign policy incoherence? How do Realists, for example, explain Moscow's decision to defend Serb positions during the Kosovo conflict in the period from spring 1998 to spring 1999, despite the fact that such an approach made military intervention led by NATO more likely – an outcome that starkly contradicted Russia's interests? Third, it is unconvincing to argue that Russian foreign policy from 1992 to 1993/94 was largely shaped by ideational factors (Gorbachev's New Thinking), and then assume that such factors ceased to play a significant role after 1993/94.

In short, while Realism is a powerful approach towards explaining why Russia's leadership eschewed an aggressive or revisionist foreign policy when the Cold War came to an end, it has an analytical weakness that would need to be addressed in order to test it. Furthermore, some important characteristics of Russia's foreign policy are difficult to be reconciled with a view of Russia in terms of a rational power-maximizing actor.

These unexplained characteristics are the focus of a second group of scholars, who can be labelled Social Constructivists. Legvold, for example, argues that the reactivism and incoherence of Russian foreign policy that characterized Russian foreign policy during the first decade after the dissolution of the Soviet Union resulted from the fact that Russia's leadership 'lacks any sort of strategic vision'.[13] And he explains this lack in terms of a 'failure to construct coherent national and state identities that are widely accepted by the population'.[14] Similarly, Lo argues that '[f]ar from any consensus emerging, the [Russian] political class was deeply divided over underlying concepts and values, policy priorities, and the means with which to realize them. [. . .] The product of this fluid interaction was a foreign policy rich in expediency, but with little unifying logic, consistency or even continuity'.[15] In other words, these scholars see the lack of a commonly shared definition of Russia's interests as the major source of incoherence and of the lack of a more or less strategic power-maximizing behaviour.

One problem of this approach is that it tends to exaggerate the extent of incoherence in Russian foreign policy during its first decade. As I will show in three case studies, while it is correct to point out to the incoherence in Russian foreign policy behaviour, there were some identifiable patterns in Russian foreign policy. Another weakness of many Social Constructivist analyses of Russian foreign policy is that they fail to specify the degree to which ideational factors mattered and do not clearly identify the link between ideas and foreign policy outputs.[16] Thus, while Social Constructivist analyses are valuable in shedding light on some important facets of Russian foreign policy, they seem prone to overstatement and lack rigour.[17]

Finally, other scholars have attempted to include domestic-level variables in the analysis.[18] The shift towards a more assertive foreign policy in 1993/94, for example, is often explained in terms of the rise of a nationalist/communist opposition in the Russian parliament. Some scholars have contended that had the West shown more concern about the domestic repercussions of its policies towards Russia during the 1990s, it could have helped strengthen Russian westernizers vis-à-vis nationalists and communists, enabling Russian foreign policy to maintain the pro-Western stance of the early 1990s.[19]

In addition, some scholars have argued that the economic winners of the transformation process are key to explaining the overall cooperative approach of Russian foreign policy during the 1990s. McFaul argues, '[m]ost important, the political and economic winners in Russia's transition are the very groups that would not benefit from war. As winners, they have actively pursued foreign policies that avoid international conflict, because they are the political and economic actors in Russia that stand to gain the most from peaceful foreign policies'.[20] Dobriansky sees a link between economic performance and Russia's foreign policy. She argues that 'more than any other traditional international-related factor, it is the dismal failure of Russia's economic and political reforms, as perceived by the Russian people, that has been responsible for the palpable worsening of US-Russian relations' in the late 1990s.[21]

The problem with most of these domestic-level approaches is that only few offer a model that specifies under what conditions and to what extent domestic-level factors mattered in foreign policy decision-making throughout the period.[22] As a result, domestic-level factors are often included to explain only residual variance. Moreover, most of these studies have focused primarily on the early 1990s.

This overview of the major approaches to Russian foreign policy is incomplete and to some extent stylized. Summarizing the state of the debate is challenging in part because many analyses of Russian foreign policy are only informed by theory to a limited degree. As a result, their findings are difficult to categorize. Yet this overview serves to contextualize the approach I propose. My main conclusion is that most of the existing approaches are incomplete, because they fail to adequately combine different explanatory variables and determine the impact of different factors. Consequently, I seek to combine different foreign policy approaches in a systematic manner by specifying the degree to which and the conditions under which their variables influenced Russian foreign policy.

Approach and hypotheses

Point of departure: The Realism of Russian foreign policy

Since the Realist approach is based on a limited number of assumptions, the study takes this approach as its point of departure. I have argued above that a major contention of Realist scholars in the field of Russian foreign policy analysis is that during the first decade after the end of the Cold War Russia's foreign policy options were significantly constrained due to the country's weak power position vis-à-vis the Western states. I agree with this observation and suggest that in cases where Russia's leadership faced a stark choice between cooperation and confrontation with the West, it chose cooperation.[23] These were cases in which external constraints were formidable; that is, the Western states were unified and determined to pursue their interest regardless of Russia's concerns. This conclusion does not mean that ideational factors and domestic factors were irrelevant in such cases, but it implies that the presence of external constraints was the single most important factor determining Russian foreign policy outputs.

Examples of Russian acquiescence in such situations are the Russian leadership's final agreement to join the Partnership for Peace programme in 1994/95, its eventual signing of the 1997 NATO–Russia Founding Act, and its participation in the 1995 Dayton peace process and in the spring 1999 Kosovo conflict resolution. Power asymmetry and Russia's dependence on the West made cooperation the only viable foreign policy strategy in these cases.[24] In the following, this first hypothesis will be called the *external dimension of Realism*, since it focuses on the constraints imposed by external factors.

This first hypothesis raises the question of what kind of Russian foreign policy behaviour we should expect in cases where the West either lacked a clearly defined policy or a united position on an international issue, that is, in cases where external constraints were not formidable. For example, this was the case with regard to the question of NATO enlargement until late 1996. While the Clinton administration was determined to enlarge NATO despite Russian concerns post 1993/94, the French wanted to grant Russia more concessions. The next chapter, 'Framework for Analysis' (Chapter 2), suggests that in addition to their emphasis on external constraints, Realists conceive of states as rational power-maximizing actors, constantly trying to improve their relative power positions in order to increase their security. I call this hypothesis the *behavioural dimension of Realism*. In other words, Realists expect Russia to maximize its relative power position in cases where external constraints were not formidable.

As already stated, analyses of Russian foreign policy which are informed by Realism suggest that both balancing and bandwagoning would fit the Realist expectation of power maximization during the 1990s. This suggestion implies, however, that the *behavioural dimension of Realism* is not falsifiable. In the context of Russia's reaction to NATO enlargement in the mid 1990s it is unclear what the power-maximizing hypothesis would imply for Russia's behaviour. Would Realists expect Moscow to balance against NATO enlargement by establishing counter-alliances, or would they expect Russia not to worry too much and to cooperate with the West so as to consolidate domestically? Chapter 2 shows that this indeterminacy is not only a problem of Realist explanations of Russian foreign policy, but that it is inherent to the Realist approach as such. The problem is that, in most cases, there is more than one foreign policy objective that is compatible with the hypothesis that states maximize power.

In addition to its indeterminacy with regard to objectives, the Realist power-maximizing hypothesis is also often indeterminate with regard to strategies. Since states operate under conditions of uncertainty, assumptions about the behaviour of other states and about how to best achieve objectives play a vital role in policy choices. Here, Realism fails again to provide concrete hypotheses. Thus, the question is how we can substantiate assumptions about state interests and strategies.

Collective ideas: How foreign policy thinking mattered in Russian foreign policy

Social Constructivists argue that state interests and ideas on strategies cannot be assumed, but must instead be endogenized. That is, analysts must derive state interests and strategic ideas from collective ideas, which are expressed in the foreign policy thinking. I argue that these collective ideas consist of three major components: ideas about the nature of international relations, ideas about the state (encompassing ideas about the state's identity, the country's international status and role, and its primary interests), and ideas relating to strategy. The first two types of ideas affect the leadership's perception of foreign policy challenges and inform its definition of the national interests. The third kind of idea informs the leadership's assumptions about the effectiveness of potential foreign policy strategies. These assumptions lead to the second major hypothesis of this study. In cases where external constraints were not formidable, collective ideas had a crucial impact on Russian foreign policy outputs. They informed the Russian leadership's perception of foreign policy challenges, shaped its definition of the country's national interests, and affected its assessments about the most efficient means to maximize those interests. In other words, changes in Russian foreign policy were to a large extent the result of changes in the Russian leadership's foreign policy thinking.

This emphasis on collective ideas in explaining foreign policy outputs necessitates an analysis of the content of collective ideas. Chapter 3, 'Evolution of the Russian Leadership's Foreign Policy Thinking', shows that collective ideas were far from static in the case of post-Soviet Russian foreign policy. Four different sets of collective ideas dominated the Russian leadership's foreign policy discourse from 1992 to 2007. From 1992 to 1993/94, the Russian leadership's foreign policy thinking was informed by *liberal ideas*. These *liberal ideas* were deeply affected by Gorbachev's New Thinking. With regard to the nature of international relations, it was assumed that the end of the Cold War had created a benign international environment, that Russia and the West would share not only interests but also values, and that positive-sum cooperation was therefore likely and natural. As for Russia's identity, the leadership perceived Russia as a *normal* or *transformed* great power that was no longer driven by a special mission. Its primary interest was to establish close or even allied relations with the West. In addition, the foreign policy leadership assumed that the Western states were interested in helping Russia succeed in its transition to democracy and a market economy and in preventing the rise of communist and nationalist forces. Consequently, it thought that the best means to maximize Russia's interests was cooperation with the West almost without qualification, in order to obtain Western support comparable to the scale of a second Marshall Plan. The Russian leadership perceived such a cooperative foreign policy as both a prudential and, given shared values, a natural choice. I will show in the case studies that this kind of foreign policy thinking largely explains why Russia indicated its willingness to join NATO in the early 1990s and why it supported the West almost without qualification in the conflict resolution during the early phase of the Bosnian crisis.

Geopolitical Realism shaped the Russian leadership's foreign policy thinking from 1993/94 to 2000. The thinking by this period was *geopolitical Realist* in the sense that Moscow conceived of the international system as competitive, states were thought to strive for spheres of influence, and Russian foreign policy was tasked with establishing Russia as an *equal* partner vis-à-vis the Western states and as a Eurasian great power. It was assumed that the best strategy to achieve these objectives was to conduct more assertive policies. Furthermore, until 1996, the thinking on strategy remained *liberal* in the sense that it was assumed that the Western states had a great interest in preventing revisionist forces from coming to power in Russia. This implied that Moscow could use the threat of the rise of revisionist forces as a lever in its dealings with the West. In the period from 1996 to 2000, the thinking on strategy became increasingly *dogmatic geopolitical* believing that Russia should balance against unipolarity in the international system, with the aim of strengthening multipolar tendencies. The means to this end included defending the role of the UN as the central arbiter in international conflicts, and globally diversifying relations. While this thinking acknowledged Russia's weak relative power position to some extent, it was based on the belief that by pursuing an active and ambitious foreign policy, and by diversifying relations and cooperating with non-Western states, Russia could enhance its international status. This increased status could then in turn be converted into political capital.

This thinking is important in explaining why during the mid 1990s the Russian leadership increasingly perceived NATO enlargement as a zero-sum game directed against Russia. Rather than acknowledging potential security gains of closer cooperation with NATO, the Russian leadership concluded that it had to oppose NATO enlargement. It also explains why Russia's leadership post 1993/94 began supporting Serb interests during the Bosnian and Kosovo conflicts despite the fact that such a stance did not provide any obvious material power or security gains. Taking into account that the thinking on strategy was based on the assumption that Russia could increase its leverage on the West by threatening that if the West did not take Russian concerns into account then this might lead to a domestic backlash, we can explain why the Russian leadership used this type of threat until 1996. Then, after 1996, the Russian leadership changed its tactic and threatened to build counteralliances and tried to diversify relations.

The Russian leadership's foreign policy thinking from 2000 to 2004 was dominated by *pragmatic geoeconomic Realism*. This mode of foreign policy thinking shared with the previous period the assumption that international relations were characterized by competition. Unlike in the previous period, however, the Russian leadership had come to see international relations not only as a geopolitical contest for spheres of influence, but also, and equally important, as a struggle for markets. Consequently, economic threats gained greater prominence in the Russian thinking about national security, and Russian foreign policy was tasked with supporting the country's economic recovery. In this sense, foreign policy thinking became increasingly geoeconomic. Furthermore, the foreign policy thinking at that time was more optimistic about the potential gains of cooperation; it became more pragmatic and it was assumed that Russia's great power status had to some extent be earned by a responsible foreign policy. This shift implied that rather than defending dogmatic positions, Russian foreign policy had to accept international realities that it could not reasonably change and to establish itself as a team player.

This set of collective ideas plays an important role in explaining why Russia's leadership toned down its anti-NATO rhetoric and changed its approach towards NATO in 2000/01, why it was willing to support the United States in its 'War on Terrorism' so promptly and substantively, and why it acquiesced in the deployment of US troops to Central Asia in 2001 benevolently.

Finally, from 2004 to 2007 the Russian leadership's foreign policy thinking became more self-conscious and ambitious, reflecting *cultural geostrategic Realism*. Consistent with the previous period, the foreign policy thinking still depicted the international system to be competitive. Now, however, this competition was not limited to geopolitics and economics, but also encompassed value systems. Furthermore, the Russian leadership had a much more optimistic assessment of the country's abilities to shape developments, and it conceived Russia's identity as being unique. While maintaining its pragmatism, the Russian leadership replaced the heavy emphasis of the previous period on establishing close relations with the United States with the desire to behave more independently and diversify relations, and the thinking was less concerned about the ramifications of its foreign policy on its relations with the West.

This set of collective ideas needs to be taken into account to explain why Moscow's approach to questions of European and international security stiffened post 2004. In this period, Moscow vociferously opposed a third wave of NATO enlargement that might encompass Georgia and the Ukraine and expressed its opposition about the planned deployment of a missile defence system in Europe.

Ideational factors exerted a significant impact on Russia's foreign policy because of the overall high degree of uncertainty that characterized the first decade and a half after the dissolution of the Soviet Union. How would the new international distribution of power affect the dynamics of international affairs? What role should Russia play? How best could Russia achieve its objectives? These uncertainties had a strong influence on both Western strategies towards Russia and Russia's approaches towards the West. In other words, during the first one-and-a-half decades after the dissolution of the Soviet Union, the Russian leadership was engaged in a cognitive process of adaptation to comprehend the new situation by testing different foreign policy objectives and strategies. To understand this process one needs to combine an analysis of external constraints with that of ideational factors.

Yet the impact of collective ideas varied. While the explanatory utility of collective ideas is high in the early 1990s, it decreases throughout the 1990s and is markedly low from 2000 to 2003/4. Post 2004, however, the impact of collective ideas rises again.

One major factor that explains changes in the extent to which collective ideas exercised an impact on Russian foreign policy is variations in structural and strategic uncertainties. During the early and mid 1990s, it was unclear what the dynamics of post-Cold War international relations would look like (which meant a high level of structural uncertainty), and it was also unclear how Moscow could most effectively pursue its interests (which implied a high level of strategic uncertainty). But with the enlargement of NATO and with the Western military interventions in the Balkans towards the end of the 1990s, structural uncertainty was reduced. The West showed that it was willing to pursue its interests despite Russian opposition. Strategic uncertainty also declined. Both close cooperation with the West and a dogmatic and ambitious foreign policy proved to be inappropriate strategies for fostering Russian interests. Thus, towards the end of the 1990s, the major parameters of the dynamic of post-Cold War international relations became clearer, and the scope of reasonable foreign policy options was narrowed down. As a result, collective ideas played a smaller role in determining Russian foreign policy outputs from 2000 to 2003/04. Yet international developments post 2003/04, such as the US inability to win the peace in Iraq, frictions in trans-Atlantic community, and high growth rates in countries such as Brazil, Russia, China, and India have increased structural and strategic uncertainties again. Also Russia's rapid economic growth and rising international demand for commodities has increased Russia's arsenal of foreign policy tools, increasing strategic uncertainty.

Explanatory and theoretical implications

The study offers explanatory and theoretical implications. From the explanatory perspective, the study supports Realist analyses of Russian foreign policy in so far as it shows that after the dissolution of the Soviet Union Russia's leadership immediately and consistently acknowledged that the country was too weak to challenge Western states and that some kind of cooperation (be it cooperative or competitive) was best for the country. In other words, focusing on Russia's weak relative material power position and on external constraints helps in parsimoniously explaining why Moscow did not choose an aggressive or revisionist foreign policy after the Cold War came to an end.

On the other hand, the analysis suggests that the process of adapting to the new post-Cold War conditions was not as smooth as some Realists would expect. Due to the relatively high level of uncertainty that characterized the first decade and a half after the end of the Cold War, it was not evident how Russia's interests should be defined in concrete terms and how Russia's leadership could most rationally achieve them. We must therefore avoid seeing material factors as realities that foreign policy decision-makers could somehow objectively comprehend. The analysis shows that the Russian leadership should rather be seen as a social actor that tested different strategies, which in turn helped it to comprehend the new situation.

From the theoretical perspective, the study has two major implications. First, it enriches the field of Russian studies by using International Relations approaches. This contribution is important since Russian foreign policy analysis is still very much characterized by an area study approach.[25] Since the end of the Cold War, some analysts have tried to bridge the gap between Russian foreign policy analysis and the wider field of international relations theory, but only few strongly theory-driven analyses have been presented.[26] This study seeks to push forward this agenda.

Second, the study seeks to contribute to International Relations theory in general. By combining Realism and a 'thin' version of Social Constructivism, it shows that both approaches can be combined, and that by doing so, foreign policy analysis can be improved. In particular, the study suggests four major findings. First, the impact of collective ideas positively correlates with the level of uncertainty in the international system. Second, the more powerful a state is, the higher the potential impact of collective ideas. Third, since primarily domestic norms and ideas determined Russian foreign policy outputs, the study encourages Social Constructivists to refocus attention on domestic norms rather than international ones. And finally, and most surprisingly from a Realist perspective, the study suggests that collective ideas can play an important role even in the realm of national security. While Realists normally claim this territory, in the Russian case, the impact of collective ideas was especially high in this realm, because questions such as the enlargement of NATO had a great impact on the Russian leadership's understanding of Russia's identity and role in the world.

Definitions and limitations of coverage

The study aims to offer a model that explains Russian foreign policy outputs. In particular, it focuses on two facets of foreign policy outputs: foreign policy *action* expressed in treaties, agreements, voting behaviour in international bodies, and other forms of diplomatic activity, and foreign policy *rhetoric* expressed in statements, which aimed to explain Russian foreign policy action or to position Russia in negotiation processes. The reason why the study puts emphasis also on this latter aspect is that most of Russia's foreign policy towards the West actually consisted of rhetoric.

With regard to actors, the study focuses primarily on the Russian foreign policy leadership rather than on the foreign policy elite as a whole. The foreign policy leadership includes actors such as the Russian president, foreign and defence ministers and their spokespersons, members of the Security Council, and some members of the presidential administration.

The study faces two significant limitations. First, while assessing the impact of foreign policy thinking on foreign policy outputs, it does not systematically analyse the factors that shaped the Russian leadership's foreign policy thinking. Second, the analysis is limited to Russia's relations with the West. To also address the sources of collective ideas and the impact of collective ideas on Russia's relations with non-Western states would go beyond the scope of this study.

Chapter outline

The study is divided into three major parts. Part I, 'Theoretical Framework and Analysis of Discourse', begins with a chapter that develops the foreign policy model of this study (Chapter 2). Its purpose is to introduce the analytical tools of the study, discuss the criteria for case selection, present the cases selected, and highlight some analytical challenges and means to address them. Chapter 3 analyses the evolution of the Russian leadership's foreign policy thinking from 1992 to 2007. Here, the content of the sets of collective ideas that informed the Russian leadership's foreign policy thinking is established.

In Part II, 'Case Study Analyses', I conduct three case studies. The aim of these case studies is to test the hypotheses and to determine the extent and conditions under which external constraints, collective ideas and domestic factors mattered. Chapter 4 deals with the Russian leadership's approach to NATO and its enlargement. Chapter 5 analyses the Russian leadership's responses to the Balkan crises. In particular, it focuses on Moscow's approaches to the Bosnian and Kosovo conflicts from 1992 to 1999. Finally, Chapter 6 studies the Russian leadership's reaction to the 11 September 2001 terrorist attacks.

Part III, 'Implications', consists of the conclusion (Chapter 7), which summarizes the findings and discusses explanatory and theoretical implications of the study.

While the argument of the study can only be fully appreciated if the whole study is read, chapters 2 to 6 are freestanding.

Part I   Theoretical Framework and Analysis of Discourse

2
Framework for Analysis

In the Introduction, I suggest that while the Realist approach provides some powerful insights for explaining Russian foreign policy, it has several weaknesses that reduce its explanatory power. I also argue that these weaknesses are not the result of flaws in the application of Realist analysis to Russian foreign policy, but rather that they are to a large extent inherent in the Realist approach as such. Consequently, as a first step, in this theoretical chapter I aim to elaborate a model to overcome these weaknesses.

In establishing the model, I seek a balance between the objectives of explanatory utility[1] and parsimony.[2] While a framework should ideally represent major dynamics as accurately as possible, the criterion of parsimony highlights the fact that an explanation that accounts for the same outcome with fewer variables is to be preferred to a more complex alternative. The reason for this preferential treatment is that parsimony and the ability to generalize findings are related to each another. Since Realism is the most parsimonious approach in International Relations, I will use the Realist approach as the starting point and add new variables where weaknesses of this approach are identified.

Realism and foreign policy analysis: Strengths and weaknesses

Realism is based on the following assumptions.[3] First, states are the main actors on the international stage. This means international organizations, multinational companies, or non-governmental organizations are not regarded as significant actors that shape the foreign policies of states.[4] Second, states are unitary actors, implying that domestic-level factors, such as regime type or individuals, do not exert a significant independent impact. Third, states are considered to be rational actors, meaning that they 'select from among available alternatives (strategies) the option that best serves their self-interest'.[5] Fourth, the international order is characterized by anarchy, creating a permanent security vacuum.

Two major hypotheses follow from these assumptions. First, the scope and ambition of a state's foreign policy is primarily determined by its relative power position. Put bluntly, the strong do what they want, and the weak suffer what they must. This hypothesis does not claim that ideational or domestic factors are irrelevant. It just suggests that the relative power position of a state primarily determines the extent to which its foreign policy is constrained by external factors and thus the scope of available foreign policy options. This implies that for analytical reasons, ideational and domestic variables can be neglected. Due to the emphasis on constraints imposed by external factors, I call this first hypothesis the *external dimension of Realism*.

While this first hypothesis is intuitive, it has one major weakness: it is in some cases indeterminate. What kind of behaviour should we expect from a relatively weak state in cases where external constraints are not formidable, that is, in cases where other states have no clearly defined policy or when the major international actors do not have a unified position on how to respond to the ambitions of this relatively weak state? Here external constraints and the distribution of power alone do not provide definitive expectations. In Gourevitch's words: 'However compelling external pressures may be, they are unlikely to be fully determining, save for the case of outright occupation. Some leeway of response to pressure is always possible, at least conceptually.'[6] And in a later article he concludes: 'if nations have choices, we need theories and research that explains how countries make these choices.'[7]

Thus, one might argue that the first Realist hypothesis needs to be qualified. Rather than arguing that the scope and ambition of a state's foreign policy is primarily determined by external constraints, it should read: In cases where a relatively weak state faces formidable external constraints, these external constraints primarily determine the state's foreign policy outputs. This modified Realist hypothesis is the first major hypothesis of this study. It should be observable in the following way: In cases where relatively weak states have to face a stark choice between cooperation and confrontation with the dominant powers, they choose cooperation.

But what kind of behaviour would Realists expect in cases where external constraints are not formidable? This question leads to the second group of Realist hypotheses, which I call *behavioural*. Two Realist answers have been suggested. *Specific Realism*[8] à la Waltz would argue that if states have some choice, they balance against power.[9] Yet this hypothesis is too contested to serve as a valid one both in cases prior to and during the Cold War.[10] Empirical evidence in the post-Cold War period further invalidates the balance against power hypothesis. If the balance against power hypothesis were true, why did Russia, or the Western European states, for example, not balance against the preponderance of US power in the first decade after the Cold War came to an end?[11]

Alternatively, another group of Realist scholars – Rosecrance has called them *generalist Realists* – does not suggest specific hypotheses about alignment behaviour, but proposes that states act rationally to increase their relative power positions.[12] Because Realists assume that striving for power is the only way of guaranteeing survival in an anarchic environment, they argue that if states behaved otherwise, they would lose ground and suffer defeats.

There are two problems with this argument. First, there is the question of how we define power maximization. Does an increase in the number of nuclear missiles, an improvement of economic competitiveness, or technological advancement count as power-maximization? Moreover, even if this were clear, the question remains of how best to achieve the power-maximization objective. Since decision-makers operate under conditions of uncertainty, they cannot know for sure which of the various strategies best serves a given objective. In practice, there is nearly always more than one foreign policy strategy that confirms the hypothesis that states maximize their power. Would Realists, for example, have expected Russia during the 1990s to focus on domestic consolidation in order to transfer economic might into international influence, or would they have expected Moscow to pursue an active and ambitious foreign policy in order to create the image of a powerful and proactive international actor, thus transferring great power status into diplomatic currency?

In the past one-and-a half decades, Realists have conducted a lively debate about how to define the power-maximizing hypothesis more precisely. An example is the ongoing debate between defensive and offensive Realists.[13] The conclusion of this debate seems to be that states choose very different strategies.[14] Consequently, this second collection of Realist hypotheses seems to point in an important direction, but its indeterminacy both with regard to the content of national interest and with regard to the means to achieve interests makes it difficult to falsify, and it therefore does not offer much analytical leverage.[15] Only conduct that undermines a state's power capabilities would falsify the hypothesis.

20 Explaining Change in Russian Foreign Policy

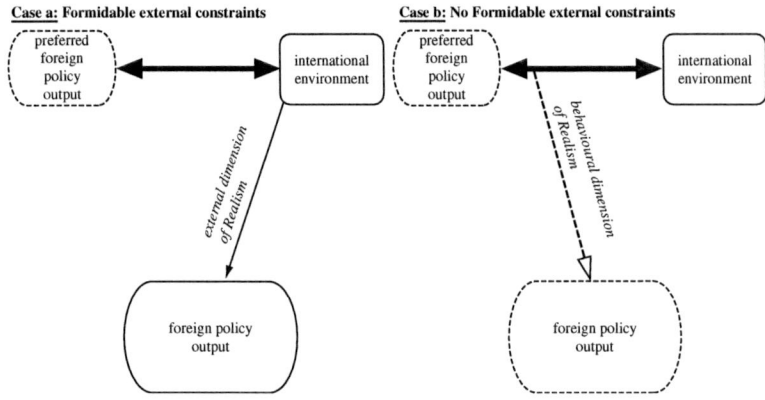

Figure 2.1 Realism and foreign policy outputs

Figure 2.1 illustrates my arguments. Consistent with Realist assumptions, it suggests that a foreign policy output is the result of the interaction between a state and its international environment (symbolized by the arrow connecting both factors). Since the *behavioural dimension of Realism* does not provide determinate expectations for the state's preferred foreign policy output, the box is drawn in broken lines. In case (a), a relatively weak state faces formidable external constraints. The arrow radiating from international environment indicates that this factor is the single most important one determining the state's foreign policy output. In case (b), a relatively weak state does not face formidable external constraints. Here the broken line of the arrow indicates that while the foreign policy output is the result of the interaction between the state and its external environment, the fact that the preferred foreign policy outcome is indeterminate leads to inconclusive expectations for the foreign policy output (symbolized by the broken lines of the box.)

This discussion raises the question of how analysts could overcome Realism's indeterminacy in cases where external constraints are not formidable. I suggest that state leaders' definitions of their country's interests and of ways to best achieve them cannot simply be assumed, but must instead be endogenized. State behaviour is too complex and non-determined to be explained by one universal assumption. In his seminal book *Perception and Misperception in International Politics*, Jervis argues that if it were evident that states seek to maximize their power, predicting the foreign policy of another state would be a simple matter. Foreign policymakers would simply have to ask themselves what they would do in place of the decision-makers of the other state. Particular worldviews, domestic constraints, leadership style, and other factors would be irrelevant. Yet he concludes that it 'is interesting [. . .] to note that decision-makers rarely feel confident about using this method. They usually believe both that others may not behave as they would and that the decision-makers within the other state differ among themselves. So they generally seek a great deal of information about the views of each significant person in the other country'.[16] In an article from 1998, he argues, 'even if security is the prime objective, this does not tell us – or statesmen – what behavior will reach it'.[17]

If this assessment of Realism's weaknesses is correct, it seems to be striking that Realism is still one of the most prominent approaches in foreign policy analysis. One explanation for this popularity might be its perceived productiveness. It seems, however, that this productiveness is often not the result of powerful and accurate assumptions, but rather of retrospective reasoning. That means that many Realist analyses of international events rely heavily on post hoc adjustments to fit the empirical data. Lebow argues that '[t]he process of backward reasoning tends to privilege theories that rely on a few key variables to account for the forces allegedly responsible for the outcomes in question. For the sake of theoretical parsimony, the discipline generally favors independent variables that are structural in nature. [. . .] In retrospect, almost any outcome can be squared with any theory unless the theory is rigorously specified. The latter requirement is rarely met in the field of international relations [. . .] Events deemed improbable by experts [. . .] are often considered "overdetermined" and all but inevitable after they have occurred'.[18]

In this discussion of the strengths and weaknesses of the Realist approach, I suggest a number of arguments. First, the Realist hypothesis about the impact of external constraints on a state's foreign policy (especially on relatively weak states) seems to be important. The weaker a state, the lesser freedom of choice it has, up to the point where its foreign policy outputs are fully determined by external constraints. Second, Realism's weakness begins when external constraints are not formidable, allowing states to choose from a variety of foreign policy options. In these cases, the Realist power-maximizing hypothesis does not offer sufficiently specified expectations about which of these options a state will choose and how it will go about achieving them. Third, to overcome this problem of indeterminacy, we must further specify state interests and ideas on strategy. Rather than assuming uniform and universal state interests and ideas on strategy, scholars must ask how the foreign policy leadership defines the country's *national interests* and how it thinks to best *achieve the national interests*, given the condition of uncertainty. The next section will therefore elaborate how Social Constructivist insights can be used to substantiate these variables.

Social Constructivism: Endogenous interests and ideas on strategy

One main Social Constructivist[19] insight is that state interests and ideas on strategy cannot be treated as unproblematic givens, but must instead be endogenized.[20] Social Constructivists argue that the 'environment in which agents/states take action is social as well as material' and that this setting provides 'agents/states with understandings of their interests'.[21] In other words, Social Constructivists conceive international life to be *social* in the sense that states relate to one another through ideas, and *constructivist* in the sense that these ideas help define who and what states are.[22] For this reason, Social Constructivists reject Realist notions of exogenously given and uniform state interests and stress the importance of ideational factors.

In order to support their argument, Social Constructivists need to suggest ways in which ideational factors impact foreign policy outputs.[23] I argue that *collective ideas* inform two crucial variables: state interests and ideas about the effectiveness of various means to achieve these interests, that is, ideas on strategy. I define collective ideas as shared expectations of behaviour held by relevant foreign policy actors. The *shared* quality of these ideas is crucial for this approach, since it assumes that the foreign policy interest of relevant foreign policy actors is not so much determined by their respective positions in the policymaking process, but by a shared way of thinking about state interests and methods to achieve them. That does not mean that all relevant actors at all times have similarly defined interests. But it suggests that on some issues, a common understanding overrides the particular interests of the relevant foreign policy actors.

In order to assess the extent to which collective ideas impacted foreign policy outputs, it is necessary to distinguish between three types of ideas: ideas about the nature of international relations; ideas about the state, which encompass ideas about the country's identity, its international status and role, and its primary interests; and ideas relating to strategy. The former two sets of ideas prescribe how the foreign policy leadership perceives a foreign policy challenge and how it defines the state's national interests.[24] One could also say that these ideas represent a state's *purpose*. Ideas relating to strategy, on the other hand, help decision-makers cope with the condition of uncertainty. They provide propositions about the likely success of various foreign policy strategies. Goldstein and Keohane argue: 'If actors do not know with certainty the consequences of their actions, it is the *expected* effects of actions that explain them. And under conditions of uncertainty, expectations depend on causal beliefs as well as on institutional arrangements for authoritative decision-making. Causal ideas help determine which of many means will be used to reach desired goals and therefore help to provide actors with strategies with which to further their objectives.'[25]

This argument does not mean that states have absolute freedom of choice or that collective ideas 'matter all the way down'. It merely states that because external constraints are often not formidable, collective ideas are important variables in explaining foreign policy outputs. Thus, in the Social Constructivist account, these ideas are as 'real' as the military forces of states or the balance of power between them.[26] It is *purpose* plus *ideas on strategy* plus the *relative power position* that primarily determine a state's foreign policy. In other words, Social Constructivists stress that states can choose how and where to direct their resources. Revolutionary powers will use them to enhance their military preparedness and against other states, whereas a status quo power might use them to increase social welfare. The direction a state chooses is determined not only by external constraints or the distribution of power, but also by the state's purpose and its ideas on strategy.[27]

From these considerations follows the second major hypothesis of this study. In cases where external constraints are not formidable (when the dominant states in the international system either do not have a policy or do not agree to a united approach), collective ideas have a significant impact on foreign policy outputs. Collective ideas about the nature of international relations and ideas about the state inform the leadership's perception of foreign policy challenges and its definition of the country's national interests, and ideas on strategy inform the foreign policy leadership's assessments about the most efficient means to maximize the state's interests.

Figure 2.2 illustrates the above discussion. Like Realists, I argue that a foreign policy output is the result of an interaction between a state and its international environment. In contrast to Realists, however, I contend that the preferred foreign policy output cannot be assumed, but instead must be viewed as the result of state interests and ideas on strategy that are impacted by collective ideas.

This view of the impact of ideational factors clashes with the Realist understanding of the role of ideas. Realists typically view ideas as 'cheap

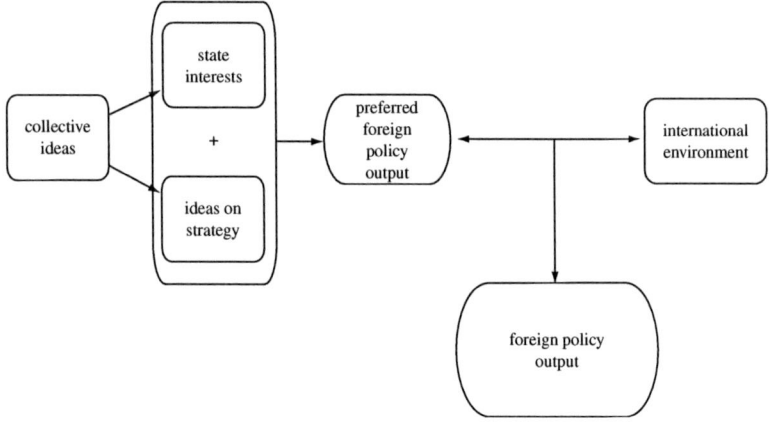

Figure 2.2 Collective ideas and foreign policy outputs

talk', which decision-makers seize upon to legitimize their interests. For Realists, these ideational factors do not exercise an independent influence: an action would happen regardless of the justification. I argue, however, that language can also persuade, that it can change how foreign policymakers define the goals they pursue and the methods to achieve them. Finnemore and Sikkink argue that '[w]hen speech has these effects, it is doing important social construction work, creating new understandings and new social facts that reconfigure politics'.[28]

If one takes the above critique of the indeterminacy of Realism seriously, this section suggests that Realism and Social Constructivism, at least in a thin version, could and should be combined in order to improve foreign policy analysis. While the inclusion of Realist insights in Social Constructivist analyses might help scholars better determine the degree to which and the conditions under which ideational factors exert an independent impact, Social Constructivism offers solutions at a point where Realism fails: it specifies how a state defines its interests and how a state chooses among foreign policy alternatives.

Methodology, methodological challenges, and ways to address them

To demonstrate the impact of collective ideas on Russian foreign policy outputs, the study first establishes the content(s) of the independent variable collective ideas from 1992 to 2007. Chapter 3 does so by analysing foreign policy speeches of the Russian leadership. From these sources, I infer dominant understandings about the nature of international relations; about Russia's identity, its international status, role, and primary interests; and about the favoured means for achieving its interests. To unravel these dominant understandings, I rely on predicate analysis, which focuses on the verbs, adverbs, and adjectives, which are used to specify nouns. As Milliken argues: 'Predications of a noun construct the thing(s) named as a particular sort of thing, with particular features and capacities.'[29] In addition to predicate analysis, I interpret statements by focusing on the following questions: Who says what, to whom, under what circumstances, and for what purpose?[30] In conducting this analysis, I make use of a broad range of speeches, statements, and interviews of the Russian leadership.

In a second step, three case studies test the extent to which Russian foreign policy outputs can be explained by Realism and Social Constructivism (Chapters 4–6). The case studies have been selected in accordance with four criteria. First, the cases should fall in the category of *least likely* cases. That means that conventional wisdom should expect little impact from the independent variable on which the study focuses.[31] Since Realists argue that ideational factors do not matter when national security is at stake, the cases should bear on national security questions, namely issues that fall into the category of *high politics* rather than *low politics*.[32] If the analysis can convincingly demonstrate the impact of collective ideas in cases where national security is at stake, the relevance of taking into account collective ideas is highlighted. Second, the cases should cover the whole period under consideration, that is, from 1992 to 2007. Third, the cases need to be researchable, which means that data should be available on foreign policy outputs, the foreign policy thinking, and the justifications of foreign policy choices. And finally, due to constraints in scope, the study only focuses on Russia's relations with the West. This implies that cases that draw upon Russia's approaches to non-Western states, such as countries belonging to the former Soviet Union, are not included.

In light of these criteria, I have selected the following cases. First, the study analyses Russia's responses to NATO and its enlargement (Chapter 4). Since NATO is a defence alliance and security issues are dominant, it is the test case where Realism should work at its best. The second case study analyses Russia's responses to the Balkan crises, in particular the Bosnian and Kosovo conflicts from 1992 to 1999 (Chapter 5). Russia's approaches to these crises are of interest because security interest overlapped with status concerns. The third case study assesses Russia's reaction to the 11 September 2001 terrorist attacks (Chapter 6). This case is of interest because Russia's leadership was forced to choose between defending what Russia considered its sphere of influence in Central Asia and maintaining good relations with the West.

One major challenge that these case studies face is the lack of archival material. If decision-making protocols were accessible, one could potentially directly derive the factors that Russia's leadership focused on in each case. The topicality and sensitivity of the cases, however, make archival research impossible, with the consequence that I rely on two other methods. The first is a congruence test between expected output and actual foreign policy output in each case study. The second is an in-depth analysis of how state officials defined Russia's national interests and justified state action in each case, and, to the extent possible, of the process that led to this decision.

The first method of congruence establishes the minimum requirement for the model of the study: The model should at least more or less accurately predict the foreign policy output in each case. Since expectations for Russian foreign policy outputs have been clearly spelt out, this test should be feasible. In cases where Russia's leadership had to face a stark choice between cooperation and confrontation with the West, the first hypothesis expects Russia to cooperate with the West. In cases where Russia did not have to face a stark choice, the second hypothesis expects collective ideas to play a crucial role. Consequently, congruence between expectation and output would strengthen my hypotheses.

Yet the congruence test alone can never be sufficient, since correlation does not imply causation.[33] Therefore, the second method of in-depth analysis of rhetoric and process is meant to further validate the results of the congruence method.[34] It is based on the obvious observation that foreign policy decisions are taken by the foreign policy leadership of a country. I stress this observation because some Realists create the impression that domestic-level factors would be redundant for foreign policy analysis. Realists argue, for example, foreign policy outputs can be explained purely with factors that are located at the system level. This statement is accurate in so far as Realists typically claim that for *explanatory reasons* the domestic level (and individual level) can be neglected since, in their view, it does not add significant explanatory leverage. Even Realists must acknowledge, however, that systemic constraints are translated into a domestic process that leads to foreign policy outputs. This reiteration of the obvious is important since it allows for a better evaluation of the validity of Realist expectations. If one wants to prove Realist hypotheses, one must show not only that Realist predictions correlate with the foreign policy output, but also that the relevant foreign policy actors were concerned with maximizing state power. This means that foreign policy thinking *always* plays a role in *foreign policy analysis*. Realists might argue that this thinking is redundant in explanatory terms, but it needs to be taken into account analytically in order to test the validity of Realist expectations.

It follows that in cases where external constraints were formidable, state officials are expected to justify their cooperative foreign policy choices in terms of Russia's dependence on Western financial assistance, or the lack of any viable foreign policy alternatives. The analytical challenge here derives from the fact that the instances when the Russian leadership had to give in to external pressure represented foreign policy defeats. Thus, it is likely that the Russian leadership tried to sell them in terms of success rather than failure. If archives were opened, we would expect to find evidence that these key foreign policy officials acknowledged – in private or in closed circles – the lack of Russian resources for challenging the West. Interviews with decision-makers and foreign policy specialists are used to address this problem. In cases where collective ideas played a vital role, one would expect officials to justify and explain foreign policy choices at least partially in terms of the dominant collective idea at a point of time. Only if both the congruence test and the in-depth methods show a correlation between prediction and evidence, do I regard a hypothesis as having been confirmed.

Another methodological challenge is that in the period under consideration, many independent variables underwent considerable change, and, as a result, changes in the dependent variable might be overdetermined. From a methodological point of view, this situation creates the problem of disentangling the respective impact of each independent variable. To address this problem, I will apply counterfactual analysis. Fearon suggests 'arguments about the relative importance of possible causes become arguments about the relative plausibility of different counterfactual scenarios'.[35] The general guideline for counterfactual analysis is that the fewer and more trivial the changes we introduce in our historical experiments, the more plausible the counterfactual becomes.[36]

3
Evolution of the Russian Leadership's Foreign Policy Thinking

This chapter analyses the evolution of the Russian leadership's foreign policy thinking from 1992 to 2007. Its purpose is to ascertain how the Russian leadership perceived the nature of international relations, how it thought about Russia's identity, international status, and role, and how it believed it could best defend the country's national interests. In analysing the Russian leadership's foreign policy thinking, the chapter seeks to trace continuities and changes over time. The analysis will lead to propositions about the content of collective ideas, whose impact will be tested in the following three case studies. I argue that the dominant collective ideas that shaped the Russian leadership's foreign policy thinking changed three times in this period: from *liberal ideas* (1992–93/94) to *geopolitical Realism* (1993/94–2000) to *pragmatic geoeconomic Realism* (2000–4) to *cultural geostrategic Realism* (2004–7).

The analysis focuses very narrowly on the foreign policy discourse of the Russian leadership and on the aspects of this discourse that concern Russia's relations with the West and involve issues of high politics.[1] Consequently, this chapter does not claim to offer a comprehensive account of the foreign policy debate in post-Soviet Russia,[2] nor does it aspire to present a complete account of the Russian leadership's foreign policy thinking.

The chapter is divided into four sections. The first three sections sequentially analyse the Russian leadership's discourse on the nature of international relations; on Russia's identity, international status and role, and its primary interests; and on strategy. The final section summarizes the findings in the form of propositions about the shifting nature of Russian foreign policy thinking.

Discourse on the nature of international relations

After the dissolution of the Soviet Union, there was a good deal of optimism about the prospects of the post-confrontational era. The first Russian foreign minister Andrei Kozyrev described post-Soviet Russia's international environment as 'favourable'. He justified this assessment by referring to the fact that there were 'neither potential adversaries nor military threats to Russian interests',[3] and that the world was going through a 'transition from the former global division and confrontation to a system of relations of global cooperation'.[4] In his view, the post-confrontational era was built on a solid foundation since it was based not on a new balance of power or system of coercion, but rather on common interests and shared values between East and West. He argued that the 'interests of Russian diplomacy and those of the democratic states are substantially the same'.[5] What these democratic states had in common was their belief that interests of the individual had to be given priority over state interests.[6]

It is difficult to establish the extent to which President Boris Yeltsin shared these positive assumptions about the nature of international relations, since he rarely spoke about foreign policy in the first years after the dissolution of the Soviet Union. Yet from the few statements he made, it seems clear that at least in the first year of Russian foreign policy, he shared this view. He argued, for example, that the post-Cold War world was much safer, that Russia no longer had enemies, and that he saw the United States and the West as a whole as not only a potential partner, but a potential ally.[7]

In short, *liberal ideas* dominated the Russian leadership's foreign policy thinking about the nature of international relations from 1992 to 1993/94. These *liberal ideas* were reflected in assumptions about a benign international context, shared interests, and values between East and West, and the prospects of positive-sum cooperation.

Yet the optimism about the prospects of the new post-confrontational era soon faded. While this disillusionment must be seen as a process, the years 1993/94 mark a turning point. Although the Russian leadership continued to argue that the post-Cold War international system was safer than the Cold War one and that the West did not pose an imminent security threat,[8] it no longer thought that shared values would automatically lead to harmonious relations between East and West. Instead, the Russian leadership increasingly questioned whether the two sides would have a common vision for the new era and emphasized the unpredictability of international affairs.[9] Especially the prospect of NATO enlargement[10] and US attempts to 'dictate' the new terms of international relations were considered unacceptable.[11] For Russia, these developments meant exclusion from involvement in both European[12] and international processes.[13]

To capture its revised view of the nature of international relations, the Russian leadership introduced the concept of multipolarity. The concept was used in two ways. First, it was employed to characterize the post-Cold War international capability distribution. The argument was that while the United States was the most powerful actor internationally, Russia and other influential centres also existed in the world, making it multipolar rather than unipolar.[14] Second, the concept of multipolarity was used to characterize the dynamic of inter-state relations: states were perceived to compete for power and spheres of influence. This element of thinking was implicit in the fear that external forces might exploit Russia's weakness in order to prevent the rise of a strong Russia.[15]

Consequently, while the foreign policy thinking in the first period from 1992 to 1993/94 had already envisioned the international distribution of power in multipolar terms (without using this term explicitly), the emphasis on the competitive nature of international politics and the need to strive for spheres of influence within the discourse on multipolarity were new features of the second period. In short, the Russian foreign policy thinking from 1993/94 to 2000 became increasingly geopolitical and Realist.

The period from 2000 to 2004 witnessed continuities and changes in the perception of the nature of international relations. As in the previous decade, the 2000 Foreign Policy Concept suggested that the likelihood of a large-scale war was low,[16] depicted the growing trend towards unipolarity in the international system as the major threat to international stability, and tasked Russia with seeking to strengthen a multipolar system.[17] The international system was again conceived in Realist terms as highly competitive. President Vladimir Putin argued in 2002 that no one was 'particularly waiting for us. [. . .] We ourselves will have to fight for a place in the "sun".'[18]

Yet despite these similarities, there was a significant difference. The Russian leadership downplayed strategic questions and emphasized economic factors.[19] NATO enlargement, for example, no longer played such a dominant role. The top items on the agenda were the threat of economic exclusion and the acknowledgement that Russia was experiencing severe international economic competition. Putin argued in his 2002 State of the Nation Address that 'bitter competition – for markets, investments, and political and economic influence – is a permanent fixture of the present-day world'.[20] While the Russian leadership had already prioritized economic issues during the 1990s,[21] in the period from 2000 to 2004, economization went deeper. Putin believed that only an economically strong Russia would be taken seriously in the international arena and that economic power could significantly expand the tools available to Russian foreign policy. Thus, compared with the previous period, there was a shift from a *geopolitical Realist* worldview to a *geoeconomic Realist* one. This shift did not mean that geopolitical questions were unimportant to Putin, but that economic issues were seen as equally significant.

In other words, from 2000 to 2004 the foreign policy thinking was again heavily affected by Realist assumptions about the competitive nature of international relations. Yet in contrast to the period from 1993/94 to 2000, Russia's leaders put more emphasis on economic issues, which is why the foreign policy thinking at that time can be characterized as *geoeconomic Realism*.

The years 2004 to 2007 witnessed two moderate but significant changes to this outlook. First, the international system was perceived in increasingly hostile and dangerous terms. In his 2006 State of the Nation Address, Putin argued that 'conflict zones are expanding in the world' and, even worse from the Russian viewpoint, these zones were 'spreading into the area of our vital interests'.[22] The Russian leadership depicted three major destabilizing factors: that the end of the bipolar world created a high level of unpredictability in international affairs,[23] that Cold War stereotypes in the West were still present,[24] and that Western states, in particular the United States, undermined international law and forced their views on other nations.[25] For the Russian leadership, these developments were alarming. It felt encircled and feared that some would like to 'once again plunder the nation's resources'.[26] The conclusion was that Russia had to regain its strength, because the 'weak get beaten'.[27]

Second, the number and kinds of perceived threats increased. While the Russian leadership maintained its geoeconomic perspective, in which economic factors were perceived to be as important as geopolitical ones,[28] the international system was now increasingly conceived to also represent an arena for the competition between value systems. Foreign Minister Sergei Lavrov argued in 2007 that the international system was characterized by competition between 'value systems and developing models'.[29] The Russian leadership was particularly concerned about Western attempts to impose democracy on countries of the former Soviet Union,[30] the Western practice of financing NGOs in Russia and in neighbouring states[31] and using information as 'weapons

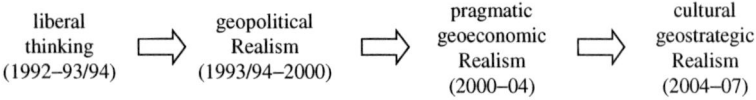

Figure 3.1 Changes in the Russian leadership's perception of the nature of international relations.

in the global competitive battle'.[32] Putin claimed that under the banner of democratization, the West tried to achieve unilateral gains and foster its own advantage.[33] Lavrov emphasized that such practices 'discredit democratic values'[34] and that they were bound to fail. He argued: 'History proves that democracy cannot be imposed from the outside.'[35]

In other words, from 2004 to 2007, the Russian leadership viewed the international system as increasingly dangerous and saw new threats. Especially the West's policies were perceived as encroachments into Russia's sphere of influence. While Moscow maintained its geoeconomic outlook, it more and more considered international politics also as representing a sphere for confrontation between value systems and information. Due to its new emphasis on values, this outlook can be labelled *cultural geostrategic Realism*.

In conclusion, the Russian leadership's thinking about the nature of international relations has passed through four distinct stages from 1992 to 2007. Figure 3.1 summarizes these findings.

Discourse on Russia's identity, international status and role, and its primary interests

After the dissolution of the Soviet Union, while talking about Russia's identity, the Russian leadership emphasized that post-Soviet Russia was a democratic and anti-Communist country. It argued that all former Soviet republics and clients, including the Russian Federation, had been victims of Soviet tyranny and had all liberated themselves from it. Speaking about the former Soviet Union, Kozyrev contended in 1992 that all the republics were 'prisoners of one huge GULAG'.[36] And in his memoirs, Yeltsin wrote that Russia and the Central and Eastern European states are 'bound by the fact that for the first time such former dissidents [then Polish President Lech Walesa, then Czech Republic's President Vaclav Havel, and Yeltsin himself] have bravely stepped into the international arena, dissidents who were hounded and persecuted in various ways'.[37]

This anti-Communist interpretation of post-Soviet Russia's identity had an impact on the perception of Russia's international status and role. While the Russian leadership, very traditionally, stressed that post-Soviet Russia was still a great power,[38] it suggested that this great power was of a very different kind than previous ones, for two reasons. First, it maintained that Russia's greatness was not so much the result of geopolitical or military factors, but of historical, social, and cultural ones. Kozyrev argued, for example, that the 'greatness of a country, especially on the threshold of the 21st century, is determined not by the size of its empire, but above all by the level of its people's well-being'.[39]

Second, with regard to Russia's international ambitions, the leadership argued that post-Soviet Russia was no longer driven by the desire to spread an ideology, even with coercive means, as it was in Soviet times. This aspect was reflected in use of the attributes *normal* or *transformed*[40] to characterize the nature of Russia's greatness. For Kozyrev, *normal* meant that 'democratic Russia wishes to establish her status through cooperation and constructive interaction with the whole international democratic community, not through political and military confrontation'.[41] Yeltsin shared this view. In his 1994 memoir *The View from the Kremlin*, the first chapter is titled 'A Normal Country'. He explains that *normal* means that post-Soviet Russia was to follow a democratic path of development and no longer regarded itself as having a special international mission.[42] Such conceptions of the sources of Russia's greatness and of the country's international ambitions reflected a clear departure from the perception of the Soviet Union as a superpower whose status was primarily based on military might and which had a global mission.

This benign characterization of the nature of international relations and the conception of Russia as a great, but *normal* power had significant consequences for the definition of Russia's primary interests. First, both Kozyrev and Yeltsin sought to overcome inherited Cold War stereotypes,[43] to further Russia's integration into Western institutions, and to seek partnership or even alliances with the West.[44] Kozyrev argued, for example, that by pursuing cooperative policies with the West, Russia was returning to the 'normal development cycle, which we dropped out for 70 years'.[45] Second, Russia had to democratize, since only then could it fully harness the benefits of being a member of the 'community of civilized nations'. In other words, especially Kozyrev saw a close relationship between internal behaviour and foreign policy achievements. To prove this relationship, Kozyrev argued that the fast recognition of the Russian Federation as the Soviet Union successor was mainly due to the fact that Russia was 'perceived as a democratic, free and peace-loving state that poses no threat to either its own citizens or other countries'.⁴⁶ And he claimed that while democratic reforms might be difficult, there was no better method to foster Russia's interests.⁴⁷ In short, both the definition of Russia's identity, international status, and role, in terms of a great but *normal* country, and of Russia's primary interests, to further international cooperation and internal democratization, show that *liberal ideas* affected the Russian leadership's thinking about identity, status, role, and primary interests in the period from 1992 to 1993/94.⁴⁸

Starting in late 1993, the optimism about Russia's ability to gain international recognition of its status as a *normal* but great power faded. In Yeltsin's first Annual Address to the Federal Assembly in 1994, he concluded: 'The Russian state has not yet assumed a worthy place in the world community.'⁴⁹ The lack of external great power status recognition triggered a quest to re-define the country's identity, international status, and role. Increasingly Russia's unique heritage as a Eurasian power, that is, as a power that synthesized both Western and Asian values, was emphasized. For example, in his 1996 Address to the Federal Assembly, rather than arguing that Russia was a member of the democratic or Western community of states, Yeltsin said: 'Russia is a unique country with its own interests and its own logic of development. From the historical point of view, Russia is a successor to the Rus, Moscow's Czarism, the Russian Empire and of the USSR. From the geopolitical perspective, Russia is in the unique position of being in Eurasia.'⁵⁰ While this less accommodating tone might have been a tactic to gain support for the presidential elections, this interpretation remained dominant even after Yeltsin's re-election. In an address to Russian diplomats in 1998, he repeated, '[w]e have started to prove in practice that Russia's geopolitical situation as an Eurasian power is indeed unique'.⁵¹

This re-interpretation of Russia's identity had significant implications for the definition of Russia's international status and role. While Russia was still perceived as a great power – Kozyrev even argued that Russia was 'doomed to be a great power'⁵² – the sources of its greatness changed. Now the Russian leadership justified the country's great power credentials primarily in terms of geopolitical factors, such as the country's nuclear arsenal, its geography, and its historical experience. The then foreign minister Yevgenii Primakov argued in 1996: 'Russia will always be a great power. This is not a question of nostalgia, it's simply a soberminded approach. At present this "greatness" is based mainly on our strategic potential, which is comparable only to America's. But that's not our country's only trump card. Take, for example, our territory, our scientific potential, the educational level of our people, and the prominent place Russia has always occupied in cultural terms.'[53] As a result, the qualifications *normal* or *transformed* were no longer used.

While it was acknowledged that Russia was in a relatively weak material power position,[54] the re-interpretation of the sources of Russia's greatness with a greater emphasis on geopolitical factors led to a more optimistic view of Russia's capabilities and the role the country could play internationally. For one, the Russian leadership argued that Russian foreign policy should aim to gain international acknowledgement as an equal partner in its relations with the West. Primakov explained in 1996 that '[i]n advocating partnership relations with our former Cold War adversaries, we proceed from the need for an equitable – and I want to put special emphasis on this – equitable and mutually advantageous partnership that takes each other's interests into account'.[55]

Furthermore, Russia's identity as a Eurasian power implied that Russian diplomacy had to develop the country's relations with non-Western countries much more determinedly. In defining the range of Russian foreign policy activities, Primakov included almost all world regions. He argued that 'if Russia wants to defend its international position as one of the most important actors [. . .] then it has to be active in all directions. This means the USA, Europe, China, Japan, India, Near East, the Asian-Pacific Region, Latin America and Africa'.[56] Primakov was supported by Yeltsin, who argued, 'despite our problems [Russian diplomacy] should be active on all directions. There is no alternative to this'.[57]

In short, the period from 1993/94 to 2000 witnessed a significant change in the understanding of Russia's identity, international status, role, and its primary interests. With this shift, Russia was perceived as a Eurasian great power, and due to the perception that Russia's greatness was mainly determined by geopolitical sources, the assessment of Russia's capabilities was more optimistic. These two factors implied that Russian foreign policy had to diversify globally and that the country had to pursue an active foreign policy to establish itself as a powerful global actor.

When Putin came to power in 2000, the emphasis shifted significantly. With regard to the definition of Russia's identity, rhetoric about Eurasianism was downplayed. The Russian leadership seemed reluctant to make a choice between West, East, or Eurasia, in order to avoid being constrained by an overtly restrictive interpretation. Asked whether Russia belonged to the East or West, Foreign Minister Igor Ivanov answered: 'Artificially opposing the West with the East as incompatible directions within Russia's foreign policy contradicts state interests.'[58]

In addition, there were also changes in the conception of Russia's international status and role. Not only did references to Russia's great power status become more infrequent, but the sources of greatness were redefined. The leadership argued that Russia could only be perceived as a great power if it were economically self-reliant. In 2000, Putin asked the rhetorical question: 'Can we hold out as a nation, as a civilization, if our prosperity continually depends on international loans and on the benevolence of leaders of the world economy?' He concluded that 'Russia needs an economic system which is competitive, effective and socially just, which ensures stable political development'.[59] At the same time, Putin was aware that the Russian economy was still far from competitive. Although Russia's weak relative power position was acknowledged throughout the 1990s,[60] in the period from 2000 to 2004, the leadership placed even more emphasis on the fact that Russia was falling behind economically. In his first Annual Address to the Federal Assembly, the newly elected President Putin argued: 'The economic weakness of Russia continues to be another serious problem. The growing gap between leading nations and Russia pushes us towards becoming a third world country.'[61] Thus, Putin saw the country's international status as closely related to its economic performance, and he had a very critical view of the state of Russia's economy. This acknowledgement represents the above-mentioned emphasis on geoeconomics in the Russian leadership's foreign policy thinking in the period from 2000 to 2004.

The foreign policy thinking also acknowledged that great power status had to some extent to be *earned* by responsible and predictable foreign policy behaviour. In his 2002 Annual Address to the Federal Assembly, Putin argued that 'the finest international standards are becoming major yardsticks of success in all spheres'.[62] Similarly, in an interview with the Russian newspaper *Trud*, Foreign Minister Ivanov argued: 'It is our aim [. . .] that our country is regarded as a beneficial partner and this will increase its impact on international events.'[63]

This redefinition of the sources of greatness did not imply that geography, the nuclear arsenal, and cultural heritage no longer played an important role in the Russian leadership's thinking about the country's great power status. The leadership came to believe, however, that only in addition to greater economic self-reliance and responsible foreign policy action could these factors boost the international standing of Russia.[64] Consequently, in a 2002 address to Russian diplomats, Putin claimed that 'it is perfectly clear now that Russia has emerged from a period of prolonged confrontation in international relations. It is no longer seen as an enemy or adversary, but increasingly as a *predictable, reliable, business-like, and equal partner*. As a matter of fact, this is all we need from the outside world. Russia does not need any preferences in international affairs'.[65]

This change in the interpretation of Russia's international status and role had an impact on the definition of the country's primary interests. Rather than gaining recognition of the country's status by means of an assertive and ambitious foreign policy, from 2001 to 2004, the Russian policy leadership believed that the country's interests could best be furthered within the framework of a close partnership with the West and the United States in particular. Putin argued: 'To reiterate, a new, close partnership between Russia and the United States is not only in the interest of our nations. It also has a positive impact on the entire system of international relations.'[66] Defending this more cooperative approach, Foreign Minister Ivanov argued in 2002: 'The thrust of that plan is that the limited resources our country has at its disposal must be used to promote our domestic reforms to the greatest possible extent. This means that we have to make sure that internal resources – human, political, financial and military – are not diverted to resolve external conflicts.'[67]

In short, in the period from 2000 to 2004, the Russian leadership toned down its rhetoric about Russia being a Eurasian great power and introduced the idea that if Russia wanted to be a great power, then this status had to some extent to be *earned* by responsible foreign policy action. This implied that Russia had to cooperate more closely with the West.

In the years 2004 to 2007, the Russian leadership's outlook changed. With regard to the country's identity, emphasis was put on Russia's distinctiveness. While the Russian leadership continued to downplay the question whether Russia was a Western, Eastern, or Eurasian country,[68] it emphasized that Russia was unique. In 2007 Putin argued, for example, 'blindly copying foreign models, will inevitably lead to us losing our national identity'.[69]

With regard to Russia's international status and role, the Russian leadership continued to argue that Russia was a great power and that the sources of greatness comprised military and economic capabilities. When it comes to the assessment of Russia's capabilities however, there were significant changes. First, in comparison to Putin's first term, during which he stressed Russia's economic backwardness, he was now much more optimistic about Russia's international position and economic power. In his 2004 State of the Nation Address, Putin concluded: 'Now for the first time in a long time, Russia is politically and economically stable. It is also independent, both financially and in international affairs.'[70] Such an assessment resembled the 2003 Military Doctrine's assessment that 'Russia's recent emergence from a state of political and economic crisis and the substantial strengthening of its positions in the world arena [. . .] is a most important trend in the world'.[71]

Second, there was a re-emphasis on military might. While traditional power factors such a nuclear capabilities did not cease to play a role in the foreign policy thinking under Putin's first presidential term, in foreign policy speeches post 2004, reference was made significantly more frequently to the fact that Russia was one of the major nuclear powers[72] and that despite its financial difficulties, it could respond to changes in the military power balance asymmetrically.[73]

On the basis of this change in the definition of the sources of greatness and in the assessment of Russia's capabilities, Russian diplomacy was tasked with becoming more independent and assertive and with looking for opportunities worldwide, even at the expense of less warm relations with the Western countries. Putin argued, 'there is growing demand from our partners abroad for Russia to play a more active role in world politics'.[74] Thus, Russian foreign policy was tasked with becoming more independent in an attempt to be seen by other non-Western states as distinct, so as to offer an alternative to the West.

A more assertive and opportunistic Russian foreign policy did not, however, imply a confrontational foreign policy vis-à-vis the Western states or an assertive policy for its own sake. It also did not rule out cooperation with the West. Yet cooperation had to deliver concrete results for Russia. Most interestingly, while in the previous period, cooperation with the West was seen as a means to increase Russia's international leverage, now the Russian leadership emphasized that the Western countries had to understand that only by cooperating with Russia could *they* achieve their objectives. Putin argued that 'there are [. . .] benefits to be gained through friendship with modern Russia'.[75]

In other words, from 2004 to 2007, the Russian foreign policy thinking about the country's identity, status, role, and primary interests became much more self-confident: Russia was a unique country, its great power status was based on a strong economy and military might, and given its improved power position, the country should pursue a more independent, assertive, and opportunistic foreign policy to defend Russian interests and to establish Russia as an independent great power that offers an alternative to the West.

In conclusion, two observations are noteworthy. First, the Russian leadership consistently perceived Russia as a great power in the period from 1992 to 2007. Yet while the post-Soviet leaderships repeatedly invoked this concept, the sources of greatness and the implications of greatness changed significantly. At first, Russia's greatness was justified

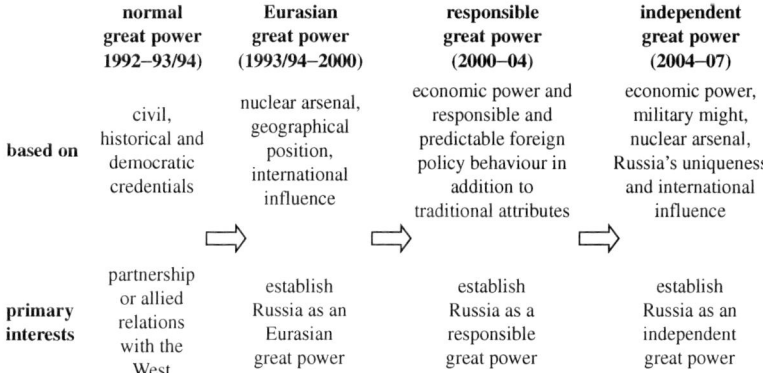

Figure 3.2 Changes in the sources of Russia's great power status and in the definition of primary interests.

with reference to its civil, historical, and democratic credentials (1992–93/94), then Russia's greatness was seen to be the result of primarily geopolitical factors (1993/94–2000), then Russia's greatness was also argued to be the result of economic performance and responsible foreign policy behaviour (2000–4), and finally Russia's greatness was seen to be the result of its economic potential, military capabilities, and uniqueness (2004–7). Second, these changes in the sources of greatness also had an impact on the definition of Russia's primary interests. The primary interests shifted from establishing partnership or even alliances with the West to establishing Russia as a Eurasian great power, to establishing Russia as a responsible great power, to establishing Russia as an independent great power.

Figure 3.2 illustrates this transition by highlighting the factors that were believed to define Russia's great power status, and what those factors implied.

Discourse on strategy

I have argued above that in the first two years of Russian foreign policy, there was an understanding that Russia's primary interests lay in establishing partnership or even allied relationships with the West and in democratization. At that time, Kozyrev believed that the best way to achieve these objectives was to cooperate with the West almost without qualification. For him, this strategy seemed to be both prudential – since post-Soviet Russia needed the West to gain access to international institutions and to ensure political, financial, technical assistance, and expert advice to support domestic reforms[76] – and also natural due to the perception of shared values. Like democratic peace theorists, he argued that 'we proceed from the premise that no developed, democratic civil society based on reasonable and rational principles can threaten us. [. . .] The developed countries of the West are Russia's *natural allies*'.[77] Consequently, replying to nationalists and communists who urged him to pursue a more assertive foreign policy towards the West, he argued: 'Democracy inside and national-communist methods outside are incompatible.'[78]

In addition to this belief, the Russian leadership thought that it could use the threat of the rise to power of revisionist forces in Russia as a lever in its relations with the West. Given the assumption of shared interests and values, the Russian leadership expected the Western states to substantially support Russia's transition towards democracy and a market economy. They referred, for example, to the need for an aid effort equivalent to the Marshall Plan to support this transition.[79] At the same time, the Russian leadership warned that if the Western states failed to help Russia's reformers, their inactivity would play into the hands of revisionist forces in Russia. If these revisionist forces were to gain power, Kozyrev warned, it would have a negative impact on East–West relations.[80]

Yet Kozyrev's optimism about the merits of an almost unqualified cooperative approach was not unanimously shared. Towards the end of 1992, Yeltsin began to criticize Kozyrev. In October 1992, he argued that Russian foreign policy should not focus too narrowly on Western countries and that Russian diplomacy should avoid being perceived as too accommodating. In a speech, he emphasized that '[t]he Russian Federation's foreign policy must be a full-scale foreign policy with multiple vectors. While developing our relations with Western countries – the US, Germany, Great Britain, Italy – we must work with equal diligence along the Eastern salient – with Japan, China, India, Mongolia'. He continued: 'We have gotten a reputation as a state that says "yes" to all proposals, whether they are advantageous to us or not. What's more, we have started tolerating slights and even insults; we let Russia be treated in ways in which no other great power could possibly be treated.'[81] This criticism had an impact on Kozyrev, who began to emphasize the need to develop relations with non-Western countries and especially with CIS member states.[82]

Although there was this shift in the strategic thinking at the end of 1992, one should not exaggerate its influence. Even Yeltsin still agreed that Russian foreign policy had to seek close relations with the West by means of cooperation. There was disagreement about the necessary degree of cooperation, but not about the need to cooperate as such. Also, the envisioned diversification of Russian foreign policy was still limited and was primarily directed towards the countries of the CIS.

After 1993/94, the balance between almost unqualified cooperation and a more assertive foreign policy tilted towards the latter. Adopting the primary objective of establishing Russia as an equal partner and as a Eurasian great power, the policy leadership argued that the way to achieve this objective was to be more assertive. Kozyrev argued in 1994 that partnership relations do 'not mean renouncing a firm – aggressive, if you will – policy of defending one's own national interests, or, at times, competition and disputes'.[83] Similarly, Primakov believed that a proactive and assertive foreign policy was the best strategy to achieve Russia's acknowledgement as an equal.[84] To justify the necessity for proactivism, he made repeated references to tsarist Foreign Minister Gorchakov and his success in re-establishing Russia's status as a great power after two devastating wars.[85] Primakov and his first deputy foreign minister Ivanov argued that, as in Gorchakov's time, the country had two major foreign policy alternatives. On the one hand, it could 'resign its great power status, quit the international scene, and [. . .] accept the rules of the game the victors force on the conquered – to become their vassal'. On the other hand, in the course that Gorchakov advocated, Russia could pursue 'changes inside the country [. . .] coupled with a vigorous foreign policy to guarantee better conditions for international renewal'.[86]

To justify the need for Russian foreign policy to become more assertive, the leadership argued that cooperative policies had proved inefficient. Yeltsin claimed in an address to Russian diplomats in 1998: 'The time of illusions has passed, never to return.'[87] The lesson learned from the first years of Russian foreign policy was that Russia had been far too accommodating in its relations with the West. In 1996, Primakov argued: 'At a certain stage [in our relations with the West] we did everything in our power to smooth those relations. But allow me to quote Mao Zedong here, who said that in order to straighten out, you have to bend. By this analogy, we bent too far.'[88] In other words, the prior policy of close cooperation was seen as misguided, and the leadership instead believed that Russian foreign policy had to defend the country's interests more assertively.[89]

In practice, this assertion meant that Russian diplomacy was tasked with ensuring that the country was involved in international decision-making, preserving the status quo by upholding norms of non-intervention and peaceful conflict resolutions, and defending the role of the United Nations as the main arbiter of international conflicts.[90]

Although there was agreement throughout this period that Russian foreign policy had to become more assertive, there was a difference in the assessment of the viabilityof using the threat of the rise to power of communist and revisionist forces. Form 1993/94 to 1996 the Russian leadership continued to argue that there was a close relationship between Western policies and the danger of the rise of nationalist and conservative forces in Russia that could also pose a threat to the West if they came to power. Kozyrev argued in 1994, 'the policies of Russian reformers and their friends abroad must be pursued taking into account how these policies are perceived inside Russia. [. . .] Russian foreign policy inevitably has to be of an independent and assertive nature. If Russian democrats fail to achieve it, they will be swept away by a wave of aggressive nationalism, which is now exploiting the need for national and state self-assertion'.[91]

Then post 1995 this threat was less frequently used and more emphasis was put on the need to balance against US dominance. Primakov argued: 'Russia must play the role to counterbalance [. . .] the negative trends [US unilateralism] that are manifesting themselves in international affairs.'[92] Yet, while the foreign policy leadership hoped that this more assertive foreign policy would lessen the perceived 'encroachments on Russia's position in the international arena',[93] it also cautioned that such an assertive foreign policy should not lead to outright confrontation with the West.[94] At some stages, Yeltsin seems to have felt the need to tone down the ambitious rhetoric. He reminded Russian diplomats: 'You all know as well as I do that the world centres of attraction and influence are marked not so much by their military might as by their high economic development. Their force of attraction is created by scientific and spiritual power.'[95]

In other words, while there was agreement in this period that Russia had to assert its interests more assertively by emphasizing international decision-making, upholding norms of non-intervention, and peaceful conflict resolution, there was a difference in the assessment of the viability of using the threat of the rise of revisionist forces in Russia. From 1993/94 to 1996 the foreign policy thinking saw this threat as a useful foreign policy means. This implies that a *liberal* train of thinking remained in the foreign policy discourse on strategy. Then post 1995 the thinking on strategy became increasingly *dogmatic geopolitical* with the result that this tactic was replaced by the task to counterbalance US dominance and diversify relations. The leadership believed that this kind of policy would increase Russia's great power status, which could then be transferred into influence.

From 2000 to 2004, the thinking on strategy became more balanced with regard to four dimensions: the extent of diversification of relations, the assessment of the potential merits of cooperation with the West, the importance of economic issues, and the question of style in foreign policy. First, with regard to the previous period's emphasis on diversifying relations, the foreign policy thinking became more cautious. While Putin still agreed that it was desirable to establish relations with almost all countries, he argued that diversification should not be treated as an end in itself, but rather as a means to increase Russia's power position. Consequently, the extent of diversification was a function of the gains, which were expected to be achieved from it. Putin asked: 'Does Russia's foreign policy remain global in its scope? The answer: It certainly does. To promote its interests [. . .] Russia needs to look for partners and allies everywhere – in Europe, Asia, Africa and Latin America. But [. . .] interaction with them should be built on an equal-to-equal basis, with real payoff to Russia.'[96]

Second, Putin emphasized the potential merits of cooperation with the West, especially with regard to challenges that both Russia and the Western countries faced. These included fighting international terrorism, the proliferation of weapons of mass destruction, and regional and territorial conflicts.[97] The Russian leadership was especially concerned about international terrorism and argued that it was the most imminent threat to international stability and that the 'civilized world' should unite in the fight against it.[98] The less pessimistic view of the merits of international cooperation was reflected in statements about new levels of solidarity between East and West. For example, Foreign Minister Ivanov argued in 2002, '[t]oday again, like during the Second World War, Russia and the US became allies, allies in the war with this dangerous threat [that is international terrorism] to the international community'.[99] While such statements should not be taken at face value, they do signify a more optimistic view of cooperation.

By pursuing policies closer to those of the Western states, Putin apparently hoped to minimize the likelihood of making inconvenient choices. This view implied that Russian diplomacy had to demonstrate that it was committed to a policy of consensus rather than of undermining Western positions. Russian foreign policy also had to become more pragmatic. Instead of the defence of dogmatic positions that Russia had no means to sustain, Putin favoured a more flexible approach, which implied, inter alia, to use Russia's veto power in the UN Security Council only in cases where vital Russian interests were concerned.[100]

This increased optimism about the merits of cooperation was, however, very different from the one that had dominated Russian foreign policy thinking from 1992 to 1993/94. Then, the foreign policy leadership saw cooperation as an end in itself, grounded in shared values. Under Putin, cooperation was treated as a means. Lynch nicely sums up this instrumental approach when he argues that 'Russian policy [under Putin's leadership] is pro-Russian and not pro-Western; the strategy of alignment is a means to an end. The most important end is revitalisation. In Putin's view, this objective is best pursued *with* the Euro-Atlantic community rather than outside it'.[101] This difference in the understanding of cooperation also explains why, in the period from 2000 to 2004, the Russian leadership was critical of the early period of Russian foreign policy. Putin argued in 2002, for example, that some people had lived 'under the illusion that the end of military-political confrontation in the world would automatically give Russia access to the world economic system, and that the world would receive us with open arms into its economic fold. Reality proved to be far more complicated'.[102]

Third, reflecting the rise of *geoeconomic* rather than *geopolitical thinking*, Putin also urged Russian diplomacy to focus more strongly on economic factors. He stated: 'The Foreign Ministry and other foreign missions need to put a greater emphasis on economic diplomacy. [. . .] It is essential to build up a system to promote and protect our economic interests abroad.'[103]

Fourth, Putin placed more emphasis on style. As a consequence of the objective of establishing Russia as a responsible great power, Putin declared that Russian diplomacy had to become more consistent and predictable. He argued: 'Having a good reputation is important not only in the economy but also in politics, and this is why we must fulfil all our long-term commitments and agreements and uphold the principles upon which our ties with other countries are based. [. . .] This approach is far more productive than rigid ideological dogma.'[104] In addition, Putin emphasized that Russian diplomats needed to be more active in shaping the image of Russia abroad.[105] Putin described what he saw as 'misperceptions' abroad: 'Our efforts to save Russia from this danger [that is international terrorism] are often interpreted in a subjective and biased manner, and serve as the occasion for various types of speculation. An important area of foreign policy activity should be insuring objective perception of Russia. Reliable information on the events in our country is a question of its reputation and national security.'[106] Therefore, he urged diplomats to take 'a more proactive line in dealing with representatives of foreign mass media'.[107]

In short, while Putin did not support the almost unqualified cooperative approach of the first period of post-Soviet Russian foreign policy, he equally rejected the aim of reasserting Russia's great power status via a *dogmatic geopolitical* foreign policy. Instead, he demanded pragmatism in cases where Russia had no reasonable chance of changing a situation. He was also more optimistic about the merits of cooperation with the West, and he urged Russian diplomats to be more proactive and to seize opportunities to improve Russia's image. All this, he argued, would foster Russia's interests and create an image of Russia as a responsible and reliable actor, thereby helping the country to assert its great power status.

Consistent with a more self-confident outlook and the objective to establish Russia as an independent great power, post 2004 the Russian leadership's thinking on strategy changed. With regard to close cooperation with the West, the Russian leadership was now more sceptical about the merits of such an approach. On the one hand, the Russian leadership continued to see benefits in cooperation with the West, especially regarding challenges that were common to both. These encompassed the fight against international terrorism, the proliferation of weapons of mass destruction, and strategic disarmament.[108] On the other hand, unlike the dominant thinking in the previous period, the Russian leadership was much more pessimistic about the potential gains of cooperation with the West. It repeatedly argued that cooperation required reciprocity and that the Western states had failed to reciprocate Russia's cooperation in the years 2000–3. Putin argued: 'The principle "I'm allowed to do it, but don't you try" is completely unacceptable for Russia.'[109] In the context of Russia–EU negotiations on the energy charter, for example, Putin's repeatedly highlighted that there was an imbalance in the gains of signing it and he asked, 'what do we get in return?'[110]

Furthermore, the Russian leadership warned that promises had to be kept. With regard to the deployment of Western forces in Central Asia, Moscow reminded the Western states that the deployment of troops was exclusively aimed to support the military operation in Afghanistan. The deployed forces should therefore not be misused for any other purpose.[111]

Acknowledging that Russia had gained too little from siding with the West in the previous years, the Russian leadership re-emphasized the importance to diversify its foreign relations.[112] Given the decline of the West's status and influence in many parts of the world, Putin stressed that Russian diplomacy had to 'break free of familiar patterns

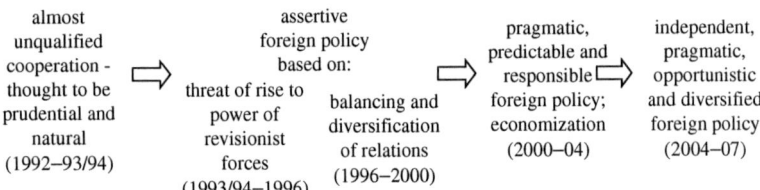

Figure 3.3 Changes in the Russian leadership's thinking on strategy.

and models and constantly re-evaluate the situation and make the necessary adjustments'.[113] While becoming more independent, assertive, and opportunistic, Putin warned, however, that Russian foreign policy should not become reckless, and foreign policy interests should not be pursued to the detriment of domestic economic and social development. This meant that a multipolar foreign policy course had to be pragmatic and deliver concrete results. It was not an end in itself.[114]

In other words, the heavy emphasis on close relations with the West of the previous period was replaced by a much more independent, assertive, and opportunistic foreign policy strategy, which assessed carefully the gains for Russia, left Atlanticism aside, and sought diversification of relations even if this meant cooling of relations with the West. Figure 3.3 summarizes the changes in the thinking on strategy.

Conclusion

The analysis of the Russian leadership's foreign policy thinking reveals significant changes throughout the period under consideration, pointing to four observations. First, the post-Soviet leadership abandoned the Marxist–Leninist ideology that had determined the Soviet Union's foreign policy and did not replace it with a new ideology. Quite to the contrary, the analysis suggests that rather than reflecting a consistent set of assumptions and prescriptions, changes in the Russian foreign policy thinking show that the Russian leadership was engaged in the complex process of coming to terms with the new post-Cold War conditions.[115]

Second, the change in Russian foreign policy thinking from the later Kozyrev period to that of Primakov should not be exaggerated. I have shown that references to Russia's great power status and to multipolarity had already been made in the first half of the 1990s. The analysis suggests that rather than introducing new terms, Primakov put more emphasis on strategic implications.

Third, while after 1993/94 the Russian foreign policy thinking became increasingly Realist, the analysis suggests that three different versions of Realism, which are all compatible with the hypothesis that states seek to maximize their power position, can be distinguished.

Fourth, there was a significant co-variation in the changes in foreign policy thinking about the nature of international relations; about Russia's identity, international status, and role; and about ideas on strategy. The following picture emerges: From 1992 to 1993/94, *liberal ideas* dominated the Russian leadership's foreign policy thinking. These *liberal ideas* were reflected in the assumptions about the benign nature of international relations; in the conception of Russia as a democratic country and as a *normal* great power; and in the assumption that the West had a great interest in the success of the Russian transition towards democracy and market economy. This belief implied that the primary interests of Russian diplomacy lay in fostering Russia's integration into Western institutions and supporting Russia's transition towards democracy and a market economy. It followed that Russia had to cooperate with the West almost without qualification both in words and in deeds. At the same time, the Russian leadership hoped to use the threat of the rise of revisionist forces as a potential lever in its relations with the West. One could say that the foreign policy thinking in this first period was very similar to Gorbachev's New Thinking. Kozyrev even argued that 'in our relations with the West as a whole, we must bring to a logical conclusion the not always consistent steps toward rapprochement that began with perestroika'.[116] This leads to the conclusion that from 1992 to 1993/94, the Russian foreign policy leadership's thinking was shaped by *liberal ideas*.

From 1993/94 to 2000, the Russian leadership's foreign policy thinking about the nature of international relations became increasingly *geopolitical Realist* in the sense that the international system was characterized as an arena for the competition for spheres of influence, and East–West relations were no longer believed to be automatically harmonious. As for the thinking about Russia's identity, international status, and role in this period, the leadership put even more emphasis on Russia's international recognition as a Eurasian great power and as an equal in the international system. The attribute *normal* was no longer used to describe Russia's great power status. The strategic implication was that Russian diplomacy had to try to establish Russia as an *equal* partner vis-à-vis the Western states by becoming more ambitious and assertive and emphasizing norms of non-intervention and peaceful resolution of international conflicts. In the period from 1993/94 to 1996, however, a *liberal* element remained in the foreign policy thinking. The use of the threat of the rise of revisionist forces was seen as an effective strategy to increase Russia's international leverage. Then from 1996 to 2000, this tactic was no longer perceived as viable and was replaced with *dogmatic geopolitical* ideas of defending principled and dogmatic positions of non-intervention, asserting Russia's special role in the region, diversifying relations, and using the threat of building counter-alliances. The impact of these ideas leads to the conclusion that *geopolitical Realism* informed the Russian leadership's foreign policy thinking from 1993/94 to 2000.

From 2000 to 2004, Russian foreign policy thinking became less geopolitical and more *pragmatic geoeconomical*.[117] Now the leadership emphasized that Russia should not defend positions that it did not have the capability to back up. This period also saw more optimism about the potential merits of cooperation, a downplaying of geopolitics, and an emphasis on the importance of economics. The thinking posited that Russia's status as a great power was a result not only of its historical legacy and geographical position, but also of both its economic performance and of a responsible and predictable foreign policy. This shift implied that Russian foreign policy had to become more pragmatic, responsible, and predictable and focus more thoroughly on the advancement of Russia's economic interests. Therefore, the Russian leadership's foreign policy thinking from 2000 to 2004 was shaped by *pragmatic geoeconomical Realism*.

Finally, from 2004 to 2007, the Russian foreign policy thinking became much more self-conscious and ambitious. While the international system was perceived to be hostile and international relations were increasingly characterized by competition also for value systems, due to the perceived improvement of Russia's relative power position, Russia was thought to have had a greater choice of foreign policy options. Disappointed by the lack of reciprocity despite cooperating with the West, the Russian leadership emphasized the need for diversification of relations and to establish Russia internationally as an independent great power that could be seen as an alternative to the West. While this did not mean a confrontational policy vis-à-vis the West or to diversify relations with non-Western states without due regard for the gains of diversification, the Russian leadership was less concerned about the ramifications of its foreign policy on its relations with the West. Due to the new emphasis on Russia's unique identity, the view that the international system was also an arena for competition between value systems and its stress on military factors, I label this thinking *cultural geostrategic Realism*.

While the sets of collective ideas presented here are stylized both with regard to the content and periodization, I suggest that these sets of collective ideas are sufficiently distinct to be useful for testing the impact of collective ideas on Russia's foreign policy outputs towards the West in the period from 1992 to 2007. The following three case studies put this test into practice.

The two following tables 3.1 and 3.2 summarize the findings of this chapter.

Table 3.1 Summary of the changing ideas about the nature of international relations and about Russia's identity, international status, role, and primary interests.

	Nature of international relations	Russia's identity, international status and role, and its primary interests
Liberal ideas (1992–93/94)	Benign – high potential for positive-sum cooperation based on shared interests and values	Russia as a great, but *normal* power, which seeks integration in Western institutions and Western support for transition towards democracy and market economy; Russia no longer has a special mission
Geopolitical Realism (1993/94–2000)	Competitive – states compete for spheres of influence and US tendencies towards unilateralism perceived as major threat	Russia as a Eurasian great power with distinct national interests; assertion of Russia's great power status; international status perceived as a means to compensate for lack of material power
Pragmatic geoeconomic Realism (2000–4)	Competitive – states compete in an interdependent world, in which economic might plays an increasingly important role	Russia as a great power by virtue of its economic might and responsible foreign policy behaviour in addition to history and material factors; mid-term aim to transform economic might into international influence so as to defend Russia's status as a great power
Cultural geostrategic Realism (2004–7)	Competitive – states compete for spheres of influence, economic influence, and value system	Russia as a great power with unique traditions; positive assessments of Russia's economic and military capabilities; objective to establish Russia as an independent great power

Table 3.2 Summary of the changing ideas on strategy

	Ideas on strategy
Liberal ideas (1992–93/94)	Almost unqualified cooperation with the West internationally and democratization domestically – this was perceived as being prudential and natural; use of threat that revisionist forces might come to power based on assumption that West had a strong interest in a democratizing Russia
Geopolitical Realism (1993/94–2000)	Defence of norms of non-intervention and peaceful resolution of international conflicts; from 1993/94 to 1996 use of the threat of the rise of revisionist forces, and from 1996 to 2000 attempts to balance against the West by diversifying relations and to establish counter-alliances.
Pragmatic geoeconomic Realism (2000–4)	Careful balance between acceptance of international realities that Russia could not reasonably change, and opportunism in cases when gains seem possible; establish Russia as a reliable partner so as to earn great power status
Cultural geostrategic Realism (2004–7)	Global search for opportunities and realization of them; attempts to establish Russia as an alternative to West; selective cooperation with the West but with careful assessment if reciprocity is achieved

Part II Case Study Analyses

4
Russia's Approaches towards NATO

The twin enlargements of NATO to the East were and are among the most contentious issues in Russia's relations with the West. Despite concerted Russian attempts to stop enlargement, to slow down the process of enlargement, and to transform the alliance into a pan-European security organization, Moscow's concerns made only a limited degree of difference. Today Russia must live with an enlarged alliance, which has a more ambitious mission and which has demonstrated its willingness to act out of area even without a UN mandate. Institutions that involve Russia, such as the NATO–Russia Council (NRC) only marginally moderate these developments.

In this chapter, I aim to shed light on the Russian leadership's responses to NATO and its enlargement. In particular, I seek to answer two questions. The first is how can we best explain change in the Russian leadership's approach towards NATO enlargement? Moscow's approach towards NATO enlargement developed in four major stages. From 1991/92 to 1993/94, Russia's leadership indicated that it wanted to join NATO in the long-term, that it did not principally object to NATO membership for the Central and Eastern European (CEE) countries, and that it envisioned the transformation of NATO into a pan-European security alliance in which Russia played an equal role. From 1993/94 to 2000, Moscow increasingly opposed NATO enlargement. To stop enlargement, the Russian leadership resorted first to a *democratic argument*, threatening that NATO enlargement played into the hands of communist and nationalist forces whose rise would foster an anti-Western foreign policy. Later, Russian diplomacy primarily used a *geopolitical argument* to counter NATO expansion, emphasizing that Moscow was determined to counterbalance NATO enlargement by redeploying forces to Russia's Western borders, strengthening security cooperation with non-Western countries, and, after the first round of enlargement, drawing 'red lines' around the Baltic states. From 2000/01 to 2004, to the surprise of Western policymakers and analysts, Moscow's approach became more accommodating when the Russian leadership indicated that it would not oppose the second round of NATO enlargement, which included, inter alia, the Baltic states, and that it sought to establish a new basis for NATO–Russia relations. Finally, from 2004 to 2007, Moscow's approach towards NATO became again increasingly assertive. While the Russian leadership viewed cooperation between NATO and Russia in the newly created NRC positively, it voiced its criticism about a third round of NATO enlargement that could encompass the Ukraine and Georgia and it put pressure on both the Kiev and Tbilisi not to foster accession. In addition, the political climate on security issues deteriorated. Examples were the dispute about the Treaty of Conventional Armed Forces in Europe (CFE) and the controversy about the construction of a missile defence system in Europe.

The second question is how can we explain contradictions in Moscow's approach towards NATO enlargement in the mid and late 1990s? While from 1993/94 to 2000 the Russian leadership carefully balanced against enlargement, it cooperated twice with the alliance. In 1994/95 it joined the Partnership for Peace (PfP) programme, and in 1997, it signed the NATO–Russia Founding Act. These instances of cooperation, especially the latter one, contradicted the hostile tone of much of the preceding rhetoric and action and thus left an impression of foreign policy incoherence.

The most prominent explanation for the Russian leadership's approach to NATO enlargement focuses on the fact that despite its sometimes-hostile rhetoric, Moscow in practice acquiesced in NATO enlargement throughout the period under consideration. Consistent with Realism, some analysts argue that Moscow's cooperation with regard to the PfP programme and the NATO–Russia Founding Act was the result of Russia's weak material power position vis-à-vis the Western states. Kubicek, for example, argues that '[t]he Russian side was basically forced to back down. [. . .] NATO's will was determined, and various Russian efforts to sabotage expansion or water down NATO were rejected. A military response clearly was out of the question'.[1] In other words, Russia behaved as if it was a rational power-maximizing actor. It cooperated with the West since it lacked a reasonable alternative choice due to the determined will of the Western states and Russia's weak relative power position.[2]

Yet while the Realist emphasis on external pressures and on Russia's lack of capabilities might offer a parsimonious explanation for these two important episodes of cooperation, it is to ask whether the focus on Realist factors alone can explain other important facets of Russia's approach towards NATO enlargement. The following analysis suggests that in the period from 1991/92 to 1993/94, Moscow took a much more conciliatory approach towards NATO than one should expect from a power-maximizing actor; that the rhetorical sabre-rattling and the cautious attempts to balance against the West that preceded the decision to join the PfP programme and the NATO–Russian Founding Act cannot be explained in Realist terms as a *prudential tactic*; and that changes in Moscow's approach to NATO enlargement post 1999 can only partly be explained in Realist power-maximizing terms.

Instead of focusing on Realist factors alone, this chapter supports the hypotheses I put forward in the Introduction about the respective impacts of external constraints and collective ideas. On the one hand, I agree with the Realist argument that when push came to shove, Moscow gave in and sought compromise with the West. Thus, external constraints are the single most important factor that explains why Russia cooperated with the West by joining the PfP programme and the NATO–Russia Founding Act. On the other hand, my argument differs from the Realist one in so far as it contends that in many instances external constraints were not formidable and that the power-maximizing hypothesis is often indeterminate. Consequently, to explain Moscow's conciliatory approach from 1991/92 to 1993/94, *liberal ideas* need to be taken into account. To explain why the Russian leadership viewed NATO enlargement in the period from 1993/94 to 2000 as a major and imminent security threat against which the country should balance, one needs to take into account a *geopolitical* worldview and damaged pride which made the Russian leadership disregard the potentially beneficial security implications of NATO enlargement and focus primarily on its geopolitical and military ramifications instead. The influence of *pragmatic geoeconomic Realism* needs to be taken into account to explain the timing and extent of foreign policy reorientation from 2000/01 until 2004. Finally, *cultural geostrategic Realism* needs to be taken into account to explain why post 2004 the Russian approach became again more assertive.

The analysis is divided into four sections. First, I show in what cases external constraints were the single most important factor explaining Russian foreign policy. Second, I assess the impacts of the *behavioural dimension* of Realism and of collective ideas on Russia's foreign policy. Finally, I summarize my findings in the conclusion.

External constraints and Russia's approach: Russia's decisions to join the PfP programme and sign the NATO–Russia Founding Act

In Chapter 2, 'Framework for Analysis', I argue that an assessment of the degree to which external factors constrained Russia's leadership is a good starting point for an analysis of Russian foreign policy. My first hypothesis predicts that Russia would cooperate with the West in cases where these external constraints were formidable. With regard to Russia's scope of foreign policy options towards NATO enlargement, there were two instances where Moscow's foreign policy choices were seriously limited by the Western states' determination to pursue their interests regardless of Moscow's concerns.

The first case of constraint was in 1994/95, when the question of whether Russia should join the PfP programme arose. Officially, NATO's PfP programme had two major objectives. It aimed to deepen the cooperation between NATO members and countries of the former Soviet bloc beyond the level of cooperation under the North Atlantic Cooperation Council (NACC).[3] Additionally, it sought to stabilize CEE after the dissolution of the Soviet Union by assisting the former Soviet bloc countries with the modernization and democratization of their forces.[4] Yet one might argue that for the West, the PfP programme's main purpose was to buy time to solve two problems. The first was the need for a compromise between enlargement proponents and opponents in CEE and Western capitals. The second was the desire of the Western states to reach a new modus vivendi with Russia prior to undertaking NATO enlargement. The PfP programme addressed both objectives, since it showed the Central and Eastern Europeans that NATO enlargement was proceeding steadily, and it signalled to Moscow that the NATO member states were willing to slow down the enlargement process in order to establish a new NATO–Russia relationship beforehand.[5]

From the Russian perspective, the PfP programme did not offer much since it proposed cooperation with the West on Western terms, and its mechanisms facilitated the rapprochement between CEE countries and NATO, therefore leaving Russia aside. Thus, the question arises why the Russian leadership agreed to join a programme with such ambiguous implications.

The most parsimonious explanation is that Russian leaders had no alternative choice. Pressured by some CEE countries to enlarge NATO and hoping to buy time, the West was determined to invite the CEE countries to join the PfP programme. In this situation, Moscow had the choice of joining it as well, or risking that NATO enlargement would proceed by ignoring Russia altogether.[6] This explanation would confirm my first hypothesis.

When the NATO–Russia Founding Act was signed in 1997, the circumstances were similar. Already in December 1994, at a meeting of NATO's North Atlantic Council (NAC), US President Bill Clinton gave his clearest public statement to date in favour of NATO enlargement. At the same time, Clinton promised Yeltsin that enlargement would happen only after NATO and Russia agreed to a new relationship[7] and only after the 1996 Russian presidential election.[8] Thus, after Yeltsin won the 1996 presidential election, Washington increased its pressure on Moscow for an agreement. In mid July 1996, US Deputy Secretary of State Strobe Talbott proposed an agreement with Russia on the following terms: NATO would issue a statement that it had no intentions of stationing nuclear weapons on the territory of the new member states; NATO would establish a new mechanism for bilateral exchange between NATO and Russia; NATO would leave the door open for Russia's future membership; and the European powers would play a greater role in maintaining European security.[9]

This agreement was far from what Russia's leadership had desired. Russia had hoped for a binding commitment that no foreign troops and nuclear weapons would be stationed on the territory of the new member states, and it wanted a right to veto out-of-area deployments.[10] Yet, despite the fact that the US terms were far from what Russia's leadership wanted, Moscow accepted them. In May 1997, Moscow signed the NATO–Russia Founding Act, which gave Russia some reassurances and created the Permanent Joint Council (PJC) for consultations between Russia and NATO.[11] The Russian leadership tried to sell the agreement as a foreign policy success,[12] but developments in the following years indicate that Russia had gained little ground. NATO was quick to locate the headquarters for Polish, Danish, and German northern forces in Szczecin;[13] the PJC did not deliver more than communiqués citing ambitions rather than substance,[14] and the PJC's weakness became apparent when it failed to serve as a mediator between Russia and NATO during the Kosovo conflict.[15] MacFarlane summarizes the dilemma for Russian foreign policy at that time: 'Western states and organizations seek to draw Russia into their networks, but on their terms, to avoid enfranchising Russia in such a way that Western flexibility of decision-making and policy would be significantly constrained.'[16] The question therefore is how to best explain Russia's acquiescence in the NATO–Russia Founding Act, which did not seem to serve Russia's interests.

The most parsimonious explanation is that again Russia had little choice in the matter. It could have either rejected this offer and gained nothing in exchange, or it could have agreed and gained minimal concessions. The basic dilemma for Russia's leadership was that it did not have the means to counter NATO enlargement and that the Western countries were more or less united on this issue. Three statements support this assessment about Russia's lack of foreign policy alternatives. The *New York Times* cites Polish Foreign Minister Bronislaw Geremek, who says that Russian Foreign Minister Yevgenii Primakov had told him: 'You have to understand we are not glad about the enlargement of NATO. But we know it will happen. Just don't ask us to be happy about it.'[17] And Yeltsin is reported to have told Clinton at their March 1997 meeting in Helsinki: 'I am prepared to enter into an agreement with NATO, not because I want to but because it's a step I'm compelled to take. *There is no other solution for today*.'[18] And in his *Midnight Diaries*, Yeltsin argues that 'Russia had nothing with which to oppose NATO'.[19]

In other words, Russia's behaviour supports my first hypothesis that in cases where external constraints were formidable, Russia cooperated with the West. This conclusion about the overriding impact of external constraints is further supported if we consider that these decisions were taken despite fierce domestic parliamentary opposition. With regard to joining the PfP programme, both centrists and nationalists/communists criticized the Kremlin's approach. The head of the Duma's Subcommittee on International Security and Arms Control Viacheslav Nikonov argued that the PfP programme would undermine Russia's attempts to consolidate the Commonwealth of Independent States (CIS).[20] More radical were representatives of the Liberal Democratic Party of Russia (LDPR) and of the Communist Party, who argued in the aftermath of Russia's signing of the PfP programme that Kozyrev had 'committed an act of treachery'.[21]

The Duma raised an even harsher protest during the 1996/97 negotiations, which resulted in the NATO–Russia Founding Act. Some delegates formed an anti-NATO deputies' association, which linked the process of NATO expansion to Western concessions on other security issues such as the upgradation of the Organization for Security and Cooperation in Europe (OSCE) or nuclear disarmament and threatened to speed up the development of tactical nuclear weapons if the West did not take its demands into account.[22] Communist Party leader Gennady Zyuganov described the NATO–Russia Founding Act as an 'Act of Russia's unconditional capitulation to NATO'.[23] In a comprehensive analysis of the domestic debate about NATO enlargement, Sergounin concludes that the enlargement issue 'has united (with few exceptions) rather than divided the Russian elites'.[24] Thus, the fact that the Russian leadership agreed to both the PfP programme and the NATO–Russia Founding Act, despite fierce domestic parliamentary opposition, highlights the overriding impact of external constraints on Russian foreign policy in these two cases where external constraints were formidable.

Yet, while the Western countries were united by 1994/95 and 1996/97 on these two issues, they had not always been so prior to the decisions. This disunity gave Russian diplomacy scope for choice, and a focus on external constraints cannot explain Russian foreign policy in these periods. Thus, two important questions remain: Why did the Russian leadership's approach towards NATO change significantly from 1992 to 2007? And why did Moscow use volatile rhetoric and carefully attempt to balance against the West prior to these two instances of cooperation?

The indeterminancy of the Realist power-maximization hypothesis and the impact of collective ideas

Liberal thinking and Russia's cooperative approach from 1991/92 to 1993/94

In explaining change in the Russian leadership's approach towards NATO enlargement, the first question is why Moscow took a positive attitude towards NATO enlargement from 1991/92 to 1993/94. This positive attitude was reflected in a number of decisions and statements. In November 1991, in the first hours of post-Soviet Russia, Moscow joined the NACC;[25] and in December 1991, President Yeltsin indicated that Russia's membership in NATO was a long-term policy objective.[26] He argued: 'I am not raising the question in such a way that admission to NATO would take place immediately [. . .]. But sooner or later history will lead us to this.'[27] Similarly, in early 1992, Foreign Minister Kozyrev stated that Russia would seek 'eventually allied relations with the civilized world, including NATO, the UN and other structures'.[28] And in early 1993, he argued that 'Russia sees cooperation with NATO as an effective mechanism for overcoming the division of Europe'.[29]

When in 1993, the so-called Visegrad countries of Czechoslovakia, Hungary, and Poland urged the alliance to admit them as new members, President Yeltsin announced in August during a visit to Warsaw and Prague that Russia had no objections to this desire. He argued that the decision 'by sovereign Poland and aimed at general European integration does not run contrary to the interests of other states, including Russia'.[30]

Yet the Russian Foreign Ministry quickly qualified this endorsement of enlargement. Despite the fact that Foreign Minister Kozyrev initially supported Yeltsin's stance,[31] the Russian Foreign Ministry maintained in September 1993 that while Russia understood the desire of Poland and of other CEE countries to be admitted as NATO members, it rejected the 'bloc approach [. . .] that we have inherited from the past'. It emphasized that Moscow favoured an approach that strengthened collective security in the context of the Conference on Security and Cooperation (CSCE) and the NACC.[32]

This emphasis on collective security and the CSCE as an alternative to NATO enlargement reflected a slight change in Moscow's approach in the second half of 1993. Yet this proposal was not a significant departure from the initial endorsement of enlargement. Russia's leadership did not conceive of NATO as a major and imminent threat, and it believed that the eventual membership of Russia in NATO was a distant but possible and desirable goal. A letter that Yeltsin sent to Washington and other European capitals in mid September 1993 supports this assessment.[33]

Since these initial statements endorsing enlargement were to some extent based on wishful thinking rather than a well-considered strategy,[34] we should not exaggerate their meaning. Yet they are still telling as expressions of the mood of the Russian leadership directly after the dissolution of the Soviet Union. Consequently, the question is how can we explain this positive attitude towards NATO enlargement in 1992 and early 1993 and this still somewhat positive attitude in the second half of 1993?

One explanation is that in this period, there was no need to take a firm position, since the enlargement question was at that time a basically hypothetical one. No Western capital was seriously thinking about it. While this argument is certainly true, it does not explain why Russia's leadership put forward a position that was more accommodating than 'necessary'. In 1993, the European alliance members were fairly critical about the idea of NATO enlargement. London was concerned that NATO enlargement would dilute the alliance and the US commitment in Europe. Paris, on the contrary, was worried that enlargement would strengthen the role of NATO, undermining France's hope of developing Europe's independent security and defence role. And Bonn was divided on the question.[35] Thus Moscow could have reasonably voiced careful objections. Such a position would not have created any negative consequences for Moscow, as Russia's leadership would not have been differing from the stances of major European NATO members. So why did the Russian leadership set forth a much more NATO-friendly view than 'necessary'?

To explain this puzzle, we need to take into account the impact of the dominant train of thought at that time. The analysis of the evolution of the Russian leadership's foreign policy thinking shows that in this period, the leadership's view was informed by *liberal ideas*. This liberal outlook was built on the assumption that with the end of the Cold War, the antagonism between East and West had come to an end, and Russia and the West would henceforth share interests and values. Furthermore, the foreign policy thinking conceived of Russia as a *normal* great power, which meant that Russia no longer sought to impose its views on other states. Such an underlying thinking correlates with the Russian leadership's behaviour and rhetoric. *Liberal ideas* and the assumption that Russia was now a *normal* non-interventionist great power appeared, for example, in Yeltsin's justification for his positive approach towards Poland's membership aspirations in August 1993. He argued that '[t]he time when Polish leaders travelled to Moscow for advice, or, on the contrary, Moscow leaders went to Warsaw to give advice what to do is gone. There are two sovereign states and decisions of each of them should be respected'.[36]

In other words, while the benevolent attitude towards NATO enlargement from 1991/92 to 1993/94 can partly be explained by the fact that there was no need to take a firm position, in order to explain why the Russian leadership took a much more positive attitude towards NATO enlargement than 'necessary', we need to take the impact of *liberal thinking* into account. In this period, the Russian leadership was driven by the desire to use the historical moment to become an equal member of the Western society of states.

The rise of dogmatic geopolitical Realism and Russia's careful attempts to balance against NATO enlargement from 1993/94 to 2000

In the period from 1993/94 to 2000, Moscow neglected the early, positive assessments of the implications of NATO enlargement, and Russia's approach towards it became increasingly confrontational. How can we explain this change in approach?

By the spring of 1994, Moscow's assessment about Western intentions had already become increasingly pessimistic. In May 1994, Yeltsin argued in his Address to the Russian Federal Assembly that 'ideological confrontation has been replaced by a struggle for spheres of influence in geopolitics'.[37] The most symbolic clash between Russia and the West occurred in the winter of 1994. As a reaction to NATO's December 1994 decision to prepare an extensive study on enlargement[38] and as a response to Clinton's above-mentioned pro-enlargement statement, at the December 1994 CSCE summit in Budapest Yeltsin warned that there was a danger that the Cold War was being replaced by a 'cold peace'.[39]

This negative view of Western intentions and the consequent opposition to NATO enlargement became the major characteristics of Russian foreign policy towards the European security environment from 1993/94 to 2000. In Yeltsin's 1995 Address to the Russian Federal Assembly, he warned that '[d]ecisions on European security that are made without Russia's participation and, even worse, against Russia, would be counterproductive'.[40] And in September 1995, he argued that NATO expansion 'is fraught with the potential for war throughout Europe'.[41] Even two months before the signing of the NATO–Russia Founding Act, Yeltsin repeated in his Address to the Russian Federal Assembly that NATO enlargement contradicted Russia's interests, would cause a split in Europe, and was motivated by the desire to force Russia out of Europe and to ensure its strategic isolation.[42] In May 1997, he even compared the political climate between Russia and the United States with that at the time of the 1962 Cuban Missile Crisis.[43]

To stop enlargement, the Russian leadership used several different strategies. From 1993/94 to 1996, Moscow applied three primary means to this end. First, Russian officials used a *democratic argument* when they warned that NATO enlargement would create a dangerous domestic backlash in Russia by sweeping communist and nationalist forces into power. In January 1994 Russian Presidential Spokesman Vyacheslav Kostikov argued that Yeltsin was concerned that 'expanding NATO by granting membership to countries located in immediate proximity to Russia's borders will elicit a negative reaction from Russian public opinion and promote the development of undesirable sentiments in civilian and military circles, and could ultimately lead to military and political destabilization'.[44] Since the outcomes of the parliamentary election of 1995 and of the presidential election of 1996 were unpredictable and since many observers were concerned that communist and nationalist forces might win ground, this threat was not hypothetical. US Deputy Secretary of State Talbott confirms that Yeltsin urged Clinton to postpone enlargement until his re-election for these reasons and that Clinton took his concerns into account.[45]

Second, Russian officials threatened that NATO enlargement would force Moscow to take military countermeasures. They warned that Russia would revise the military doctrine, build up Russia's defence capabilities,[46] withdraw from the CFE,[47] and direct its nuclear weapons towards countries that had applied for NATO membership.[48]

Third, in addition to the application of rhetorical threats, Russia's leadership tried to undermine NATO enlargement by suggesting that the C/OSCE[49] was a much more adequate European security organization since it was more inclusive and as a security organization better equipped to address the new challenges of the post-Cold War era. The biggest advantage of the C/OSCE from the Russian point of view was that Moscow had an equal say in it. Thus, in September 1994 Moscow proposed the ambitious 'Programme to Increase the Efficiency of the CSCE', which aimed at transforming the CSCE into a pan-European security organization with its own governing body and with the responsibility of coordinating the major Euro–Atlantic institutions – including NATO, the EU, the Western European Union, and the CIS.[50] This idea was consistently, yet unsuccessfully, advanced until the December 1996 OSCE Lisbon Summit. While the Western states were willing to upgrade the CSCE to become the OSCE, they did not agree to a transformation of it.[51]

From 1996 to 2000, the Russian leadership's approach of opposing NATO enlargement changed, becoming more *dogmatic and geopolitical*. During this period Russian diplomacy relied primarily on the following three means to oppose NATO enlargement. First, Moscow threatened that NATO enlargement would force Russia to take adequate countermeasures. Defence Minister General Igor Rodionov warned in 1996 that 'a situation similar to what we had during the Cold War, when the confronting groups of forces were deployed against each other and were maintained at a high level of combat readiness for attack' could reoccur.[52] Similarly, Foreign Minister Primakov argued in 1996 that Russia would take 'adequate measures in terms of military construction'.[53]

Second, the Russian leadership threatened to create counteralliances to oppose NATO enlargement. Primakov argued in 1996 that Russia would be forced 'to remedy the geopolitical situation [. . . by] finding new partners and allies'.[54] The envisioned integration of Belarus into the Russian Federation must partially be seen in this context.[55] In March 1997, in a joint statement by Yeltsin and Belarusian President Alyaksandr Lukashenka, the countries proclaimed that they were 'united in their rejection of NATO's plans to advance eastwards'.[56] And the timing of the visits of the premier of India and of the foreign minister of China to Moscow shortly before the March 1997 Helsinki NATO Summit also signified Russian attempts to threaten the West with the build up of new alliances to counter NATO enlargement.[57]

Third, after the signing of the NATO–Russia Founding Act and after the alliance had invited the Czech Republic, Hungary, and Poland to join, the Russian leadership drew 'red lines' around the Baltic states, arguing that Russia could not tolerate NATO countries on its borders.[58]

How can we best explain Moscow's perception of NATO enlargement as a major and imminent threat and its decision to carefully balance against NATO enlargement in this period? One explanation treats Russia's increasingly confrontational behaviour as a prudential and well-calculated tactic to enhance Russia's leverage in the bargaining process, which is consistent with what I call the *behavioural dimension* of Realism. By carefully balancing against NATO enlargement, the Russian leadership hoped to undermine the Western consensus and, at best, stop the enlargement process, or, at least, gain some concessions. Yeltsin supports such a view when he recalls: 'Paradoxically, I think that our tough stance on the eastern expansion of NATO [. . .] played a role in gaining us this new status [in the G7].'[59]

How convincing is this interpretation of Russia's increasingly confrontational approach? As indicated above, in 1993, the European allies were still highly reluctant about the idea of NATO enlargement. This attitude changed slowly over the following years. The dilemma of the US administration was that in order to get the European allies to agree to NATO enlargement, it had to find a new modus vivendi with Russia. Yet to achieve this new modus vivendi, Washington needed to put pressure on Moscow, which could only be done if the allies stood united in favour of enlargement.[60] This causal relationship gave Russia important leverage, which Moscow tried to exploit by attempting to drive a wedge between Western European allies and the United States so as to undermine the Western consensus. In his memoir *Russian Crossroads*, Primakov argues that in the summer of 1996, he was in talks with French President Jaques Chirac about a 'chained' process of NATO enlargement. This meant to first reform NATO, then to establish a special relationship between Russia and NATO, and only then to begin talks on NATO enlargement.[61] These consultations caused great concern in the United States. US Deputy Secretary of State Talbott feared in the summer of 1996 that Foreign Minister Primakov was 'looking for (and, I fear, finding) weak spots on the NATO front; he'd like to exploit these to see if he can slow down or even stop enlargement, or extract from us concessions that would make a mockery of our determination – that new members of the Alliance have all the rights and protections of current members'.[62]

Although Moscow was in the end unable to stop the process of enlargement, these developments support the interpretation that Russia's attempts to carefully balance against NATO enlargement allowed it to gain concessions that it would not have received otherwise.

Yet, while the balancing tactic might have delivered some gains, it did so at considerable costs. The application of threats played into the hands both of the CEE countries, which could reasonably argue that Russia still posed a serious threat to their security, and of hardliners in Western capitals, who pushed for enlargement to contain an unpredictable Russia. Asmus reports, for example, that in a meeting with the then US Ambassador to the UN Madeleine Albright, Supreme Allied Commander General John Shalikashvili and State Department Adviser Charles Gati, Polish President Lech Walesa argued that the PfP programme was a big mistake and that delaying NATO enlargement would only encourage Russian imperial tendencies: 'To tame the bear you must put him in a cage and not let him run free in the forest.'[63] This concern was recognized in Russia. Foreign policy analyst Aleksei Pushkov argued that 'the East European countries built their policies of rapprochement with the West on the basis of pitting themselves against Russia'.[64] In other words, these costs must be counted against the gains achieved by carefully balancing against the West. Depending on how much weight one attaches to the costs and gains of this approach, it remains questionable whether these balancing attempts were a prudential strategy aimed at maximizing Russia's relative power position.

In retrospect, we can ask whether Russia might not have gained more by conducting a more cooperative policy with regard to NATO. Already in 1993/94, the US leadership envisioned a plan to 'compensate' Russia for NATO enlargement by offering, inter alia, a special consultative forum between Russia and NATO. US Deputy Secretary of State Talbott argued in a memorandum in October 1993 that if 'our administration decides to proceed on an NATO-plus-V3 [NATO plus the so-called Visegrad countries Czechoslovakia, Hungary, and Poland], then let's take Yeltsin up on his proposal for a security arrangement of some kind between the Russian Federation and NATO'.[65] Similarly, a US National Security Council memo to the US President from spring 1994 entitled 'Advancing our European Security Agenda: Working with Russia and the Central and East Europeans (CEE)' suggested the creation of a separate cooperative relationship with Russia as NATO expanded.[66] While this counterfactual analysis does not imply that Russia could have achieved much better terms of agreement with NATO during the 1990s, it suggests that an agreement might have been achieved at a lower political cost.

These costs weaken the argument that prudential and well-calculated power-maximizing considerations are key to explaining Russia's approach. They rather seem to be post hoc rationalizations of Russian foreign policy.

Furthermore, one might ask from the Realist perspective whether NATO enlargement in this period should have been perceived as a threat to Russia at all. On the one hand, it is arguable that NATO enlargement posed a threat to Russia. First, containment of the Soviet Union had been the major reason for NATO's creation during the Cold War. But while the Cold War came to an end with the dissolution of the Soviet Union and of the Warsaw Pact, NATO continued to exist. Did this not imply that NATO's new opponent was Russia? Second, many members of the Russian foreign policy elite believed that Western capitals and Moscow had agreed in the late 1980s that if Moscow allowed German reunification within NATO, the alliance would not be enlarged eastwards.[67] If the Western states had broken this crucial promise, how could they be trusted any longer? Third, NATO demonstrated in Bosnia and later also in Kosovo that it – in contrast to Russia – had the capacity to deploy forces effectively, and, even worse, that it would use force without a UN mandate. Fourth, since it was highly unlikely that Russia would become a member of NATO, the alliance's enlargement meant that Moscow would be excluded from Europe's most effective defence and security organization and be left with fewer potential allies of its own. Finally, NATO was a cooperative institution aiming at mutually beneficial outcomes, with the consequence that the costs of competing with NATO's power increases were much higher for Russia,[68] since collective defence in an alliance is cheaper than national defence.[69] Since Realists are interested in material power capabilities rather than intentions, from their point of view, NATO enlargement posed a threat to Russia.

Yet on the other hand, NATO enlargement arguably posed only a very hypothetical threat to Russia, and may have even brought Moscow some security gains. First, NATO never used the threat of force to coerce Russia.[70] Thus, it is unconvincing to argue that because NATO used force in the former Yugoslavia, it might do the same against Russia. Second, NATO needed the agreement of all its member states to use force, which made an attack against Russia highly unlikely. Third, Russia possessed second-strike nuclear capabilities, so nuclear deterrence still worked. Fourth, it seems reasonable to agree with US Deputy Secretary of State Talbott that NATO enlargement was at least as much a political as a military project and was designed to stabilize CEE rather than to hold Russia in check.[71] This assessment is supported by the fact that while the civil US administration favoured enlargement, during much of the 1990s, the Pentagon was against it. US military officials thought that enlargement would weaken the cohesion of NATO and that it would disproportionately increase US obligations in comparison to limited strategic military gains.⁷² And finally, NATO enlargement had a positive effect on Russia's security. Russia always feared a revisionist Germany and a fragmented Europe, where nationalization of security policies could lead to instability. The continued existence of NATO and its enlargement minimized both threats.⁷³

This discussion suggests that NATO enlargement had ambiguous implications for Russia's security. Given this ambiguity, what kind of security interest would Realists predict for Russia? Would they expect Moscow to treat NATO enlargement as a major and imminent threat or as a hypothetical one, since it was highly unlikely that NATO would be used as an instrument against Russia, and enlargement even offered some positive security implications? If we take into account the other challenges that Russia faced throughout the 1990s, it is even more surprising that NATO enlargement should have been perceived as a major threat. Between 1989 and 1995, Russia's gross national product had halved, and it did not begin to recover until 1999.⁷⁴ Prime Minister Primakov argued in September 1998 that the economic crisis posed a threat to Russia's integrity that was 'not a theoretical or hypothetical issue' and that Russia was facing 'a very serious threat of our country being split up'.⁷⁵ Furthermore, Russia was confronted with more immediate threats on its southern borders and from separatist tendencies within Russia, as the 1997 Concept of National Security stressed.⁷⁶ Would Realists not expect Russia to focus first and foremost on economic recovery, political consolidation, and the threats emanating from the south, with the mid-term aim of translating political stability and economic power into military might? Such an approach would imply that Russia had to accept enlargement, to build stable relations with the alliance, and to conduct a 'maximally economical foreign and defence policy' in order to carry out internal reconstruction.⁷⁷

While the Realist perspective suggests that the Russian leadership should have seen NATO enlargement as undesirable, the Realist power-maximizing hypothesis does not sufficiently rank a number of potential threats. As a result, I conclude that it is indeterminate as to whether NATO enlargement should have been perceived as a major and imminent or as a hypothetical threat. Consequently, it is to ask how we can better explain Moscow's decision of choosing an increasingly confrontational approach to NATO enlargement.

I suggest that the increasingly confrontational approach in the period from 1993/94 to 2000 can only be explained by taking into account the collective ideas that informed the Russian leadership's foreign policy thinking in this period. The analysis of the evolution of the Russian leadership's foreign policy thinking in Chapter 3 suggests that in this period, the Russian leadership's foreign policy thinking became increasingly *geopolitical Realist* and was concerned with the preservation of Russia's Eurasian great power status. The dominant themes at the time were concerns about traditional military security threats and the perception of Russia as not merely a *normal* great power, but as an equal great power.

By taking into account these kinds of collective ideas, it becomes clearer why the enlargement of NATO caused such concern for Russia's leadership. While the Warsaw Pact had been dissolved and Russian forces had withdrawn from CEE, its former adversary enlarged its sphere of influence. The Russian leadership perceived this development as a humiliation,[78] which made it overlook the fact that NATO enlargement also offered security gains. In other words, without taking into account the force of damaged pride, the fact that the Western countries behaved like victorious powers, and the perception that NATO enlargement undermined Russia's great power status, we cannot explain the overemphasis on the challenges posed by NATO enlargement vis-à-vis its positive security implications.[79]

The Russian leadership's explanation for why the West wanted a weakened Russia reveals the extent to which *geopolitical Realist ideas* affected the Russian leadership. Defence Minister General Igor Rodionov explained that NATO enlargement was pursued by the Western states to get closer to Russia's natural resources: 'Russia's gigantic territorial expanses and its colossal natural resources [. . .] have long attracted the gaze of those who dream of lording it over our land.'[80] Rodionov's successor, Igor Sergeyev, similarly characterized NATO's 1999 war against Yugoslavia as a threat to Russia itself[81] and repeated Rodionov's assertion that the United States pursued NATO enlargement in order to control world markets and resources.[82]

This preoccupation with geopolitics and great power status recognition is also an important factor in explaining why Russia's leadership made the agreements to both the PfP programme and the NATO–Russia Founding Act conditional on the formal acknowledgement of the country's special status. Before Moscow agreed to join the PfP programme, Yeltsin argued that a partnership between Russia and NATO 'by virtue of its scope and substance, should be different from relationships with other countries'. He added that '[t]he idea is to conclude a special agreement with NATO in keeping with Russia's place and role in world and European affairs and with our country's military power and nuclear status'.[83] In the end, NATO agreed to grant Russia such a special status.

A special protocol to the PfP programme acknowledged Russia's 'unique and important contribution [. . .] as a major European, international and nuclear power'.[84] Russian Ambassador to Belgium Vitaliy Churkin emphasized that this recognition was unique: 'NATO doesn't have a document of this sort with a single other country. [. . .] Therefore, our relations with the alliance are unique in both content and form.'[85]

The same preoccupation with acknowledgement of great power status was reflected in the Russian leadership's desire to conclude an agreement with NATO before accession negotiations with the Central and East European NATO membership candidates began in 1997. As a result, Russia and NATO agreed to the NATO–Russia Founding Act in May 1997, two months before the first three NATO membership candidates were officially invited to start accession negotiations at NATO's Madrid Summit in July 1997.[86] Furthermore, Russia was granted a seat in the G7. Despite the fact that membership in the G7 (similar to the signing of the above-mentioned special protocols) did not provide significant substantial gains, for Yeltsin, membership in this prestigious club symbolized a great foreign policy success since it increased Russia's international status.[87]

Collective ideas also play an important role in explaining why the Russian leadership used the threat of the rise to power of revisionist forces as a means to counter NATO enlargement from 1993/94 to 1996 and why after 1995, this *democratic argument* was increasingly replaced by the *geopolitical argument* that NATO enlargement would force Russia to create counteralliances. This change from the *democratic argument* to the *geopolitical argument* correlates with the change in the leadership's thinking on strategy. The analysis of the evolution of the Russian leadership's foreign policy thinking in Chapter 3 suggests that Moscow's thinking on strategy in the period from 1993/94 to 1996 was shaped by *liberal ideas*. These *liberal ideas* led policymakers into thinking that the West based its policies towards Russia on the assumption that Western moves would have an impact on Russian domestic politics and that changes in the Russian domestic distribution of power might lead to an undesirable Russian foreign policy. Such assumptions cannot be explained by Realism.

The analysis of the Russian leadership's discourse on strategy then suggests that from 1996 to 2000, the Russian leadership's thinking on strategy moved away from liberal assumptions and towards the idea that Russia had to assert its interests by applying threats and by seeking to carefully balance against the West. In short, while the *behavioural dimension* of Realism is too indeterminate to explain Russian strategies towards NATO enlargement, by taking into account collective ideas in the Russian leadership's thinking on strategy, we can explain changes in the Russian approach towards NATO enlargement.

In conclusion, in this analysis of Russia's approach to NATO from 1993/94 to 2000, I suggest three general observations. First, it is implausible to conceive the increasingly confrontational policy of that period as predominantly a well-calculated tactic to enhance Russia's bargaining power. Such an interpretation rather seems to represent a post hoc rationalization by Russian foreign policy makers and it underestimates the costs of the increasingly confrontational approach. Second, the *behavioural dimension* of Realism cannot sufficiently explain the Russian leadership's perception of NATO enlargement as a major and imminent rather than a hypothetical threat. I suggest that while Realism can explain why NATO enlargement should have been perceived as undesirable and why close cooperation between NATO and Russia was unlikely, we need to take into account collective ideas to explain the degree to which the Russian leadership saw NATO enlargement as a threat. A geopolitical view and great power status considerations are important factors in explaining why the Russian leadership focused primarily on the negative ramifications of NATO enlargement, neglected positive security implications, and paid so much attention to ensuring that Russia's great power status was recognized in special protocols. Third, collective ideas also help explain why the Russian leadership chose to use the *democratic argument* to persuade the West to respond to its concerns from 1993/94 to 1996, and why it used the *geopolitical argument* from 1996 to 2000.

Pragmatic geoeconomic Realism and Russia's conciliatory approach from 2000 to 2004

It came as a surprise to many Western decision-makers and analysts that the Russian leadership's approach towards NATO and its enlargement became increasingly conciliatory from 2000 to 2004. The reorientation was noticeable already in 2000/01, even before the 11 September 2001 terrorist attacks. Despite the tensions between Russia and NATO over the war in the former Yugoslavia, at a meeting with NATO's Secretary General Lord George Robertson in February 2000, acting Russian President Vladimir Putin expressed Russia's willingness to expand its relations with NATO.[88] In a BBC interview in March 2000, he even argued that he did not rule out the possibility of NATO membership for Russia, if Moscow's views were adequately taken into account.[89] By mid 2000, the NATO–Russia dialogue had been resumed, both sides were engaged in active conference diplomacy, and Moscow's attitude with regard to the question of the Baltic states' membership in NATO had even changed. In March 2001, President Putin broke with the former policy of drawing 'red lines' around the Baltic states and argued that while NATO enlargement to the Baltic states would have a negative impact on Russian security, all states had the right to choose whom they wanted to ally with.[90] As a result of this foreign policy reorientation, Russia's reactions to the second round of NATO enlargement in April 2004 were sober. President Putin argued that NATO–Russia relations 'are developing positively'. And rather than claiming that NATO posed a threat to Russia, he emphasized that NATO was not adequate as an organization to address contemporary security challenges. He claimed that Russia has 'no concerns about the expansion of NATO in terms of the security of the Russian Federation', but 'today's threats are such that with the expansion of NATO, they will not disappear'.[91]

This new approach towards NATO had three major implications. First, it opened the door for the establishment of the NRC. At the 7 December 2001 PJC meeting, the establishment of this council – which was to replace the PJC – was officially announced, and it came into being at the NATO–Russia Summit in May 2002 in Rome. The NRC distinguished itself from the PJC in so far as Russia and NATO members meet as equals 'at 27' (instead of in the bilateral 'NATO plus 1' format under the PJC) and decisions are taken jointly. It can therefore be seen as an improvement of Russia's position vis-à-vis NATO.[92] Second, the Russian Ministry of Defence established a diplomatic mission to NATO and set up Russian Military Branch Offices at NATO's two top military command headquarters, while NATO expanded its military mission in Moscow. Third, a secure telephone link was established between the NATO secretary general and the Russian defence minister.[93]

The creation of the NRC and these other developments should, however, not be interpreted as a return to something like Gorbachev's New Thinking. As Putin and Defence Minister Sergei Ivanov repeatedly stressed, they still viewed NATO enlargement as a mistake. Thus, while Moscow acknowledged that it had no means to stop enlargement and stated that it did not see NATO enlargement as a serious threat, it still did not agree to the enlargement rationale as such. This position also explains why cooperation in the NRC was not easy, leading to tensions at times. For example, before the Baltic states joined NATO, Russia's representatives urged the alliance to delay enlargement, criticized Russian minority issues in the Baltic states,[94] and demanded that the alliance refrain from deploying NATO forces in these three countries.[95] And when the three states were finally admitted in April 2004, Russian officials criticized the deployment of four Belgian F-17 fighter jets to an airfield in Lithuania and the flight of AWACS reconnaissance aircraft in Baltic airspace about 120 kilometres from the Russian border.[96]

Yet, despite the fact that NATO–Russia relations were still far from friendly, Moscow's approach towards NATO from 2000/01 to 2004 had changed significantly in comparison to its approach in the mid and late 1990s. Russia's leadership no longer conceived of NATO as an imminent and major security threat, it acknowledged some potential security gains of cooperation with NATO, and, most importantly, the relative significance of NATO in Russia's approach to European security decreased.[97] Foreign policy analyst Sergei Karaganov argued in July 2001: 'For a certain time, Russia's approach towards Europe was predominantly focused on this issue [NATO enlargement] alone. As a result the Russian government diverted foreign political resources from many other issues, some of which were much more relevant.'[98]

Thus, the question at hand is how can we best explain this significant yet tentative foreign policy reorientation? One important reason for this change was the acknowledgement of foreign policy failure. The application of threats in the 1990s had proved to be unproductive. NATO was enlarging, the Kosovo conflict had shown that the alliance would use force even without a UN mandate, and in NATO's 1999 Strategic Concept, the alliance even envisioned military involvement beyond Europe's borders.[99] All these developments demonstrated that Russian attempts to counter NATO enlargement by balancing against it had reached an impasse and that a new approach was needed.

Second, Primakov's attempts to find new non-Western allies had proved to be a failure as well. The union with Belarus was of little success and did not pose a credible threat to the West. The situation was similar with regard to the Ukraine and to the collective security arrangements within the CIS.[100] Light concludes that the value of cooperation for the other CIS members and even for the Russian government itself was rather questionable.[101] And finally, while Russia's attempts to develop 'strategic partnerships' with China, India, and Iran produced some financial gains due to the trade of military and nuclear equipment, they did not lead to the formation of a credible counterweight against NATO enlargement.

Third, if Russia's leadership had hoped to be able to drive a wedge between the EU and the United States, the years 2000 and 2001, and especially Europe's reaction to the 11 September 2001 terrorist attacks, had shown that this rationale would not work. Valery Zhurkin argued in 2001 that '[a]ttempts to view cooperation between Russia and the

European Union as an alternative or a counterbalance to the policy of NATO and United States may be described as wishful thinking'.[102]

Yet, while the acknowledgement of foreign policy failure and changes in the international context point to a more conciliatory stance, the timing and extent of reorientation is striking. Describing the domestic climate in Russia in 1999, Arbatov argues that '[s]erious discussions took place concerning military conflict with NATO. All of a sudden, the apocalyptic scenarios of the Third World War [. . .] returned to the table as practical policymaking and military operational planning issues [. . .] reviving the worst instincts and stereotypes of the Cold War'.[103] While this characterization of the mood of the Russian foreign policy elite might be somewhat dramatized, Light, White, and Löwenhardt support the general conclusion that the 1999 war in the former Yugoslavia increased the Russian foreign policy elite's scepticism about the prospects of Russian–Western cooperation. They argue that at the end of the 1990s, there were only 'few genuine liberal westernizers left and none of them remain in policy-making positions'. They also point out that 'Pragmatic nationalists claimed that as a result of Kosovo, those who were in favour of Russia "going into Europe", or becoming more European, had suffered a great blow'.[104] This implies that the timing and extent of the reorientation of Russian foreign policy was not predetermined by the acknowledgement of foreign policy failure, or by changes in the international context. Quite to the contrary, elite surveys show that at the end of the 1990s, the elite was sceptical about a more pro-Western policy.

Again, I argue that we need to take into account collective ideas. In particular, changes in three spheres play an important role in explaining the timing and extent of policy reorientation. First, the analysis of the evolution of Russian foreign policy thinking in Chapter 3 suggests that in the period from 2000/01 to 2004, the Russian leadership put greater emphasis on strengthening Russia's economy. It thought that cooperation with the West would be the best means to this end. Thus it acknowledged that a prolonged hostile climate between Russia and the West was counterproductive.

Second, the foreign policy thinking of this period was pragmatic rather than dogmatic. This outlook implied that Russia had to accept developments that it could not reasonably prevent. This pragmatism explains why the Russian leadership stopped trying to balance against the second round of NATO enlargement, why it no longer drew 'red lines' around the Baltic states, and why it no longer tried to drive wedges between Europe and the United States.[105]

Finally, while Russian foreign policy thinking in this period was still concerned with the preservation of Russia's great power status, the leadership thought that this status could not simply be assumed, but rather had to be *earned* by responsible and predictable foreign policy action. Since Russia's leadership wanted this recognition from the Western states, Moscow had to act in accordance with Western interests. Putin's approach towards the CEE countries in the years 2001 to 2003 is telling in this regard. On a state visit to Poland in 2002, he not only laid flowers at a monument to Poland's Second World War resistance army and visited another to victims of the 1956 Soviet intervention, but he also acknowledged that Russian foreign policy had made mistakes with regard to the CEE countries. When asked whether the involvement of Warsaw Pact forces in Hungary and Czechoslovakia were mistakes, Putin replied: 'In my opinion, those were huge mistakes. And the Russophobia which confronts us in Eastern Europe today stems precisely from those mistakes.'[106] Similarly, in July 2003 Foreign Minister Ivanov argued that Russia's approach to CEE during the 1990s had resulted in a 'lost decade', and suggested that many potentially beneficial possibilities had been neglected.[107]

In short, while the acknowledgement of foreign policy failure and changes in the international context are significant to understanding why it was important for the Russian leadership to change its approach to NATO enlargement after 1999, we also need to take into account a change in the Russian leadership's foreign policy thinking to explain the timing and extent of the reorientation in Russia's approach towards NATO enlargement in the period from 2000/01 to 2004.

Cultural geostrategic Realism and Russia's cautious assertive approach from 2004 to 2007

In the period from 2004 to 2007 Moscow's approach to NATO became cautiously assertive.[108] With regard to whether Russia intended to join NATO, the Russian leadership made it unambiguously clear that it had no such intention. In 2005 Putin ruled out joining NATO since NATO membership would mean 'giving up part of our sovereignty, and [. . .] restrictions in passing political decisions'.[109]

With regard to Russia's overall view on a third wave of NATO enlargement, Moscow made very clear that it strongly opposed a new round of enlargement that would bring NATO even closer to its borders. On the one hand, it maintained its approach not to negate the rights of NATO to enlarge and of the states to join NATO, but to argue instead that the enlargement of NATO would not help solve current challenges to

European and international security and that it would have negative ramifications on Russia's security.[110] Putin emphasized that in particular the deployment of NATO forces on the territory of new NATO member states posed a threat to Russia and represented a violation of reached agreements.[111]

On the other hand, Moscow vociferously expressed concerns that the new wave of enlargement should not encompass countries that Russia considered vital parts of its sphere of influence, such as the Ukraine and Georgia. While Moscow did not again draw 'red lines' around these two states as it did in the mid and late 1990s with the Baltic states, it argued that accession of the Ukraine would be 'especially sensitive' for Russia, that the majority of Ukrainians did not want to integrate with NATO, and that accession would presuppose annulling the Ukraine's 'commitments concerning the [Russian] Black Sea Fleet based in Sevastopol'[112] in Crimea.[113]

In addition to using rhetorical pressure, there are indications that Moscow supported anti-NATO protests in Crimea during NATO's *Sea Breeze* manoeuvres in spring 2006 to put pressure on the Ukrainian government not to pursue accession. As part of the protests, the unloading of a US vessel sailing under a NATO flag was prevented and in June 2006, the Crimean parliament declared the peninsula a 'NATO-free zone'.[114] In a similar fashion, the Russian leadership opposed Georgia's NATO membership aspirations. Foreign Minster Sergey Lavrov questioned the accession rationale when he asked: 'Who is the threat to [. . .] Georgia?',[115] and the Russian leadership made clear that it had countermeasures at hand. Defence Minister Ivanov argued in September 2006 that two brigades of Russian forces had been deployed at the borders with Georgia.[116]

In short, consistent with the approach taken in the previous period, the Russian leadership did not negate NATO's right to further enlarge to the East as such, and it did not vociferously draw rhetorical 'red lines' around the Ukraine and Georgia. In contrast to the previous period, however, Moscow clearly articulated its opposition to a third wave of NATO enlargement and used its leverage to put pressure on the Ukraine and Georgia to undermine their accession negotiations. Such an approach suggests that the Russian leadership came to believe that the hollow sabre-rattling of the 1990s proved insufficient and that Russia's only means to halt further enlargement was to rely on substantial levers directed primarily at the accession candidates rather than existing NATO member states.

With regard to Russia's engagement in the NRC, the Russian leadership's approach was ambivalent. On the one hand, it repeatedly declared that it viewed cooperation between Russia and NATO member states in this forum as positive. In January 2005 Putin summarized: 'In just a very short time we have taken a gigantic step from past confrontation to working together and from mutual accusations and stereotypes to creating modern instruments for co-operation.'[117]

On the other hand, no new quality of cooperation between Russia and NATO has emerged in practice and the substantial results are fairly thin.[118] This mismatch between rhetoric, on the one side, and actual cooperation, on the other, indicates that the Russian leadership took an ambivalent approach to the NRC. While Moscow valued cooperation in the NRC since it engaged here with NATO member states at eye level, it did not consider cooperation as a means to bring Russia closer to NATO with the eventual aim of becoming a NATO member. The Russian leadership viewed cooperation with NATO in purely instrumental terms. Consequently, Russia refused to develop an Individual Partnership Action Plan with NATO, which would have encompassed support for democratic transformation and constrained Russia's internal policies.[119]

Finally, what significantly distinguishes this period of NATO–Russia engagement was a deteriorating climate at the general political level concerning European security. One example was arms control. NATO insisted that Russia had to fully implement political commitments it undertook at the 1999 Istanbul OSCE Summit, which would entail withdrawal of all troops, military equipment, and ammunition stockpiles from Georgia and Moldova's Russian-speaking separatist region of Trandsniester before NATO members sign the Adapted Treaty on Conventional Forces in Europe. Russia, for its part, insisted on the immediate ratification of the Agreement, extension of the CFE regime to the new NATO member states Estonia, Latvia, and Lithuania, and the lowering of treaty limits for NATO to compensate for the military potential acquired by the alliance as a result of its two waves of enlargement.[120] In his 2007 Annual Address, Putin even threatened to declare a moratorium on its observance of the CFE treaty until all NATO members ratify and 'observe' it.[121]

Another example of the deteriorating political climate was Moscow's expression of severe concerns about the US plan to construct a missile defence system in Europe.[122] The US administration justified the creation as the need to prevent a potential attack from rogue states such as Iran. The Russian leadership consistently condemned the deployment of such a system, arguing that the Iranian missile programme did not pose a threat to Europe and the United States, that the deployment made necessary an 'asymmetrical response',[123] and that it would destroy the 'balance of power' in Europe.[124]

In short, from 2004 to 2007, the Russian approach towards NATO became cautiously assertive. On the one hand, the Russian leadership continued cooperation in the NRC. On the other hand, it voiced concerns about a third wave of enlargement much more vociferously than it did in the period from 2000/01 to 2004, it applied pressure on the Ukraine and Georgia to undermine their attempts to get closer to NATO membership, and the general political climate on questions of European security deteriorated. Thus, the question is how to explain these changes in Moscow's approach towards NATO.

One factor to explain this change is that the balance sheet of the consequences of the rapprochement between Russia and the West in the period from 2000 to 2004 was imbalanced. While Russia went a significant step into the Western direction, supported the war in Afghanistan against the Taliban and al-Qaeda, and took a muted line towards the 2003 Iraq invasion, post 2004 Moscow felt increasingly endangered by NATO's determination to enlarge to an area that Russia considered its special sphere of influence. Furthermore, NATO globalized its outreach and despite Russia's involvement in the NRC, Moscow felt isolated when it came to important questions such as the construction of a missile defence system in Europe. Thus, the rapprochement provided insufficient returns for Russia. But what does this acknowledgment of foreign policy failure from a Realist perspective imply about Russia's approach?

As argued above, Russia had only limited means to counter NATO enlargement. Especially an assertive foreign policy represented an ambiguous foreign policy instrument. While an assertive foreign policy might have increased the price for NATO enlargement, its use offered proponents of enlargement evidence to justify their claims in favour of enlargement. Thus, from a Realist perspective, it is not clear what strategy would have maximized Russia's interest most.

To explain why the Russian leadership chose this more assertive strategy, I suggest that the dominant thinking at that time needs to be taken into account. *Cultural geostrategic Realism* conceived the international system in increasingly hostile terms, saw especially Russia's 'near abroad' as an arena for competition also for value systems, stressed Russia's uniqueness, and was more optimistic about the country's capabilities, both in financial terms and in terms of its defence capabilities.

If one takes this set of collective ideas into account, it becomes understandable why the Russian leadership, on the one hand, continued to cooperate with the West in the NRC. In contrast to the dialogue with the EU, here Russia's unique status was acknowledged and it met NATO members at eye level. Furthermore, discussions in NATO focused primarily on security issues and not on values, as it was often the case in Russia–EU negotiations. Also dialogue in the NRC, as insufficient as it might be, was better than US unilateralism.[125]

On the other hand, the more positive assessment of Russia's capabilities and a re-emphasis on geostrategic questions explain why the Russian leadership felt more optimistic about its ability to oppose a third wave of enlargement and why it was willing to take a firmer line on other questions which related to European security. In addition, the view that international relations became increasingly an arena also for the competition between value systems made Moscow especially concerned about potential NATO memberships of countries that the Russian leadership considered as those belonging to its new sphere of influence. The Russian leadership saw the revolutions in Georgia, the Ukraine, Kyrgyzstan, and Uzbekistan as a great danger to Russia, which necessitated a clear policy of deterrence. Yet, the pragmatic element of the foreign policy thinking explains why the Russian leadership did not fall back on the tactic of rhetorically threatening the NATO to enlarge, but why it instead targeted its opposition mainly against the accession candidates.

Finally, a more optimistic assessment of Russia's capabilities to provide for its own security explains why Moscow no longer indicated that it might join NATO as it did in 2000. Putin self-consciously argued that: 'the economic state of the country and the defence potential are such that our security from outside is guaranteed'.[126] Furthermore, joining NATO would have meant joining it on NATO's terms. Taking into account that Russia's leadership depicted Russia's identity as being unique, integration on Western terms was not desirable according to the Russian viewpoint.

In other words, while the lack of reciprocity to some extent explains why the Russian leadership changed its approach towards NATO, collective ideas play an important role in explaining the direction and extent of reorientation post 2004.

Conclusion

The analysis of Russia's approaches to the European post-Cold War security agenda points to four general observations. First, the foreign policy of post-Soviet Russia changed significantly from that of the Soviet Union. I agree with Baranovsky, who argues that the belief in a fundamental antagonism between East and West vanished and that some kind of partnership – be it submissive, cooperative, or competitive – was judged to be in Russia's interest.[127] This belief was reflected in the fact that Russia's leadership at no time conducted an aggressive or revisionist foreign policy and never followed the calls of nationalists or communists to act on the threat of redeploying troops to its Western borders to oppose NATO enlargement.

Second, the first hypothesis about the extent to which external constraints affected Russian foreign policy was confirmed in the cases of Russia's decisions to join the PfP programme and the NATO–Russia Founding Act. The fact that the Russian leadership took these decisions despite fierce domestic parliamentary opposition shows the overriding impact of external constraints in cases where those constraints were formidable.

Third, to explain change in the Russian leadership's approach towards NATO enlargement, we need to take into account collective ideas. To explain why Moscow took a more positive stance than 'necessary' towards NATO enlargement from 1992 to 1993/94, we need to take into account *liberal ideas*. Moscow's increasingly confrontational approach from 1993/94 to 2000 is only insufficiently understandable in terms of Realist power-maximizing behaviour. To explain the Russian leadership's assessment of NATO enlargement not only as a potential but as an imminent and major security threat and to explain the Russian leadership's desire to gain acknowledgement of Russia's great power status, we need to take into account the rise of *geopolitical Realist thinking*. To understand the timing and extent of policy reorientation from 2000/01 to 2004, we need to take into account *pragmatic geoeconomic Realism*. The pragmatism of this thinking made Moscow stop opposing developments it could not reasonably prevent. And the acknowledgement that Russia's status as a great power had to be earned to some extent explains why the Russian leadership decided to act in accordance with Western interests to foster Russia's economic integration. Finally, to explain the direction and extent of reorientation post 2004, we need to take into account *cultural geostrategic Realist thinking*. While still impacted by pragmatism, this set of collective ideas emphasized Russia's uniqueness, had a more optimistic assessment of Russia's capabilities, placed higher importance on geopolitical factors, and viewed international relations also as an arena for competition between value systems. In short, these cases support the hypothesis on the impact of collective ideas.

Fourth, the extent to which collective ideas mattered changed. There was less scope for the impact of collective ideas from 2000 to 2003/04. Russia's experience with NATO enlargement throughout the 1990s showed that it had very limited capabilities to prevent the process. With this realization and given Russia's limited number of reasonable foreign policy alternatives at that time, a continuation of the approach of opposing NATO enlargement was unlikely to be beneficial. Thus, the explanatory leverage of collective ideas in this period decreased. Post 2004, the impact of collective ideas, however, was higher again. While the lack of reciprocity pointed to a change in Russia's approach, to explain the direction and extent of reorientation, ideational factors play a significant role.

5
Russia's Responses to the Balkan Crises (1992–1999)

The crises in the Balkans, and in particular the conflicts in Bosnia and Kosovo, were formative for Russian foreign policy in the 1990s. They forced the Russian leadership into making crucial choices: What role was Russia to play in Europe? Did Moscow still regard the former Yugoslavia as Russia's special sphere of influence? Would Moscow sanction the interference of external actors in the internal affairs of a country? And more generally, how would Moscow use these conflicts to shape Russia's relations with the West?

The Russian leadership's responses to these questions have changed over time. In the period from 1992 to 1993/94, Moscow cooperated closely with the West, and there was a high degree of agreement between the two sides on both the nature of the Bosnian conflict and the question of how to address it. Then from 1994 to autumn 1995, the perceptions of the nature of the conflict and of the best methods to solve it increasingly diverged, escalating to a rhetorical clash between Russia and the West in August/September 1995. Yet surprisingly, despite this escalation, the Russian leadership cooperated closely with the West during the Dayton negotiations in the autumn of 1995 and in the implementation of the resulting arrangements.

A similar pattern of interaction characterized the country's approach towards the Kosovo conflict. From March 1998 to mid April 1999, the Russian and Western perceptions of the nature of the conflict and of strategies to address it increasingly drifted apart. Relations deteriorated when NATO decided to intervene militarily in March 1999. Yet starting in mid April 1999, the Russian leadership again began to cooperate with the West, finally even endorsing the Western terms of a settlement.

Consequently, this chapter seeks to answer four questions. First, why did the Russian leadership get involved in the Balkan conflicts despite the fact that involvement did not promise any obvious direct power or security gains? Second, how can we explain the Russian leadership's almost unqualified cooperative approach towards the West in the period from 1992 to 1993/94? Third, how can we explain the increasingly confrontational approaches towards the West from 1994 to September 1995 during the conflict in Bosnia and from March 1998 to mid April 1999 during the Kosovo conflict? And finally, how can we explain the Russian leadership's eventual close cooperation with the West in both cases, despite the preceding hostile rhetoric?

Analysts offer different explanations for the Russian leadership's behaviour during these conflicts. One group focuses primarily on why Russia's leadership cooperated closely with the West in autumn 1995 and in spring 1999 despite the preceding hostile rhetoric and argues that these instances of cooperation are best explained by Russia's weak relative power position and its financial dependence on the West.[1] In other words, in these two instances Russia's leadership simply had no choice but to cooperate if it did not want to loose Western support for the country's consolidation.

Yet if cooperation was the most prudential foreign policy strategy in these two instances, then why did Moscow conduct an increasingly confrontational foreign policy from 1994 to September 1995 during the conflict in Bosnia and from March 1998 to mid April 1999 during the conflict in Kosovo? Kubicek suggests that these instances of cautious balancing can be understood as attempts to reassert Russia's influence in the Balkans and to subordinate NATO to other international organizations.[2] From this point of view, Russia's cautious balancing behaviour is seen as an essentially prudential power-maximizing tactic.

One might ask, however, whether these attempts of balancing were actually power maximizing at all. During both conflicts, the Russian leadership's attempts to dilute pressure on the warring parties made an escalation of the situation on the ground more probable. As a result, Western intervention (even militarily and led by NATO), which was not in the Russian interest, became increasingly likely.

On the other side of the spectrum are scholars who argue that Russian diplomacy was not guided by any consistent set of priorities. Kremeniuk, for example, argues that Russian foreign policy was ad hoc and had no underlying strategy at all. He argues that the vacillations between partnership and confrontation show that 'Russia was not following a straight road of realism and a sober assessment of its aims. It rather progressed along a road of immediate responses to the situations'.[3] In other words, scholars such as Kremeniuk do not see any logic in Russian foreign policy.

In this chapter, I put forward a middle position. With regard to the first question of why Russia involved itself in the conflicts, I argue that while the crises did not pose imminent challenges to Russia's security or promise direct power gains, they posed significant indirect threats. Russia's involvement can therefore be explained in Realist terms. From the Realist perspective, Russia's leadership should have been interested in preventing the escalation of the conflicts so as to reduce the likelihood of Western military interventions justified on humanitarian grounds and led by NATO. Yet while the Russian leadership's interests can be explained in Realist terms, the Realist power-maximizing hypothesis is indeterminate for predicting what kind of approach would have been most effective in achieving this objective. On the second question of why the Russian leadership from 1992 to 1993/94 cooperated with the West almost without qualification, I argue that the Realist perspective cannot explain the extent of cooperation. Here we must consider the impact of *liberal ideas* on Russian foreign policy thinking. Furthermore, to explain the increasingly confrontational approaches in the periods 1994/95 and 1998/99, we need to take into account the impact of a *geopolitical* kind of *Realism* on the Russian leadership's foreign policy thinking. The Russian leadership's desire to establish Russia as a Eurasian great power and its belief that Moscow could influence the West by protesting against Western interventions are important factors explaining why the Russian leadership decided to cautiously balance against the West in these periods despite the fact that such an approach would increase the likelihood of military intervention. Finally, the Russian leadership's close cooperation with the West in the autumn of 1995 and in the spring of 1999 is best explained by external constraints. In both cases, the Russian leadership had to face the stark choice of either cooperating with the West or confronting it.

In short, while the analysis supports the Realist hypothesis on the impact of external factors on Russian foreign policy in the periods of autumn 1995 and spring 1999, it challenges the claim that when external constraints were not formidable, Russian foreign policy can best be understood in terms of a power-maximizing behaviour. Instead, I suggest that in cases where external constraints were not decisive, we need to take into account the impact of collective ideas. This finding supports my second hypothesis. The analysis implies that had the Russian leadership been less preoccupied with the desire to re-establish Russia as a Eurasian great power by conducting increasingly confrontational policies in the periods 1994/95 and 1998/99, it might have played a much more constructive role in the process of conflict resolution, which in

84 *Explaining Change in Russian Foreign Policy*

turn might have compelled the Serbs to give in more quickly and, as a result, might have made it unnecessary for Russia to conduct embarrassing and costly policy reversals. In other words, Russian foreign policy might have gained more by conducting itself in a less ambitious manner.

The chapter is divided into four major sections. First, I elaborate to what extent the *behavioural dimension* of Realism, with its emphasis on rational power-maximizing behaviour, can explain Russia's interests in the conflicts and how it responded to them. Second, I assess to what degree ideational factors need to be taken into account to explain the Russian leadership's approaches. Third, I show in what cases external constraints were the single most important factor explaining Russia's diplomacy. And finally, the conclusion summarizes the findings of this case study.

The indeterminacy of the Realist power-maximization hypothesis

The first question is why Moscow got involved in the Bosnian and Kosovo crises at all. From the Realist point of view, one might ask why Russia, or for that matter any other Western state, should have bothered about the Balkan crises at all. From a purely material point of view, neither the Bosnian Serbs' campaign for a Greater Serbia and desperate attempts of Bosnian Muslims to defend themselves against the Serbs and later the Bosnian Croats[4] nor the Kosovar Albanian campaign for greater autonomy[5] had a direct impact on Russia's power position or its security. Russia was linked to neither the Bosnian Serbs nor the Federal Republic of Yugoslavia (FRY) in any a strategic alliance. Thus, there was no Russian obligation to support either of the two parties. Furthermore, Bosnia and the FRY were far away from Russia's borders, so refugees from the conflict were unlikely to flee to Russia. The destabilization of the region might have constituted a problem for Russia, but it would have been of much greater concern for the South Eastern European and Western European states. Given that during the 1990s Russia had to face the difficult consequences of economic reforms, and that in 1998 it was confronted with its deepest financial crisis since the dissolution of the Soviet Union, it is surprising from a Realist point of view that Russia's leadership should have paid attention to these two crises at all.[6]

The Balkan crises represented, however, potential indirect threats to Russia's security in three ways. First, there was the danger that the escalation of these conflicts could trigger intervention by Western states on the basis of human rights concerns. If Western states and the international community came to regard a humanitarian crisis as a legitimate reason for intervention in the Bosnian and Kosovo cases, then this position could give them reason to intervene in some states of the Commonwealth of Independent States (CIS), which had major human rights problems, but which constituted Russia's traditional sphere of influence.[7] Thus, from the Realist point of view, Russia's leadership had an interest in preventing the setting of a precedent for such intervention. Second, the situation, particularly in Kosovo, where a Muslim population strove for greater autonomy or even independence, bore some resemblance to that in Chechnya. Thus, the Russian leadership's fear of separatism and disintegration within its own territory should have led to oppose any precedent that would provide international legitimacy for secession.[8] Third, Russia's leadership should have had a great interest in preventing NATO, in which it had no role, from interfering in a region it considered to belong to the Russian sphere of influence.[9]

What implications does this assessment of the indirect nature of threats have for Russian interests? Given Russia's difficult financial and economic situation throughout the 1990s, it seems reasonable to conclude that from the Realist point of view, Russia's leadership would be expected to focus on more pressing security concerns. However, to the extent that diplomatic resources were available, Realists would expect Russia's leadership to oppose an intervention led by NATO, which would legitimize intervention on humanitarian grounds and maybe even secession.

Given such defined Russian interests, how would Realists expect the Russian leadership to act to foster Russia's interests? The Western states' determination to intervene in these conflicts was mainly a response to the humanitarian situation on the ground. Potential bilateral levers that Russia's leadership could use to affect the situation on the ground included its political ties with the FRY, energy supplies, and debts. Multilaterally, Russia played an important role in the UN Security Council, the Contact Group,[10] and the OSCE. Realists expect Russia to behave like a rational power-maximizing actor. In the context of the Balkan crises, this expectation implies that the Russian leadership should have applied the most effective means to prevent the intervention of Western states. But what would have been the most effective means?

On the one hand, the Russian leadership could have closely cooperated with the Western states in order to put pressure on the Bosnian Serbs and on Serbian President Slobodan Milosevic and thus prevent the Western states from intervening.[11] The problem of such an approach was, however, that the Russian leadership needed to be cautious that the Western states would not rely too heavily on NATO and that its cooperation would not be taken for granted (this was a lesson learned from the flaws of the Gorbachevian New Thinking approach). Furthermore, there was the risk that by cooperating with the West, Russia would implicitly sanction interference in the internal affairs of a country if the Serbs proved to be too resistant to external pressure. On the other hand, the Russian leadership could have balanced against the Western states to try to increase its leverage and the price for its cooperation. Yet the danger of this approach was that siding with the Serbs might have led to an escalation of the situation on the ground, which would have made a Western intervention more likely.

Consequently, while both a policy of outright confrontation and a policy of almost unqualified cooperation with the West are unreasonable from the Realist point of view, the power-maximizing hypothesis fails to spell out what degree of cooperation would be most rational. This indeterminacy is the result of Realism's underdetermination of strategic assumptions. As a result, the next section takes into account collective ideas and tests whether they can explain the Russian leadership's responses to the crises.

Collective ideas and Russia's responses to the Balkan crises

Liberal thinking and Russia's almost unqualified cooperation from 1992 to 1993/94

The Bosnian crisis was to a large extent a consequence of the break-up of the Socialist Federal Republic of Yugoslavia. When the conflicts in Slovenia and Croatia came to an end, Bosnia and Herzegovina declared sovereignty in October 1991, and in February/March 1992, held a referendum to determine whether its citizens wanted to opt for a status outside the FRY – the successor to the Socialist Federal Republic of Yugoslavia. Two of the three major populations, that is, Bosnian Muslims and Bosnian Croats, overwhelmingly supported independence, but the Bosnian Serbs rejected it. They wanted Bosnia and Herzegovina to be part of a Greater Serbia, or at least to be divided into three independent states. When in April 1992 the European Community and the United States recognized the Bosnian government under the leadership of Alija Izetbegovic, the Bosnian Serbs set up a parallel government under the leadership of Radovan Karadzic and decided to divide the country by force. Because the Bosnian Serbs were able to maintain the weaponry of the former FRY army, they were disproportionally stronger, and by the end of 1992, they controlled 70 per cent of the territory. The conflict became even more complicated when the Bosnian Croats abandoned their alliance with the Bosnian Muslims against the Bosnian Serbs and launched their own landgrab. In their desperation, the Bosnian Muslims called upon the international community for help.

From 1992 to 1993/94, the Russian leadership's reaction to the conflict was characterized by almost unqualified cooperation with the West. Examples of this close cooperation in 1992 were the Russian leadership's support for UN Security Council Resolution 757 of May 1992, which imposed economic sanctions and tightened the arms embargo against the FRY;[12] Moscow's approval of the extension of the United Nations Protection Force (UNPROFOR) to Bosnia in September 1992 to deliver humanitarian aid;[13] and its backing of a no-fly zone for all military aircraft over Bosnia in October 1992.[14] Furthermore, Russia's leadership even agreed that NATO should police the no-fly zone as long as both the UN and NATO sanctioned the actual use of military force under the so-called dual-key command procedure. Such a Russian approach was not self-evident, since Moscow's strategy towards the other Balkan crises before 1992 was characterized by a reluctance to intervene and take sides.[15]

While Russian foreign policy in 1992 was marked by the absence of any independent foreign policy proposals, 1993 witnessed the first tentative attempts to develop a more independent approach. Increasingly, Russian officials blamed Croatia for the escalation of violence and demanded the extension of sanctions against it,[16] and Moscow objected to a US initiative to lift the arms embargo against Bosnian Muslims.[17] However, one should not see this increasing independence of Russian foreign policy as a reversal of Moscow's initial, almost unqualified cooperative foreign policy. Russia was not the only state that criticized Croatia's role in the conflict, and it was not alone in objecting to the lifting of sanctions against Bosnian Muslims.[18] Additionally, Moscow fully supported the Vance Owen Peace Plan,[19] supported the tightening of economic sanctions in April 1993 when the Bosnian Serbs failed to show their support for this proposal,[20] and seized the opportunity and impressed the Western states with a new four-point plan when the proposal failed in the spring of 1993.[21] These points were reflected in the 22 May 1993 13-point Joint Action Plan that was put forward by the United States, Russia, Great Britain, France, and Spain.[22] US Senator Richard Lugar commented on Russia's proactive foreign policy: 'Due to an almost total vacuum of American leadership, you have the Russians, of all people, doing the most active diplomacy. The reversal of roles is rather breathtaking.'[23] Although this assessment might be somewhat exaggerated, it supports the judgement that while Russian foreign policy became more independent, this new independence and activism was very much within the parameters of what the Western states regarded as a reasonable approach to the conflict. Thus, the period from 1992 to the end of 1993 can be characterized as a time of close cooperation between Russia and the West.

Realists would need to explain this almost unqualified cooperative stance either with formidable external constraints that 'forced' Russia's leadership to cooperate or show that close cooperation was a prudential power-maximizing strategy. Yet neither hypothesis is supported by evidence. With regard to the former argument, while the Western states wanted to do something for the Bosnian Muslims and blamed the Serbs for the escalation of the conflict, they disagreed on exactly what to do. This disunity implies that Russian decision-makers had scope for choice, and it is conceivable that the Russian leadership could have opted to do nothing (that is not to get involved in the conflict at all) or to more assertively defend Serb positions, as it would do later. Thus, external constraints were not formidable and cannot explain Russia's almost unqualified cooperative foreign policy.

But what about the Realist power-maximizing hypothesis? I have argued above that while the Realist power-maximization hypothesis is indeterminate with regard to strategies, a policy both of outright confrontation with the West and of almost unqualified cooperation seems unreasonable from the Realist point of view. Thus, what is striking about this period is the extent of Russian cooperation. Why did Moscow break with its pre-1992 stance in the Balkan conflict? Why was it willing to criticise the Yugoslav leadership despite the fact that former Yugoslavia was traditionally regarded as Russia's sphere of influence? Why did Moscow simply follow the Western lead?

The extent of cooperation can only be explained by taking into account the Russian leadership's foreign policy thinking in the period from 1992 to 1993/94. In the analysis of the evolution of the Russian leadership's foreign policy discourse in Chapter 3, I suggest that in this period, the Russian leadership's foreign policy thinking was dominated by *liberal ideas*. These ideas were heavily influenced by concerns to uphold human values, and they assumed that close cooperation with the West was not only in Russia's interests, but also natural. These ideas do not only correlate with Russia's approach to the Bosnian conflict, but are also reflected in the Russian leadership's rhetoric. The Russian leadership refused to view the conflict in terms of a geopolitical rivalry between Russia and the West. Instead, it viewed the conflict as a local one and blamed the Serbs.[24] Foreign Minister Kozyrev defended the May 1992 tightening of sanctions against the FRY by arguing that Belgrade had 'brought upon itself the United Nations sanctions by failing to heed the demands of the international community'.[25] After Russia decided to support a tightening of sanctions against the Serbs in April 1993, Russian President Boris Yeltsin similarly argued: 'The Russian Federation will not protect those [the Serbs] who set themselves in opposition to the world community.'[26] Furthermore, the idea that close cooperation was the best means to foster Russian interests was reflected in Kozyrev's statement that 'Russia must not go back to a policy of obstruction'.[27]

By taking into account the impact of collective ideas, we can also explain why the Russian leadership used the threat of the rise of revisionist forces as a lever to increase its bargaining power vis-à-vis the West. A good example of the effectiveness of this threat was the US decision to postpone a UN Security Council vote on harsher sanctions against Serbia in April 1993. At that time Yeltsin was under domestic pressure since he needed to win a referendum on his presidency and his policies. He was afraid that a condemnation of the Serbs would play into the hands of communist and nationalist forces. Therefore he warned that 'the Serbs are communists [. . .] and they're working with our communists who are at my throat!'[28] As a result, the UN Security Council agreed to postpone the vote.[29]

Thus, both Russian foreign policy action and rhetoric reveal the extent to which Russian foreign policy was shaped by *liberal ideas* and show that these ideas are important to explaining Russia's willingness to cooperate with the West.

The impact of the Russian leadership's foreign policy thinking was even stronger than domestic politics. In early 1992, the Supreme Soviet already had begun to criticise the Russian leadership's approach to the Bosnian crisis. It demanded that the Russian leadership refuse to support UN resolutions that blamed only the Serbian side[30] and argued that sanctions had either to be extended to Croatia[31] or eased for the FRY.[32] To underscore these demands, members of the Supreme Soviet visited Serbia to meet with the leaders of Serbia and the FRY and with Bosnian Serb leader Karadzic.[33] Thus, one can conclude that while domestic political pressure might have played a role in the timing of some decisions, overall the Russian leadership pursued a foreign policy based on *liberal ideas*, rather than one driven by domestic political pressures.

90 Explaining Change in Russian Foreign Policy

The rise of geopolitical Realism and Russia's increasingly confrontational approaches in 1993/94–1995 and 1998/99

Although Russia's approach from 1994 to September 1995 never became anti-Western and Moscow never challenged the West in a confrontational manner, in this period, Russia's foreign policy became increasingly independent and embraced a more assertive national agenda, laying more emphasis on the protection of Serb interests and rejecting NATO's threat of the use of force and the actual use of force. A similar pattern of behaviour also characterized Moscow's approach during the Kosovo crisis from March 1998 to mid April 1999. The following two sections explain why the Russian leadership chose this more independent and assertive foreign policy in these two periods.

Russia's approach to the Bosnian conflict from January 1994 to September 1995

Differences in the Russian leadership's approach to the Bosnian conflict post 1993 can be detected by comparing Moscow's foreign policy prior and post 1993 with regard to three dimensions: the question of sanctions, the Russian leadership's diplomatic initiatives, and its attitude to the use of force. With regard to sanctions, there was already a slight shift in Moscow's approach in 1993. Then the Russian leadership began to demand a more equal application of sanctions also against Croatia and objected to the lifting of sanctions against the Bosnian Muslims. Yet Moscow put forth this new approach reluctantly, and the Russian leadership was careful that its demands and objections were raised in concert with other Western states. This caution changed in the period from 1994 to September 1995 when Russia's leadership vehemently demanded that sanctions against the FRY be eased.[34] Since the Western powers assumed that Bosnian Serb forces were supported by the FRY and these forces were making substantial territorial gains, they perceived the demand to ease sanctions against Belgrade as a sign that Russia had abandoned its neutral role in the conflict and was increasingly siding with the Serbs.

With regard to diplomatic initiatives and the use of force, Russia's position increasingly contradicted the Western one. When on 5 February 1994 a mortar shell killed 68 and wounded more than 200 people in Sarajevo, NATO issued an ultimatum to all forces fighting within 20 kilometres of Sarajevo to hand over their heavy weapons within ten days and threatened to subject all weapons found after the deadline to NATO air strikes. Russia's leadership reacted to this ultimatum with reservations. While the Russian Foreign Ministry condemned those guilty of this atrocity and supported the demand that heavy weapons be withdrawn, it criticized the means used to achieve this end (ultimatum backed by force). Foreign Minister Kozyrev urged the Western states to react rationally and cautiously and warned that failing to do so might turn this incident into a repetition of Sarajevo in 1914.[35] A similar concern was reiterated two months later. When in April 1994 NATO planes attacked Serb positions around the UN safe-area Gorazde[36] in response to an assault by Serb forces, the Russian Foreign Ministry argued again that these attacks were counterproductive.[37]

Excluded from the decision-making process in NATO and understanding that Russia would not be able to convince the Western powers to nullify the February 1994 ultimatum, Moscow decided to initiate an independent mission with regard to the Sarajevo crisis. Russian Special Envoy Vitaliy Churkin delivered to Serb President Milosevic and Bosnian Serb leader Karadzic a proposal from Yeltsin that the Bosnian Serbs withdraw their heavy weapons to positions 20 kilometres from Sarajevo within the time limit set by NATO, while 400 Russian peacekeepers were transferred to Sarajevo.[38] Both leaders accepted this proposal. In the end, the heavy weapons were withdrawn and the February crisis was resolved without the use of force. While it is difficult to assess whether NATO's threat of the use of force was the decisive factor or whether Russia's diplomatic intervention convinced the Bosnian Serbs to withdraw, this event was celebrated in Russia as an example of a successful independent Russian foreign policy. Yeltsin argued in February 1994 that 'unlike the NATO bloc, which gave the Serbs an ultimatum, Russia had asked the Serbs to withdraw their heavy weapons [. . .], this was in psychological terms a subtly calculated move that worked.'[39] Similarly, Churkin argued that the crisis was solved because firstly, the 'phrase "a request from Russia," had a powerful psychological effect [. . .]. Secondly, the letter was signed by the Russian president'.[40]

For Yeltsin, this proactive foreign policy was an example of how Russian foreign policy could combine a focus on Russia's distinct national interests with the aim of gaining recognition of Russia's great power position. He argued: 'Up to now, our foreign policy has been lacking in initiative and creativity. Russia's brilliant peacekeeping initiative in the Bosnian conflict is, unfortunately, only an exception so far. [. . .] We are fond of repeating that [Russia] is a great country. And that is indeed the case. So then, in our foreign-policy thinking let us always meet this high standard.'[41]

Yet as Russia's leadership would soon discover, its leverage was limited, and the impact of Churkin's enumerated 'psychological effect' proved to be weak. When Churkin negotiated a ceasefire between Serb and Muslim forces at Gorazde in April 1994, Russian diplomacy celebrated it as another success, only to find out shortly thereafter that the Bosnian Serbs had not followed through. As a result, the Russian leadership finally lifted its objections to a second round of NATO air strikes, which then seem to have convinced the Bosnian Serbs to back down. Expressing his disappointment, Churkin argued: 'The Bosnian Serbs must understand that in Russia they are dealing with a great power, not a banana republic. Russia must decide whether a group of extremists can be allowed to use a great country's policy to achieve its own aims. Our answer is unequivocal: "never".'[42]

While the rest of the year 1994 witnessed some instances of cooperation with the West – Russia, for example, supported the July 1994 peace proposal, which gave 51 per cent of Bosnia to the new Muslim–Croat Federation and 49 per cent to the Bosnian Serbs[43] – overall Moscow continued to defend Serb interests and tried to convince the Western leaders to distinguish more carefully between Milosevic and Karadzic. Foreign Minister Kozyrev went so far as to describe Milosevic as the 'leader of the peace party'.[44]

The most severe test of Russia's relations with the West during the Bosnian crisis arose, however, in the summer of 1995, when NATO bombed targets and threatened 'unprecedented levels' of air strikes in response to Bosnian Serb attacks on the UN safe-areas of Gorazde, Tuzla, Bihac, and Sarajevo.[45] At first, Russia's response was restrained. In late May 1995, Yeltsin defended air strikes and argued that they had to be seen as a reaction to the Bosnian Serbs' unwillingness to cease military action in the safe areas.[46] Furthermore, in June 1995 Russia abstained from a UN Security Council vote that sanctioned the creation and deployment of a NATO Rapid Reaction Force to better protect UN peacekeepers, indirectly backing the NATO mission.[47] In July 1995, however, Russia's foreign policy became more reserved. When NATO used air strikes to repel the Bosnian Serbs offensive around Sarajevo, Srebrenica, and Zepa, the Russian foreign ministry characterized them as 'senseless',[48] and Defence Minister Grachev condemned them as 'madness'. He argued that political methods of influencing the Bosnian Serbs were still 'far from exhausted'.[49] When the Croatian forces took advantage of the Bosnian Serbs' preoccupation with NATO and conquered the Krajina in early August 1995, Russia's relations with the West deteriorated. Foreign Minister Kozyrev accused the West of complicity in the Croatian attack.[50] The situation escalated fully at the end of August 1995, when NATO responded to a Sarajevo marketplace massacre with air strikes of unprecedented magnitude without prior consultations with Russia. Moscow denounced the air strikes as proof of NATO's partiality in the conflict,[51] and the Russian government even argued that the air strikes 'called into question the survival of the current generation of Bosnian Serbs, who are in effect threatened with genocide'.[52]

In other words, the Russian leadership's behaviour throughout 1994, especially its support for the July 1994 peace proposal, reveals that on the one hand the Russian leadership did not want to conduct a foreign policy of outright confrontation with the West. On the other hand, its approaches in February and April 1994 and during the summer of 1995 indicate that Russia's and the West's perception of the nature of the conflict and the means to solve it significantly diverged. Thus, the question is how can we best explain this divergence?

One explanation is that it was not Russia's approach that changed, but the approach of the Western states.[53] This point is especially valid with regard to the United States. President Bill Clinton had to face a Republican-dominated Congress that criticized the administration's passivity in this conflict.[54] This pressure was exaggerated by the start of campaign for the November elections, and Clinton feared that he would be discredited as a weak president who did nothing to stop the humanitarian crisis in Bosnia.[55] Thus, he was forced to act in Bosnia. Dobbs argues that '[a]s the crisis deepened, a Pax Americana came to be seen as the least unpalatable option'.[56] This change in priorities led to the nomination of Richard Holbrooke as a special envoy. In other words, the increasing discrepancy between the Russian and the Western approaches to the conflict can partly be explained by a significant priority change in the West, most importantly in the United States.

But even if it were the case that the new US course represented the more drastic departure from a former consensus, why did the Russian leadership not follow this change as most Western European states? Why did it instead decided to carefully oppose the West?

Collective ideas need to be taken into account to explain Russia's decision to take a defiant stance. I argue in Chapter 3 that from 1993/94 to 1996, *geopolitical Realism* shaped the foreign policy thinking. This foreign policy thinking conceived the nature of international relations as competitive, implying that Russia had to define its interests independently and defend them. Furthermore, this thinking was affected by great power nostalgia and damaged pride. While in the previous period the leadership had seen Russia as a great but *normal* power, it now perceived Russia as a Eurasian great power that had a right to claim spheres of influence, that needed to be recognized internationally as a major great power, and that deserved to be involved in international decision-making. If one takes into account these collective ideas, it becomes understandable why the Russian leadership increasingly sided with the Serbs. It was not so much that Moscow wanted to increase Russia's material power position – as Realists would argue – but that Russia's leadership used this conflict to demonstrate and re-establish Russia's independence and status as a great power.

The impact of damaged pride and the desire to gain great power status recognition can be illustrated, for example, by Moscow's concerns of being excluded from the Western decision-making processes in February and April 1994. In fact, it seems that both in February and April, Russia's leadership was more concerned about the fact that Russia was not involved in the processes that led to the issuing of ultimata than it was about the substance of these ultimata. With regard to the February 1994 threat to subject all weapons found within 20 kilometres of Sarajevo to NATO air strikes, Russia's leadership argued that the North Atlantic Council (NAC) was not the right forum to issue such far-reaching threats, and that this decision should have been left to the UN Security Council.[57] Yeltsin argued on 15 February 1994: 'We won't allow this problem to be resolved without Russia's participation.'[58] And two months later during the April 1994 crisis, Yeltsin complained: 'I have insisted and continue to insist that such questions as the bombing of Serbian positions must not be decided without preliminary consultations between the United States and Russia.'[59] Kozyrev argued that trying 'to make such decisions without Russia is a big mistake and a big risk'.[60] Thus, the real problem for Russia's leadership seems to have been the lack of Western respect for Russia's great power status and its involvement. This was clearly expressed by Deputy Prime Minister Sergei Shakhrai who argued that the 'bombing of Serbian positions [. . .] is a slap in the face of *Russian prestige*'.[61]

In addition to explaining why the Russian approach became increasingly confrontational, taking into account the impact of *liberal ideas* on the thinking on strategy helps to explain the puzzle of why Russian diplomacy continued to use the threat that if the West did not pay more attention to Russia's interests, this neglect would foster the rise of nationalist and communist forces in Russia. In response to the demands of the leader of the Liberal Democratic Party of Russia (LDPR) Zhirinovsky, who had threatened that if Foreign Minister Kozyrev did not change Russia's foreign policy and support the Serbian side, he would be ousted, Kozyrev warned, 'certain political forces are seeking to draw Russia into a global catastrophe'.[62] And later in 1994, he argued that '[t]he opposition has succeeded in exaggerating this feeling toward the Serbs, toward Belgrade. Now, whatever the reason is, it is a fact of life that a considerable part of Russian public opinion believes that Serbs are the closest people to Russia in the Balkans, and they have to be protected. We have to take that into account'.[63] While it is difficult to say whether the rise to power of nationalists and communists was a real threat at that time, the Russian leadership used the threat as an explicit warning with regard to the Western states to take Russia seriously and involve it.

In summary, the analysis of Russia's behaviour from 1994 to 1995 suggests that only by taking into account *geopolitical Realist ideas* can we explain the increasingly confrontational approach of the Russian leadership. This leads to the next question of whether collective ideas also play an important role in explaining Russia's approach to the Kosovo conflict from March 1998 to mid April 1999.

Russia's approach to the Kosovo conflict from March 1998 to mid April 1999

When the Socialist Federal Republic of Yugoslavia disintegrated in the early 1990s, a movement within Kosovo for greater autonomy or even independence gained momentum. One major reason for the Kosovar Albanian discontent was Serb President Milosevic's 1989 decision to rescind most of Kosovo's former autonomy. This policy change denied the Kosovar Albanians the special status for the territory that they had enjoyed since the adoption of the 1974 constitution. As a result, the Kosovar Albanians established parallel state structures and appealed to Western states for support. The West missed a unique opportunity to deal with this issue during the Dayton negotiations of November 1995.[64] Having failed to gain Western support, the Kosovo Liberation Army (KLA) was formed and increasingly used coercive means to foster its aim of regaining autonomy or even independence by attacking Serb police forces in Kosovo. This campaign led to an escalation of violence. The first peak of the crisis was reached in February/March 1998 when Serb police forces killed over 60 Kosovar Albanians in Srbica and other villages in the Drenica Valley region as an attempt to counter 'terrorist attacks'. The victims included at least 11 children and 23 women.[65]

The international community reacted hesitantly. On 9 March 1998, the Contact Group unanimously condemned Serbia's disproportional use of force against the Kosovar Albanians and urged Milosevic to cease all action by Serb security forces against the civilian population, to withdraw Serb special police forces from the territory, to allow an OSCE mission to Kosovo, and to begin a large-scale constructive dialogue with the Kosovar Albanians. Yet, while the Contact Group agreed to make these demands, it failed to agree on measures to enforce them. On the one hand, the Russian leadership supported an embargo on arms deliveries to Belgrade and a ban on the sale of special police equipment. On the other hand, it neither agreed on the question of a moratorium on government guarantees for investors in the Yugoslav economy nor on the issue of denying entry visas to Yugoslav officials.[66] These reservations were partly shared by Italy and France, who also argued that too much pressure would have a counterproductive impact on Belgrade's willingness to engage in dialogue with the Kosovar Albanians.[67] Since the United States and Britain demanded much tougher sanctions, the states in question reached compromises, such as the UN Security Council Resolution 1160 of 31 March 1998.[68]

This pattern of basic agreement of the international community with regard to objectives and disagreement with regard to means, played into Milosevic's hands. The consequence was that the KLA became more determined to use coercive means to promote its objectives and to gain international attention. It was quite successful in doing so. In May 1998 KLA fighters were able to win ground in large areas in central Kosovo, which made Serb forces increase their pressure on the Kosovar Albanians.[69] The deteriorating situation in Kosovo forced the Western states to consider additional measures. At a NATO defence ministers' meeting on 11 June 1998, the ministers directed NATO military authorities to undertake an air exercise in Albania and Macedonia with the aim of demonstrating NATO's capability to project power rapidly into the region, and they asked them to develop a full range of military options to support the resolution of the conflict.[70] On 15 June 1998, NATO started its air exercise *Operation Determined Falcon*.[71]

Moscow reacted with disappointment to the air exercise because it had not been informed about it in advance.[72] Such disregard was seen as a violation of the principles of the NATO–Russia Founding Act of 1997. As a consequence, Yeltsin invited Milosevic to Moscow. Both statesmen reaffirmed the need for the preservation of the territorial integrity of the FRY and denounced any forms of terrorism, separatism, and armed actions against civilians. Furthermore, Milosevic pledged that he was willing to solve the problem with 'political methods on the basis of the equality of all citizens and ethnic communities in Kosovo' and said that a form of autonomy should be discussed with the Kosovar Albanians.[73] The outcome of this talk was celebrated in Moscow as a success of Russia's negotiation strategy over the Western use of force.[74]

After NATO's air exercise and the Yeltsin–Milosevic talks, Serb police forces were restrained during June and July 1998. The KLA used this situation to fight back Serb policy and paramilitary forces, so that by mid July 1998, it had claimed as much as 40 per cent of Kosovo. As a result, in late July 1998 Serb military, paramilitary, and interior police forces launched a major offensive that forced 100,000 Kosovar Albanians to flee their homes in August alone. By September 1998, 250,000 Kosovar Albanians were internally displaced or refugees, and the UN Security Council passed Resolution 1199 that repeated the demands of a cessation of attacks against civilians, withdrawal of security forces, and the start of a meaningful dialogue with the Kosovar Albanians with international involvement.[75] The resolution, however, once again lacked an enforcement mechanism due to Russia's opposition.[76]

Frustrated by the UN Security Council's inability to impose more decisive sanctions and threats, the Western states increased their pressure by using NATO. The NAC approved the issuing of an *activation warning* (ACTWARN).[77] The ACTWARN was not a decision to use force, but it enabled the alliance to prepare for such a decision in short order. Russia's leadership voiced objections to this decision and tried to reactivate the roles of the Contact Group and of the OSCE.

Since the Western states were not united on what legal basis would justify the use of force, they decided to opt for yet another diplomatic attempt to solve the crisis. In October 1998, Holbrooke was sent to Belgrade to negotiate. Should Milosevic not agree to the Western demands, he threatened, the West would consider the use of force. Since this mission opened a new door for a peaceful resolution, Moscow supported the initiative by sending a high-level delegation to Belgrade to put additional pressure on Milosevic to agree to this proposal.[78] An agreement was finally reached on 15/16 October 1998 and UN Security Council Resolution 1203 of 24 October 1998 called on both sides to comply with the Holbrooke–Milosevic agreement and established the OSCE Kosovo Verification Mission.[79] While the Western states threatened to use force in the case of Belgrade's non-compliance, Moscow claimed credit for the success of Holbrooke's mission because it had sent the high-level delegation. Lynch argues, '[i]n this, Russia sought to offset NATO's claims that the threat of imminent air strikes had secured Belgrade's agreement'.[80]

This agreement had a positive impact on the Kosovar Albanians' situation. By the end of November 1998, almost all displaced persons inside Kosovo had either returned to their villages or had found temporary shelter elsewhere, and humanitarian agencies and other international organizations were granted access to Kosovo.

This easing of the tension did not, however, last very long. On 15 January 1999 in Racak, Serb forces killed 45 Kosovar Albanians, including women, children and elderly persons, and destroyed parts of the village. The head of the OSCE mission William Walker termed the massacre 'an unspeakable atrocity' that constituted 'a crime against humanity'.[81] Racak provoked a new round of more decisive international negotiations. The Contact Group decided on a meeting on 29 January 1999 that representatives of the FRY, the Serb government, and the Kosovar Albanians had to meet in Rambouillet to begin negotiations with the direct involvement of the Contact Group, and insisted that an agreement must contain substantial autonomy for Kosovo while maintaining Kosovo in the FRY and thus safeguarding the FRY's territorial integrity.[82]

The outcome of the negotiations in Rambouillet was disappointing. By the end of the first Rambouillet round in February, the Serb side had agreed to the fundamentals of the political deal. Yet it rejected its implementation by a 28,000 strong NATO force. As a consequence, no agreement between the parties was reached, and even the Kosovar Albanians did not sign the accords. When the negotiations were resumed on 15 March 1999, the Kosovar Albanian delegation signed the Rambouillet Accords under Western pressure, but Belgrade refused to do so with the result that the negotiations reached a deadlock.[83]

Although the Russian leadership agreed to the basic terms of the Rambouillet Accords, its contributions to the talks were of little help and the Russian delegation did not put pressure on the Yugoslav representatives. Quite to the contrary, Russian diplomats decreased pressure on Belgrade by arguing that only a provisional agreement would be possible at that point, and they constantly questioned the legitimacy of the Kosovar delegation by raising the issue of the terrorist background of KLA representatives.[84]

After the failure of the Rambouillet negotiations, the Western states faced a dilemma: diplomatic pressure and observer missions had proven to be inefficient. A comprehensive embargo might have been an effective means, but without the support of the Russian leadership, such an embargo could not work. Thus, the Western states thought that they had only one last and most aggressive option left if they did not want to lose credibility: the application of military force. Consequently, on 24 March 1999 NATO unleashed a set of air strikes against the FRY without Russia's consent or consultation and without a UN Security Council Resolution explicitly authorizing the attacks. President Clinton stated that the alliance's objective was to 'demonstrate the seriousness of

NATO's purpose so that the Serbian leaders understand the imperative of reversing course'.[85]

The initial rhetorical reaction of Russia's officials was harsh. On 24 March, at an emergency meeting of the UN Security Council shortly after bombs began to fall, the Russian UN Ambassador Sergei Lavrov demanded an immediate cessation of 'this unacceptable aggression'.[86] President Yeltsin condemned NATO military action and warned that 'Russia has a number of extreme measures in store, but we [the Russian government] decided not to use them so far'.[87] In addition to this, on 24 March 1999, Prime Minster Primakov, en route to Washington to negotiate IMF financial assistance, turned his plane around; Russia's leadership recalled its chief military representative from NATO's European military headquarters, expelled NATO representatives from Moscow, ended all cooperation with NATO's Partnership for Peace programme, and deployed a surveillance ship to the Ionian Sea.[88] Finally, Russian diplomats tried to organize international opposition against NATO's air operation. Two days after the bombing campaign started, Russia introduced a draft UN resolution, co-sponsored by non-Security Council member states Belarus and India, calling for a halt to NATO attacks and a resumption of negotiations. In the vote, China and Namibia supported the motion, but the other 12 member states opposed it. The critical point for Russian diplomacy was that not only Western states turned down the motion, 'non-aligned' states such as Argentina, Bahrain, Brazil, Gabon, Gambia, and Malaysia did so as well.[89] Adam Roberts argues that this vote provided an indirect international legitimization of NATO's actions.[90]

Yet despite the heated rhetoric and atmosphere and against the demands of some Russian nationalists, Russia's leadership reacted cautiously. It did not break off relations with the West fully, it did not send troops to Serbia, and it did not provide Serbia with military equipment. In this sense, Moscow's foreign policy action was more cautious and restrained than its rhetoric.

In short, the conflict resolution from March 1998 to March 1999 was characterized by a growing gap between Russia's and the West's perceptions of the nature of the crisis and of adequate means to respond. For the Western states, the humanitarian disaster was alarming. The deteriorating situation in Kosovo in late 1998 and early 1999 made them conclude that diplomatic pressure or economic sanctions would not be sufficient to change Belgrade's policy, especially if Russia's leadership did not support them. As a result, they concluded that both sides needed to be forced to the negotiation table and that an agreement needed to be enforced. Russia's leadership, on the other hand, maintained that the

West should not use force and that the UN and the Contact Group should deal with the conflict. Yet since these two bodies were not able to find a common denominator, the warring parties used the opportunity to create facts on the ground.

Consequently, if one assumes that from the Realist perspective the Russian leadership's major concern should have been to prevent the escalation of the conflict so as to avoid a military intervention led by NATO, then the puzzle is why Russia's leadership did not put more pressure on Milosevic. Though Russia's leverage on Belgrade was limited and even a more constructive Russian policy might not have prevented the use of force, Russian pressure might have forced Milosevic to capitulate earlier.[91]

Different answers have been offered to explain this puzzle. First, Baev argues that an ambitious and non-cooperative stance gave Russia most leverage.[92] Since NATO lacked a UN mandate for military action and since the Russian and Chinese leaderships were reluctant to agree to coercive means, the West would have needed to pay high side-payments for agreements from these two countries. From this perspective, the Russian leadership behaved as if it were a Realist power-maximizing actor.

Yet how realistic was the notion that Moscow could extract Western concessions by taking a defiant stance? The Western response to the escalation of the conflict in autumn 1998 and its determination in Rambouillet showed that the Western states were more determined than ever not to fail again in Yugoslavia. And, as Goldgeier and McFaul emphasized in October 1998, there were strong indications that 'NATO would act no matter what the Russians might say'.[93] Furthermore, did not Russia's Bosnian experience show that it should not overestimate its leverage? Despite Moscow's opposition to the use of force, NATO unleashed air strikes in the summer of 1995. As a result of this campaign, the Russian leadership was marginalized as a diplomatic and military factor.[94] Thus, while a confrontational stance potentially increased Russia's leverage, the dangers of overplaying this card were considerable. This ambiguity casts doubt on the claim that the Russian leadership's ambitious approach can primarily be explained in terms of a power-maximization strategy.

A second explanation for the Russian leadership's unproductive behaviour is that by putting pressure on Belgrade, Moscow would have indirectly acknowledged that the Kosovar Albanians had a legitimate claim to greater autonomy. This step, in turn, might have undermined Russia's own policy with regard to Chechnya. US Secretary of State Madeleine Albright argues: 'My own feeling was that Russia's position was shaped less by solidarity with their fellow Slavs than by the possibility that international action there would serve as a precedent for outside intervention in Russia, where Chechen separatists regularly clashed with the arms.'[95] And US Deputy Secretary of State Strobe Talbott paraphrases Russian Foreign Minister Ivanov, who explained in a phone conversation with Albright in winter 1998: 'Madeleine, don't you understand we have many Kosovos in Russia.'[96]

Yet this argument does not seem conclusive, either. First, even the Russian leadership declared that greater autonomy was also what they envisioned for Kosovo.[97] Second, if the Russian leadership worked against a solution on the basis of greater autonomy, it ran the risk that the situation would escalate further and that this deterioration of the situation would make a NATO-led military intervention necessary. This intervention might have resulted in secession – an outcome far more undesirable from the Russian perspective than that of greater autonomy. The Independent International Commission on Kosovo concludes that Russia's 'rigid commitment to veto any enforcement action was the major factor forcing NATO into an action without mandate'.[98] Such a military intervention, with the potential result of secession, must have clearly been the worst-case scenario for Russia's leadership. Thus, the real question for Russian policymakers was not whether they liked the idea of granting the Kosovar Albanians greater autonomy, but rather how they could prevent Western military intervention. And it seems that they could only do so by putting pressure on Milosevic bilaterally and/or by using the UN, the Contact Group, and the OSCE as means. Russia's leadership, however, chose obstructionism. Thus, the argument that Moscow might have been afraid of indirectly legitimizing outside interference in an internal affair by cooperating with the West does not seem convincing.

A third explanation combines the arguments that the Russian leadership might have simply exaggerated its leverage on Western foreign policy and that it might have thought that even if NATO intervened militarily, the political ramifications for Russia would be limited. US Ambassador to Russia James Collins supports the former argument. He argues that Moscow's inability to anticipate the Western determination to act on behalf of the Kosovar Albanians constituted a significant intelligence failure.[99] And with regard to the latter assumption, US Envoy to Kosovo James Dobbins argues that in fact most Western leaders thought that the military conflict would be short – similar to the NATO military campaign in Bosnia.[100]

How convincing is this explanation? With regard to the former argument about intelligence failure, we might ask how the Russian leadership could not have realized that the Western states were increasingly determined to act, since Western leaders communicated this intention repeatedly through various channels to the Russian leadership.[101] And with regard to the latter argument, while it is likely that the Russian leadership did not think that the military intervention would take long, it is still to ask why it preferred even a short military intervention to a diplomatic solution. In short, this explanation is also unconvincing.

Fourth, one might argue that Russia's leadership did all that it could, but that Milosevic was too resistant. It is true that bilateral diplomatic pressure failed to affect Milosevic. The June Yeltsin–Milosevic meeting and the following escalation of the conflict in the autumn of 1998 is a good example of Milosevic's stubbornness.[102] Yet one might ask why Russian diplomacy did not use a potentially stronger lever, such as that of energy supplies. In the second half of 1998, Russian companies made $211 million on oil and gas trade with Yugoslavia,[103] and Serbia was in debt to Gazprom for $325 million.[104] Since Gazprom was highly intertwined with the Russian state, it would have been a powerful tool to put pressure on Milosevic.[105] The contention that Moscow would have been able to apply such sanctions is supported by the fact that in the summer of 2000, Russia stopped the delivery of gas when Serbia's debts reached the $400 million mark.[106] There is, however, no evidence that Russia's leadership threatened to use energy supply as a lever in 1998/99. Thus, it is striking that the Russian leadership was so reluctant to support the Western countries despite the fact that Moscow had a potentially strong economic lever.

How are we to explain this stance? In other words, how are we to explain the fact that Moscow defended Belgrade's point of view even though from the Realist perspective, 'standing up for Milosevic is damaging both to Russian national interest abroad and at home. [. . .] it neither helps with Russia's near-term problems nor makes or breaks Russia as a Great Power' as Goldgeier and McFaul have argued?[107] And, as Russian Foreign Minister Ivanov stated, if Russia wanted to 'prevent a precedent to be set in which one or another military potential is used in crisis situation without the consent of the UN Security Council',[108] why did it choose to obstruct the political conflict resolution in 1998/99?

I suggest that to explain this puzzle, we need to take into account collective ideas. Similarly, as in the period from 1994 to September 1995, here again the Russian foreign policy thinking was shaped by *geopolitical Realism*. This set of collective ideas depicted international relations as an arena where states compete for spheres of influence in a geopolitical contest. Furthermore, the United States was perceived as the major threat to international peace and stability due to its unilateral policies. At that time the thinking on strategy was based on the strategic assumption that the best means to counter these unipolar tendencies was to cautiously balance against them. This *geopolitical thinking* was present not only in foreign policy action, but also in the rhetoric during the time of the Kosovo crisis. Not only did conservatives and nationalists call Milosevic a strategic partner,[109] but even Foreign Minister Ivanov stated in October 1998 that the Balkans 'represent a zone of special interest'[110] for Russia. In a discussion with US Deputy Secretary of State Talbott, he even referred to the domino theory, which was used during the Cold War, when he warned that the conflict in Yugoslavia could lead to a new world war.[111] This thinking, in terms of spheres of interests and in zero-sum categories, stands in stark contrast to the rejection of such attitudes in the years 1992 to 1993/94.

Furthermore, consistent with the view that the United States posed the greatest threat to international peace and stability, Ivanov claimed that the rationale behind NATO's behaviour was obvious: to enforce US political, military, and economic dictates and to strengthen a unipolar world where Washington could 'control everybody's fates'.[112] The Russian leadership was especially concerned about NATO's discussions of a strategic concept that widened its responsibility to areas beyond Europe and the North Atlantic and which was adopted in April 1999.[113] Consequently, Ivanov concluded that the Western states would use the 'myth of a humanitarian catastrophe'[114] to justify their actions and warned that all states that did not follow the US lead could be threatened in the future.[115] In his *Midnight Diaries*, written a year after the Kosovo crisis, Yeltsin continued to argue that the Kosovo conflict was not simply a local conflict, but a Western, and especially US, attempt to impose its will on a nation under the cover of a humanitarian intervention. He argues: 'If we accept such rules of the game, we risk creating a global crisis of democratic values. Soon the force of only one country or one group of countries will decide everything in the world. Instead of the mentality of a world peacemaker, we are seeing the psychology of a world enforcer and a dictator country.'[116] Such an overemphasis on the United States is striking, given that major European states were members of the Contact Group and that NATO, rather than a unilateral United States or a coalition of the willing, intervened in the conflict.

Russian diplomat Oleg Levitin supports the assessment that *geopolitical thinking* impacted Russian foreign policy. He argues that Primakov was a 'prisoner to imperial nostalgia' and 'beguiled' by the concept of multipolarity in international relations.[117] As a result, Russia's leadership gave a high value to the preservation of a close relationship with Milosevic in order to maintain its role as a great and independent power in the Balkans. This perspective was so strong that it created a taboo in Moscow about reassessing whether Russia's strategy really promoted the country's national interest, and it led Russian diplomacy to obstruct the Western states rather than actively work with them towards a solution to the conflict. The statement of Boris Mayorsky, Russia's chief mediator in the Rambouillet talks, that 'in general we never tried to persuade anyone to sign the document',[118] confirms Levitin's view.

In addition, there was also a shift in the Russian leadership's thinking on strategy during this period. While the above discussion has shown that during the years 1994 and 1995, the Russian leadership used the *democratic argument* to increase its leverage, from 1996 to 1999, the Russian leadership used the *geopolitical argument* during the Kosovo conflict. This change in strategy correlates with the change in the leadership's thinking on strategy from *liberal ideas* to *dogmatic geopolitical* ones. In March 1999, Foreign Minister Ivanov argued that Europe had not been as close to such a serious rift since 1945,[119] and Defence Minister Sergeyev warned similarly that the Kosovo conflict could lead to another 'cold war'.[120]

This analysis does not suggest that the Russian leadership was pleased about the crisis or that it was glad that Milosevic 'offered' Moscow an opportunity to demonstrate Russia's great power attributes by defending a multipolar world. Yeltsin often tried to calm down the rhetoric. However, the evidence supports the conclusion that Moscow's approach to this question cannot be explained by power-maximizing considerations. Instead, we need to take into account the collective ideas that dominated the Russian leadership's foreign policy thinking at that time and affected the definition of the Russian leadership's objectives and strategies. During that time, the foreign policy thinking viewed the international arena as a space of geopolitical contest and it emphasized the need to balance against US hegemony. Hence, this case is a confirmation of the hypothesis that *geopolitical Realism* affected Russian foreign policy during this stage of the conflict.

External constraints and Russia's foreign policy

So far the analysis has suggested explanations for Russia's cooperative foreign policy in the years 1992 to 1993/94 and the increasingly confrontational policies of the years 1994 to September 1995 and of the years 1998 to mid April 1999. The next section seeks to explain why

Russia cooperated closely with the West in the autumn 1995 Dayton negotiations on Bosnia and again from mid April to June 1999 with regard to the Kosovo crisis. In both cases the Russian leadership's sudden cooperation came as a surprise due to the volatile rhetoric and confrontational foreign policy action preceding each of these decisions.

Russia's cooperation during the Dayton negotiations (autumn 1995)

The above discussion of Russia's behaviour during the Bosnian crisis has shown that by the summer of 1995, Russia's leadership had realized that the United States was determined to act, while Russia's impact on the conflict was waning. NATO air strikes had a significant impact on the situation on the ground. The Bosnian Serbs were pushed back to roughly 49 per cent of territory stipulated by the Contact Group's plan, and NATO's August 1995 operation *Deliberate Force* forced the Bosnian Serbs to withdraw their heavy weaponry from around Sarajevo, which finally ended the siege of the Bosnian capital.[121] At the same time, Moscow's leverage was diminishing. An example was Yeltsin's August invitation of Serb and Croatian presidents Milosevic and Tudjman to Moscow to find a peaceful solution. Almost immediately after Tudjman accepted Yeltsin's invitation, he backed out, with the result that Yeltsin and Milosevic met alone and achieved little beyond the expression of Russian sympathy for the Serb president's difficult position. Defence analyst Pavel Felgenhauer summarized the dilemma of Russian foreign policy at the end of August 1995: 'Moscow has no real levers for influencing the situation in ex-Yugoslavia. Russia may be a great power, but not in that region, at least not in 1995.'[122]

This episode supports my first hypothesis on the impact of external constraints on Russian foreign policy. This hypothesis argues that in cases where the Russian leadership had to make a choice between confronting and cooperating with the West, it chose cooperation. This was precisely the case in autumn 1995. The West was determined to bring the Bosnian conflict to a halt. It assumed that the only way to do so was to use NATO to put pressure on the Bosnian Serbs. The fact that this strategy starkly contradicted Russian objectives did not create a major concern for Western, and especially US policymakers. At the same time, Russian foreign policy was at an impasse. As shown above, at that time Moscow had no leverage with the Bosnian Serbs, and no leverage to prevent NATO from intervening. In this case, it could have either supported the Bosnian Serbs or it could have sided with the West by trying to play at least a symbolic role in the process of conflict resolution and to salvage its relations with the West. The Russian leadership chose the latter option. This change of strategy constituted a major reversal in Russia's approach to the Bosnian conflict. As a result, despite the Russian leadership's harsh criticism about the Western use of force in the summer of 1995 and despite its de facto exclusion from the negotiation processes that led to the Dayton Peace Accords in November 1995, Russia's leadership was eager to participate in implementing the accords and agreed to place 1400 peace-keeping forces de facto under US control in NATO's Implementation Force IFOR (later Stabilization Force, or SFOR).[123] Russian journalists Georgii Bovt and Natal'ia Kalashnikova concluded that '[e]verything is proceeding as if Boris Yeltsin had never made any harsh statements with confrontational overtones about NATO, and NATO had never responded to them with perfect equanimity'.[124]

Faced with such a foreign policy defeat, the Russian foreign policy leadership's aim was to save face by claiming that the Dayton Peace Accords were to a large extent the result of Russia's diplomatic activity.[125] At that stage, Moscow's main concern seems to have been to uphold Russia's image as a great power. Holbrooke describes an interesting episode in this regard. He recalls that in October 1995, Foreign Minister Kozyrev suggested to him that the three Balkan presidents should visit Moscow prior to the Dayton negotiations. The aim of this visit would not be to engage in substantial negotiations between them and Yeltsin, but to enhance Yeltsin's prestige on the eve of the elections for the Russian parliament. Holbrooke argues, '[t]he Russians promised that if we agreed to this meeting, they would restrict it to a "photo opt" with Yeltsin'.[126] At a meeting between Yeltsin and Clinton in late October 1995, Clinton agreed to this face-saving solution, knowing that the three Balkan presidents thought that such a meeting with Yeltsin would be 'exhausting, unproductive, and politically undesirable' and that it would even delay the start of Dayton by one day. Yet Clinton wanted to support Yeltsin.[127] Eventually, the meeting did not take place, because Yeltsin was hospitalized.[128] This episode demonstrates that Yeltsin clearly understood that he had no leverage to substantively affect the negotiations and that he was highly concerned with finding a face-saving compromise so that he could at least show that he was procedurally involved.

In short, Moscow's cooperative behaviour in the autumn of 1995 supports my first hypothesis on the extent to which external factors shaped Russian foreign policy. When push came to shove, the Russian leadership gave in and sought cooperation with the West. The result was a swing in Russian foreign policy that contradicted prior policy. The extent of the swing exemplifies the weakness of the *geopolitical Realist* thinking that dominated Russian diplomacy at the time. It shows that a policy that does not match capabilities with ambition is likely to produce inconsistency.

This U-turn in Russian foreign policy took place despite fierce domestic opposition, and despite the fact that Yeltsin's opponents were likely to use it against him in the December 1995 Duma elections. In the course of 1995, the Bosnian issue was hotly debated in the Russian Duma, the Russian lower house, which adopted a number of resolutions that called upon the government to unilaterally lift economic sanctions against Serbia, to violate the international embargo, and to impose sanctions against Croatia.[129] Furthermore, deputies repeatedly called on the government to relieve Kozyrev of his duties.[130] The fact that the Russian leadership pursued this policy change despite domestic opposition supports the hypothesis of the overriding impact of external constraints in cases where they were formidable.

Russia's cooperation in finding a solution to the Kosovo conflict (mid April 1999 to June 1999)

A similar pattern of behaviour occurred in the period from mid April 1999 to June 1999 with regard to the Kosovo crisis. Despite the heated rhetoric, in mid April 1999 Yeltsin significantly shifted Russian foreign policy when he nominated former Prime Minister Viktor Chernomyrdin as his special envoy.[131] The most important step after Chernomyrdin's nomination was a meeting between him and Clinton on 3 May 1999. This meeting opened a month of intense diplomacy between a newly created troika, consisting of US Deputy Secretary of State Talbott, Russian Special Envoy Chernomyrdin, and Finnish President Martti Ahtisaari, who represented the European Union.[132] They were able to agree quickly on the least contentious issues: that Yugoslavia's territorial integrity and sovereignty were not in question; an interim administration was to be established by the UN; refugees were allowed to return; and the entire package would have to be endorsed by the UN Security Council.

Five issues were contested: first, whether all Serb military, paramilitary, and police forces needed to be withdrawn; second, when the bombing would be stopped; third, whether the international military force to be deployed in Kosovo had NATO at its core; fourth, who could participate in the international force; and finally, whether Russia would get its own sector in Kosovo.[133] Chernomyrdin's aim in these talks was to moderate the Western demands in Belgrade's favour. Finally, however, he gave in on almost all substantial questions.[134] Even on the most controversial issue, concerning the question of how Russian troops were to be incorporated into NATO's Kosovo Force (KFOR) command structure, Moscow gave in on 18 June 1999 and accepted that Russian forces would remain under Russian tactical command but under the general operational control of NATO's force commanders, and that it had to distribute its forces among the US, French, and German sectors rather than have a sector of its own.[135] Milosevic accepted these terms of the settlement when he realized that he could not expect Russian military backing and that his political support was already exhausted.[136] By siding with the West, Russia played an important role in bringing the conflict to an end at that time.[137] The conflict came to a formal end when the military agreement was signed at Kumanovo air base in Macedonia on 9 June 1999, which led to the UN Security Council Resolution 1244 on the following day.[138]

The question therefore is how can we best explain this sudden reversal in Russian foreign policy in mid April 1999? Again, the situation was characterized by its aggravation. NATO's decision to use military force was the worst-case scenario for Moscow, since it meant that Russian diplomacy had failed to accomplish any reasonable goal. It had failed to prevent the Western states from legitimizing the Kosovar Albanians' strife for greater autonomy, protect Serb interests, portray Russia as an influential great power, constrain NATO from playing a major role in the conflict, and become a genuine partner to the West.[139] In this situation, Russia's leadership had to make a choice: was it willing to back up its pro-Serbian rhetoric by supporting Serbia substantively against the West, or did it want to cooperate with the West to salvage relations and to play a role in the final conflict resolution?

Consistent with my first hypothesis on the impact of external constraints, Russia's leadership chose cooperation rather than confrontation in this situation where external constraints were formidable. In other words, faced with a stark choice, Moscow's major concerns were to save good relations with the West, secure the economic and strategic benefits of being in a close relationship with the West, and avoid being humiliated by siding with Serbia, which was expected to finally give in to Western pressure. While it is difficult to find any official statements that would explicitly justify Russia's cooperative behaviour in terms of its dependence on the West, there is some indirect evidence that supports this conclusion. First, in the summer of 1998, Russia had to face its most serious financial crisis, and it was desperately in need of new IMF loans. Negotiations about them were conducted throughout the first half of 1999, and a final agreement was reached in July 1999.[140] This timing suggests that to some extent, the IMF decision to support

Russia might have depended on Russia's behaviour. Second, US Deputy Secretary of State Talbott argues that Yeltsin wanted a deal with the West before the June 1999 EU and G7/G8 Cologne Summit so that he would be 'well received' there.[141] This aim was achieved, which also supports the conclusion that the Russian leadership prioritized its relations with the West over relations with the Serbs when it faced a stark choice.

Again, it is worth highlighting that the Russian reversal took place despite opposition from the Russian legislature, which criticized the Russian leadership's cooperative course. In reaction to NATO's decision to launch the military campaign against Serbia, the Communist Party, and representatives of the LDPR advocated an aggressive policy against the United States and its allies, expressed solidarity with the Serb people,[142] and sent unofficial delegations of nationalist and communist deputies to Belgrade to guarantee Milosevic Russia's support.[143] In March/April 1999, this domestic criticism constituted a serious danger to Yeltsin, since the Duma was considering a variety of impeachment charges against him, and a vote on impeachment with an unclear outcome was scheduled for mid April 1999.[144] The fact that Yeltsin decided to cooperate with the West in mid April 1999 despite this strong domestic opposition indicates that even in these politically difficult situations, external constraints were the decisive factor.

Conclusion

This analysis suggests that in order to explain Russian foreign policy with regard to the Balkan crises, Realism and Social Constructivism need to be combined. While Russia's reversals in autumn 1995 and in spring 1999 can best be explained by the force of external constraints, Russia's almost unqualified cooperative approach in the period from 1992 to 1993/94 and its increasingly confrontational approaches from 1994 to September 1995 and from March 1998 to mid April 1999 can only be explained by taking into account the impact of collective ideas. The problem for Realist explanations of Russian foreign policy in cases where external constraints were not formidable is that the *behavioural dimension* of Realism with its power-maximization hypothesis is too indeterminate. Thus, the analysis supports my hypotheses about the impact of Realist and ideational factors.

In addition to this, the analysis raises a number of questions and observations. First, in retrospect it seems that the Russian leadership's increasingly confrontational approaches in the years 1994/95 and 1998/99 were unproductive. By decreasing pressure on the Serbs, Russian foreign policy made military intervention led by NATO more likely. This created conditions in which Russia's leadership had to face a stark choice and thus make policy reversals. While the analysis has shown that Russia's leverage on the Serbs should not be exaggerated, it suggests that Russia's leadership could have done more both bilaterally and multilaterally. A more constructive approach might not have prevented military intervention, but it might have compelled the Serbs to give in more quickly. This argument suggests that Russian foreign policy itself created conditions that were difficult for it to navigate in. These awkward conditions made the rapid policy reversals necessary, and they were perceived as diplomatic defeats that revealed Russia's weakness.

Second, the analysis suggests that a foreign policy based on the desire to gain great power status acknowledgement is flawed if ambitions exceed capabilities.[145] The dash of Russian paratroopers to Pristina is another example that demonstrates the weakness of this approach. In June 1999, Moscow accepted the terms of the settlement for Kosovo and agreed to the role it would play in the international force there. Yet before the first NATO troops had even entered Kosovo, Russian troops moved into Pristina, deploying to the airport. While this move caused extreme irritation in NATO's headquarters,[146] it had no military or diplomatic utility, as Yeltsin himself admits in his *Midnight Diaries*.[147] In addition, the operation was so badly conducted that the paratroopers soon faced a shortage of supplies.[148] The operation simply demonstrated the importance of symbolic action for Russian foreign policy. This symbolism is nicely expressed by the words of a general who was cited in the Russian daily *Kommersant*: 'In Pristina we have been the first, like once in Berlin.'[149]

Finally, the analysis suggests that the Russian leadership had good reasons to be concerned about the Balkan crises from the Realist point of view. While the conflicts did not pose direct threats to Russia's security, they represented indirect threats. Since the study gives preference to parsimonious explanations, the fact that Russia became involved in these conflicts at all is therefore mainly explained in these Realist terms. However, this involvement can partly also be explained by the Russian leadership's perception of Russia as a great and major European power. Such an interpretation of Russia's identity did not allow Russia's leadership to remain inactive in a situation where the Western states had become involved. The essence of this thinking is reflected in a statement by Churkin, who argued that '[w]e are not only a world power but also a *European* country and *naturally* it is in our interest that there should be peace in Europe'.[150]

6
Russia's Response to the 11 September 2001 Terrorist Attacks

The Russian leadership's reaction to the 11 September 2001 terrorist attacks on the United States was swift, and Western policy makers and analysts were surprised by the extent to which Moscow cooperated with Washington in the 'War on Terrorism' in general and supported the US-led military campaign against the Taliban and al-Qaeda in Afghanistan in particular. Not only did Russia's leadership express solidarity with the American people, it also backed the United States diplomatically by voting for UN Security Council Resolution 1373; it provided Washington with intelligence; it supplied the Northern Alliance with military equipment and advice; and it benevolently acquiesced in the deployment of Western troops to Central Asia – an area that Moscow considered its special sphere of influence. Even more surprising, the Russian leadership granted this support without making cooperation conditional on explicit side-payments. Such a cooperative response to a US-led military intervention starkly contradicted the Russian leadership's reactions to Western military interventions in previous years. Thus, in this chapter, I seek to answer the question of how we can best explain the Russian leadership's cooperative foreign policy in this case.

In the academic debate, there seems to be a consensus that the Realist paradigm explains this puzzle. Grachev argues, for example, that the Russian leadership simply did not have a viable alterative to cooperation since 'any choice other than this purely pragmatic political decision would have led to a dead end'.[1] Trenin makes a similar argument about the lack of foreign policy alternatives with regard to the Russian leadership's acquiescence in the deployment of Western troops to Central Asia. 'If Moscow had attempted to "not allow Americans onto the territory of the CIS," it would hardly have been successful.'[2] And former US Deputy Secretary of State Strobe Talbott argues that the Russian leadership's decision to cooperate with the United States can be explained by the fact that a defeat of the Taliban served Russian interests at a small cost.[3] While most of these experts also acknowledge President Vladimir Putin's courage in making such an accommodating foreign policy choice, they explain Russia's behaviour predominantly either by external constraints that were so formidable as to leave Russia little choice, or by essentially rational power-maximizing behaviour.[4]

The explanation put forward here differs from the prevailing Realist mainstream in so far as I argue that only with hindsight does the Russian leadership's decision to cooperate closely with the West appear to be rational and almost inevitable. While I agree that external constraints offer a compelling and parsimonious explanation to why the Russian leadership responded with some kind of cooperation rather than with a confrontational foreign policy, external constraints alone are too indeterminate to predict the actual extent of cooperation. Furthermore, I will show that the rational power-maximizing hypothesis also fails to explain why the Russian leadership decided to cooperate with the West open-endedly and did not make its cooperation conditional on explicit side-payments. I will conclude that only by taking into account the impact of collective ideas in general, and *pragmatic geoeconomic Realist thinking* in particular, can we explain the kind of cooperative foreign policy. The view that it was better to go along with developments, rather than to try to defend principled and dogmatic positions; the desire to establish Russia as a responsible great power; and the acknowledgement of potential positive-sum gains of cooperation in the foreign policy thinking at that time explain important facets of the Russian response. These ideas shed light on the questions of why the Russian leadership used this opportunity to redefine Russia's image abroad; why it cooperated with the West without asking for explicit compensations; and why it responded so benevolently to the deployment of Western troops to Central Asia. In this sense, the response to 11 September was more than merely an attempt to use the US intervention to defeat a common enemy, as Talbott suggests.[5]

This chapter is divided into four major sections. First, I assess to what extent the Russian leadership's reaction can be explained by focusing on external constraints. Second, I ask what the power-maximization hypothesis can add to our understanding of the Russian leadership's foreign policy. I follow this analysis with an assessment of the respective impact of ideational factors. Finally, in the conclusion, I summarize the major findings of the case study.

External constraints and Russia's response

In Chapter 2, 'Framework for Analysis', I suggest that the impact of external constraints is a good starting point for the analysis of Russian foreign policy. In cases where external constraints were formidable, my first hypothesis expects the Russian leadership to cooperate with the West. This hypothesis leads to the following questions: What kind of challenge did the terrorist attacks against the United States represent for Russia? What foreign policy options did the Russian leadership have? How did it respond? And finally, to what extent can the Russian leadership's actual policy choices be explained by external constraints?

With regard to the first question about the type of challenge the terrorist attacks posed, I argue that while the attacks did not represent a direct challenge to Russia, their indirect implications had a bearing on Moscow. First, there was the question of how Russia's leadership would respond diplomatically to the US declaration of a 'War on Terrorism'. Second, Moscow had to decide whether and to what extent it supported the US war against the Taliban and al-Qaeda in Afghanistan. And third, the Russian leadership needed to choose how to respond to the US request to use Central Asian airspace and airbases.

With regard to these indirect challenges, Russia's leadership had four potential assets at its disposal. First, from the diplomatic point of view, Russia's status as a permanent member of the UN Security Council gave Moscow an instrument to legitimize or delegitimize the 'War on Terrorism' in general, and a war against the Taliban and al-Qaeda in Afghanistan in particular. Second, Russia had the experience of fighting a war in Afghanistan, and it had some intelligence about potential targets in Afghanistan and about the dynamics inside the Taliban movement.[6] Third, due to close ties with the Northern Alliance and due to the fact that the Northern Alliance fought primarily with Soviet-era weapons, Russia's leadership had means to substantively support a military operation against the Taliban.[7] Finally, due to its role in Central Asia, Russia's leadership had some leverage on the Central Asian states. While Moscow was not able to prevent Central Asian states from offering airspace and airbases to the United States, the Russian leadership could have made such cooperation more difficult for them.

Consequently, Russia's leadership had considerable assets at its disposal that it could have used either to support or to undermine the US war against the Taliban and al-Qaeda. In fact, this was the first time in post-Soviet Russian history that the Russian leadership had something to offer by way of support that the United States badly needed.[8]

If the Russian leadership had considerable assets at its disposal, the next question is how could it have potentially reacted to the indirect challenges outlined above? Four reasonable ideal-type responses were available, and they can be imagined as being located along a continuum. On one extreme is an *almost unqualified cooperative response*. Not only could Russia's leadership have offered the United States moral and diplomatic support – condemning the terrorist attacks and legitimizing the US war against the Taliban and al-Qaeda in Afghanistan by supporting, inter alia, UN Security Council resolutions – but it could also have actively supported the war effort through means such as intelligence sharing, military assistance to the Northern Alliance, and encouraging of the Central Asian states to participate in the US 'War on Terrorism'. This wide-ranging cooperation, based on assumptions about shared interests and values, would have been offered without asking for any side-payments and without taking advantage of the situation.

On the other extreme of the continuum would have been an *almost confrontational response*. Moscow could have interpreted the attacks as a consequence of the unilateral and 'arrogant' behaviour of the United States in international affairs. In this sense, it could have perceived the events as a tragic, yet 'just reaction to a flawed US foreign policy'. Following this line of reasoning, Moscow could have used its veto power in the UN Security Council to delegitimize US military intervention in Afghanistan; withheld intelligence to the United States and material supplies to the Northern Alliance; and threatened the Central Asian states to cooperate with the United States.[9] While such a response would not have prevented US military intervention in Afghanistan, it would have made that intervention more costly.

Somewhere in the middle between these two extremes, tilting slightly towards the almost unqualified cooperative response, we can imagine an *open-ended instrumental response*. Like the almost unqualified cooperative response, this kind of reaction would have entailed moral, diplomatic, and substantive support for the US campaign against the Taliban. Yet differently, this response would not have been based on notions of shared interests and values, but on the implicit instrumental expectation that far-reaching support for the United States would deliver the most dividends in Russian–US relations in the mid-term. Furthermore, this kind of response would have tried to utilize the US campaign in order to foster Russia's own interests in Afghanistan and the momentum created by the 'War on Terrorism' in order to internationally delegitimize acts of terrorism and gain support for Russia's campaign against 'international terrorism' in Chechnya.

Finally, one could imagine a fourth response, that of *conditional cooperation*. Such a reaction would also be intermediate, but tilting slightly towards the confrontational end of the spectrum. It would have led Russia's leadership to condemn the terrorist attacks, but show more reluctance in supporting the US war against the Taliban and al-Qaeda in Afghanistan. Russia's leadership could have argued that Washington should not act unilaterally and that the UN should play the role of the central arbiter. It could have made cooperation with regard to intelligence sharing and the provision of military supplies to the Northern Alliance conditional on *explicit* concessions on other issues. Furthermore, it would have received attempts to station Western troops in Central Asia with suspicion. Acknowledging that Moscow would not be able to prevent the deployment of Western troops to Central Asia, this approach would imply that Moscow would threaten Central Asian states to cooperate with Washington with the aim of gaining explicit promises that Western troops would be stationed there only for a limited time. Such an approach would have been conceptually similar to Russia's behaviour during the Kosovo crisis prior to mid April 1999.[10]

I argue that the Russian leadership's actual response is best reflected in the characteristics of the *open-ended instrumental response*. This conclusion can be inferred by analysing the Russian leadership's rhetorical and diplomatic response; the extent of support for the anti-terrorist operation against the Taliban both with regard to intelligence sharing and military support to the Northern Alliance; and the extent of Russia's facilitation of the deployment of Western troops to Central Asia. First, the Russian leadership's rhetorical and diplomatic reaction was swift and far-reaching. Directly after the attacks, President Putin called US President George W. Bush to express his condolences and to offer the dispatch of rescue workers;[11] the Russian Ministry of Defence cancelled a military exercise in the airspace above the Atlantic, Arctic, and Pacific oceans;[12] Russia's Foreign and Federal Security Services apparently cooperated with US intelligence services to obtain information on possible perpetrators;[13] and in a Russian television broadcast on 11 September, Putin condemned the attacks, expressed his condolences and argued that the whole civilized mankind was challenged by the events.[14]

This highly cooperative attitude was also reflected in Russia's diplomatic activities in the following weeks. Rather than trying to delay or to block UN Security Council Resolution 1373, which backed the US military campaign against the Taliban, Russia supported it.[15] In so doing, the Russian leadership gave the US operation legitimacy and helped Washington to act decisively. Furthermore, Arbatov argues that Putin played an important pro-US role at the October 2001 Asia-Pacific Economic Cooperation (APEC) Summit in Shanghai, where the anti-terrorist coalition became increasingly strained and anti-US feelings grew. By publicly defending the war in Afghanistan, President Putin helped to balance out Chinese and Iranian concerns.[16]

Second, with regard to the extent of the Russian leadership's support for the anti-terrorist campaign in Afghanistan, two phases need to be distinguished. During the first week and a half after the attacks, the Russian leadership was reluctant to define a clear position. While it expressed solidarity with the American people and emphasized its readiness to assist the United States in investigating the terrorist attacks,[17] it hesitated to support the US military campaign in Afghanistan.[18]

Yet after these days, the contours of the Russian leadership's response became increasingly explicit. First, Moscow's attitude towards intelligence sharing changed. On 21 September 2001, Foreign Minister Igor Ivanov announced that Russian intelligence services were providing the United States with information on the location of terrorist training camps in Afghanistan.[19] Putin's address to the Russian public on 24 September 2001 reiterated this position.[20] While it is difficult to assess the extent and quality of actual intelligence sharing, some evidence suggests that intelligence cooperation was significant and valuable. Woodward contends that Russian intelligence provided 'extensive on-the-ground intelligence, especially about topography and caves in Afghanistan'.[21] In addition, Russian intelligence seems to have offered insights into terrorist networks operating in Central Asia, the Caucasus, and worldwide.[22]

That intelligence cooperation has been beneficial can be inferred from the fact that the momentum in intelligence cooperation was maintained in the months after 11 September.[23] One example for this continued cooperation was the May 2002 transformation of the Russian–US working group on Afghanistan[24] into a working group on counterterrorism in general.[25] In an interview with the Russian newspaper *Trud* in December 2001, Director of the Russian Foreign Intelligence Service (SVR) Sergei Lebedev praised international intelligence cooperation in the fight against terrorism.[26] Thus, while there was certainly a good deal of nervousness on both sides about exposure, it is reasonable to conclude that the level of cooperation between US and Russian services was significant.

Furthermore, Russia's leadership also supplied the Northern Alliance with military equipment, technicians and advisers. In October 2001, Russia apparently delivered forty T-55 tanks, eighty BMP-1, and BMP-2 infantry fighting vehicles, several dozen armoured personnel carriers, multiple rocket launchers, anti-aircraft rockets, and light arms.²⁷ The significance of this support should not be underestimated. Lawrence Freedman argues that when the strategic bombing campaign of the first few weeks failed to achieve the envisioned results, the Bush administration had to rely much more heavily on the Northern Alliance.²⁸ Due to the fact that the Northern Alliance fought primarily with Soviet-era weapons, the US ability to supply military equipment to the Northern Alliance was limited and Russia's cooperation even more essential. Thus, while it is difficult to assess the extent to which Russia's support to the Northern Alliance contributed to the success of the US military operation in absolute terms, Moscow seems to have done a considerable amount in this sphere.

Third, with regard to Moscow's reaction to the US request to use Central Asian airspace and airbases, Moscow apparently also supported the United States in this matter. On 14 September 2001, Defence Minister Sergei Ivanov initially ruled out the dispatch of Western forces to Central Asia, arguing that Central Asia 'is within the zone of competence of the CIS Collective Security Treaty'.²⁹ But on 19 September 2001 Foreign Minister Ivanov indicated that every country had the right to decide for itself whether or not to provide access to bases or any other form of cooperation to the United States.³⁰

To assess the extent to which Moscow facilitated the use of Central Asian airspace and airbases, one would need to know more about how developments unfolded. The critical questions are first, whether the United States consulted Moscow before, simultaneously, or after Washington approached the Central Asian states and second, whether there were consultations between Moscow and the Central Asian states. In other words, did Russia's leadership face a fait accompli, or did it have some real choice in the matter?

To answer the first question, the then Deputy Assistant Secretary for European and Eurasian Affairs at the US State Department Steven Pifer reports that Washington consulted Moscow simultaneously as it approached the Central Asian states. This tactic was the result of two considerations. On the one hand, Washington saw no reason to ask Moscow for a permission to consult with independent Central Asian states. On the other hand, the US leadership wanted to have the Russian leadership on board and did not want to surprise Moscow.³¹

Unfortunately, we do not know much about the extent of consultations between Moscow and the Central Asian states. Only in the case of Tajikistan is there clear evidence that Dushanbe's offer of airfields to the

United States was the result of prior consultations with Moscow and in fact of active Russian persuasion. A statement by the Chief of the Tajik Foreign Ministry Information Department Igor Sattarov reveals Tajikistan's dependence on Russia. He argued that '[w]e cannot tackle these issues without consultation with our allies, in particular with Russia'.[32] The Tajik leadership was concerned about the repercussions of US engagement in Afghanistan because of the potential destabilizing impact on its borders.[33] Tajik President Emomali Rahmonov therefore called upon Russia to secure the country's borders.[34] Only after Moscow had signalled that it was reinforcing its border troops was Tajikistan willing to offer airbases to the United States.[35] Thus, in the case of Tajikistan, Russia seems to have actively facilitated cooperation between Dushanbe and Washington. Yet due to the fact that Tajikistan was at that time a de facto Russian protectorate, we cannot transfer the findings about the consultations from this case to the question of whether other Central Asian states also consulted with Moscow prior to agreeing to provide the United States their airspace and airbases.

Thus, if we take into account the fact that Washington did not 'ask' Moscow for permission to approach the Central Asian states before consulting with them, and if we assume that only in the case of Tajikistan did a Central Asian state 'ask' Moscow explicitly for permission to cooperate with Washington, it seems that Russian diplomacy had to face what amounted to a fait accompli.[36]

Yet even if it is correct that Russia's leadership had little choice, Moscow's benevolent acquiescence in Uzbekistan's and Kyrgyzstan's offers of assistance was striking. While Moscow obtained from Washington the promise that Western forces would be deployed to the region only for the period of the military operation in Afghanistan, it is striking that the Russian leadership agreed to such an imprecise promise and did not try to obtain more explicit guarantees that Western forces would not be based in Central Asia without time limits, or that it did not ask for other side-payments. Due to the strategic importance of these three countries and due to the fact that alternative staging areas for the US operation (for example, in Pakistan) were endangered by fundamentalist Muslim groups, Moscow made an important contribution to the success of the US military operation in Afghanistan by acquiescing so easily in the deployment of Western forces to the region.[37]

This analysis leads to the final question of whether the Russian leadership tried to benefit from the unfolding developments or whether it cooperated with the United States without trying to take advantage of the situation. Evidence suggests that Russia's reaction was instrumental.

The Russian leadership hoped to use the 'War on Terrorism' to legitimize its own campaign in Chechnya, it tried to foster its own interests in Afghanistan, and it wanted to change the 'terms-of-trade' in Russian–US relations.

In short, this decision suggests that while Russia's response was certainly aimed to foster Russian interests, it was surprisingly swift, far-reaching, and substantial. With regard to all dimensions, Russia's leadership could have reasonably offered less to the United States. In this sense, Moscow has overfulfilled US expectations in terms of contributions. Talbott recalls: 'virtually everything that President Bush asked for, Putin not only said yes, but he said I will do more than that.'[38] Furthermore, evidence suggests that the Russian leadership did not make cooperation conditional on explicit side-payments. Consequently, the Russian leadership's actual behaviour best reflects what I have called an *open-ended instrumental cooperative approach*. While Western and Russian officials' claims that Russia's decision to join the anti-terrorist coalition symbolized the true end of the Cold War[39] have exaggerated the meaning of Russia's response, the extent of cooperation symbolized a radical turn in Russian foreign policy.[40]

Can external constraints explain this radical turn? Due to the indirect nature of the challenge posed by the 11 September terrorist attacks, external constraints do not explain the extent of Russian cooperation. Russia was not coerced into supporting the US military campaign both diplomatically and substantively in such a far-reaching and swift fashion. This means that an explanation based on external constraints alone is insufficient. What external constraints do explain, however, is why Moscow did not choose an *almost confrontational response*. If the Russian leadership had chosen such an approach, the country would have become a pariah state, while most other nations showed solidarity with the United States. To interpret such a tragic event in terms of a 'just reaction to US arrogance' and to undermine the US military campaign in Afghanistan would have isolated Russia in the Western community.

As a result, the next section assesses the extent to which the *behavioural dimension* of Realism, which emphasizes cost–benefit calculations to increase the relative material power position of a state, can explain the extent and nature of Russian cooperation. To increase analytical clarity, the questions of why Russia benevolently acquiesced in the deployment of Western troops to Central Asia and why it diplomatically and substantively supported the US operation in Afghanistan, are treated separately.

The indeterminacy of the Realist power-maximization hypothesis

Russia's benevolent acquiescence in the deployment of Western troops to Central Asia

On the basis of Realist power-maximization assumptions, some analysts argue that the Russian leadership's benevolent acquiescence in the deployment of Western troops to Central Asia was a rational response to the decline of Russia's power position in Central Asia and the rise of radical Islamic movements in the region. From this perspective, the Russian leadership's approach towards Central Asia developed in the following way. During the 1990s, Russian diplomacy in the 'near abroad' was characterized by attempts to build regional cooperative security structures. Yet by the late 1990s, Russia's role had eroded significantly. While the May 1992 Collective Security Treaty (CST) between Armenia, Kazakhstan, Kyrgyzstan, Russia, Tajikistan, and Uzbekistan (and later Georgia, Azerbaijan, and Belarus) was extended for a further period of five years in April 1999, its impact waned when Uzbekistan, Georgia, and Azerbaijan withdrew from it and created their own subregional group GUUAM in 1997.[41] When Putin came to power, the Kremlin initially acknowledged the ineffectiveness of cooperative security structures and tried to pursue a more limited regional strategy in building bilateral and selective political, military and economic relations. This did not mean that Moscow lost interest in the region; quite to the contrary, the Russian Foreign Policy Concept of 2000 prioritized relations with CIS member states,[42] and President Putin chose the Central Asian states as the destination of his first foreign visits as newly elected president. But the changes showed a recognition of Russia's limited influence. On the basis of these developments, Herd and Akerman conclude that even before 11 September 'Russian influence was waning, despite Russia's rhetoric of integration, while Western influence was on the increase'.[43]

Furthermore, not only was Moscow's ability to influence developments in the region declining towards the late 1990s, but Russia and the region had to face a new and growing terrorist threat posed by the Islamic Movement of Uzbekistan (IMU). This threat became prominent in 1999 when the IMU tried to invade Uzbekistan's Ferghana Valley and occupied several villages in southern Kyrgyzstan.[44] Lieven suggests that given Russia's weak hand and the rise of this new challenge, it was rational for the Russian leadership to use the momentum created by 11 September to initiate positive-sum cooperation with Washington in the region. He claims 'coping with a large-scale Islamist upheaval in Central

Asia [. . .] would be beyond its [Russia's] strength [. . .]. Equally, the US alone can never maintain the stability of Central Asia without Russian help or against Russian hostility'.[45] In other words, from this perspective, Russia's benevolent reaction to the US intention of deploying troops to the region was a rational response aimed at increasing Russia's power position in difficult circumstances.

Yet one can argue that it is not entirely accurate to characterize Russia's influence in the region prior to 11 September as limited, nor is it self-evident that cooperation with the United States in the region was in Russia's interest. Since the years 1999 to 2001 witnessed some degree of Russian reassertion, a characterization of Russia's power position as in decline does not accurately describe trends in Russia's relations with Central Asia. Dannreuther argues that Russia's improved economic position after 1999 helped Putin to 'add some economic muscle to his political initiatives',[46] which increased Moscow's ability to influence the Central Asian states. One example was that in 2000 Russia wrote off Kyrgyzstan's energy debts once Russian was made the second official language of the country.[47]

And contrary to the above claim that cooperation with the United States was the most prudential means to mutually counter the new threat of Islamic terrorism in the region, Islamic terrorism was the factor that strengthened Russia's role in Central Asia. That implies that it should have been in the Russian interest to limit US interference in the region. Due to the common threat of Islamic terrorism, during the late1990s and in 2000/01, Russian diplomacy was increasingly successful in creating and reviving regional security institutions that went beyond the CIS and did not include the United States. Examples were the Shanghai Five[48] memorandum of December 1999, which provided for closer cooperation against terrorism and cross-border crime;[49] the Yerevan summit in May 2001, where the CIS members of the CST signed a protocol to set up a Collective Rapid Reaction Force in Central Asia; and the June 2001 transformation of the Shanghai Five into the Shanghai Cooperation Organisation (SCO) with the inclusion of Uzbekistan.

Consequently, one can argue that Russia's influence was far from waning prior to 11 September and that it must have been in the interest of Russia to limit US interference in the region at a time when it was able to build regional structures designed for the maintenance of regional stability. While it would have been unreasonable for Russia to attempt preventing the deployment of Western troops to the region, one can argue that it would have been most prudential from the Realist perspective to try to limit the deployment of Western troops, to gain guarantees that the deployment would be time limited, or to ask at least for compensation. Developments in 2004/05 support the conclusion that the US would try to keep its bases in Central Asia for as long as possible.[50]

This discussion suggests that the benevolent nature of Russia's acquiescence in the deployment of Western troops to Central Asia does not seem to be as self-evident and rational as some scholars suggest. The problem of the Realist power-maximization hypothesis is that due to its indeterminacy, it does not help us to assess Russia's power position and to weigh the costs and benefits of helping or hindering the deployment of Western troops to the region. Was Russia's power position in the region waning or increasing? Would Russia gain more by cooperating with the United States or by trying to limit US engagement in Central Asia? Without supplementary assumptions, the Realist power-maximizing hypothesis is underspecified and cannot offer sufficiently concrete expectations. Thus, this section concludes that the power-maximizing hypothesis is unable to explain why the Russian leadership acquiesced benevolently in the deployment of Western troops.

Russia's diplomatic and substantive support of the war in Afghanistan

The next question is whether the Russian leadership's decision to support the war against the Taliban in Afghanistan both diplomatically and substantively can be explained in terms of a rational relative power-maximizing strategy. I suggest above that Moscow could have reasonably contributed less to the effort. So the question is, why did it offer such far-reaching diplomatic support and cooperation in the fields of intelligence sharing and military assistance to the Northern Alliance?

Direct pay-offs

As highlighted in the introduction, Realists suggest that Russia's far-reaching cooperation can best be explained by the fact that the defeat of the Taliban and of al-Qaeda was also in the Russian interest. Some evidence supports such an explanation. Afghanistan had already been a region of concern for Russian policymakers for a long time before 11 September. Chechen rebels were allegedly trained in Afghanistan and supported by the Taliban and al-Qaeda. Consequently, since 1996, when it became clear that the balance of power in Afghanistan between President Rabbani and the Taliban was shifting towards the latter, Russian diplomacy supported the president and the Northern Alliance.[51] During the second half of the 1990s, Russia arranged transportation of Iranian aid, provided military aid and advice,[52] and during 2000 and

2001, Russia's leadership implemented UN Security Council Resolution 1333,[53] issuing a decree banning the sale of arms, ammunition, spare parts for military equipment, and dual-use technology to the Taliban on 6 March 2001.[54] Thus, from the Realist perspective Moscow's far-reaching support of the US war against the Taliban can be seen as a logical continuation of its approach towards Afghanistan prior to 11 September. Foreign Minister Ivanov explained Russia's support for the US operation in exactly these terms: 'We've said before the attacks that there are dangers for Russia lurking in the Caucasus and along the border with Asia. [. . .] In the wake of 11 September [. . .] Russia's natural reaction [. . .] was to cooperate with the international coalition in order to accomplish first and foremost its own objectives.'[55]

Yet, while there were considerable direct pay-offs resulting from the support of the US war, the defeat of the Taliban would have also had undesirable consequences for Russia. First, as argued above, the rise of radical Islamic groups in Central Asia first and foremost strengthened Russia's position in Central Asia. The reason for this dynamics was that the Central Asian governments assumed that Russia had a stronger interest in countering Islamic terrorism and that it would offer military support, while US commitment to the region seemed to be based on less stable ground. Islamic terrorism was thus the common threat that strengthened Russia's role in Central Asia. Consequently, from the Realist perspective, a manageable threat from the Taliban and al-Qaeda was in fact in Russia's interest, allowing it to defend its position as Central Asia's security provider. From this perspective, before 11 September, Moscow seems to have supported the Northern Alliance not necessarily to defeat the Taliban and al-Qaeda, but rather to hold them in check. Ivanov's above-cited statement can be read as a post hoc justification of Russian foreign policy at a time when the Russian pro-US foreign policy became domestically contested.

Second, by allowing the United States to deploy forces to the region, Russia ran the risk of being pushed out of the region. Former Russian Foreign Minister Yevgenii Primakov argued that 'the presence of US military bases in proximity to the Caspian cannot but be regarded as an attempt to strengthen US positions in choosing transportation roots for Caspian oil'.[56] Thus, by supporting the deployment of Western forces in Central Asia, Russia's leadership was helping the United States increase its influence in the region. Communist Party leader Gennady Zyuganov even concluded: 'The strategic encirclement of Russia is being completed with the full consent of Putin and his team.'[57]

Consequently, this discussion suggests that from a Realist perspective, Russia's leadership was confronted with a dilemma. While the destruction of a major support basis for Chechen rebels could only be achieved by the defeat of the Taliban and al-Qaeda, the preservation of a limited and manageable Islamic threat to the region was linked to a great extent to the existence of the Taliban and al-Qaeda. Thus, both objectives were mutually exclusive. Furthermore, the defeat of the Taliban and al-Qaeda would only be achieved by providing the United States a gateway to Central Asia. Due to the fact that the Realist power-maximizing hypothesis does not specify how to calculate costs and benefits, it fails to say whether the defeat of the Taliban movement and al-Qaeda or the survival of them would have maximized Russia's relative power position and how to assess the danger of a stronger role of the United States in the region. One would need to know more about threat assumptions and priorities to decide whether it would have been more rational for the Russian leadership to choose a policy of *conditional cooperation* or of *open-ended instrumental cooperation*. In short, the *behavioural dimension* of Realism fails to explain why Moscow chose *open-ended instrumental cooperation* instead of *conditional cooperation*.

Indirect pay-offs

In addition to the direct pay-offs, Realists argue that there were also potential indirect pay-offs from *open-ended instrumental cooperation* with the United States: Russia might have hoped to gain international diplomatic support for its military campaign in Chechnya and implicit concessions on other contentious issues in Russia's relations with the West. How convincing are these arguments?

International diplomatic support for Russia's military campaign in Chechnya. Another Realist explanation for Russia's far-reaching cooperation is that the Russian leadership hoped to change the international perception of its military campaign in Chechnya and to achieve an international diplomatic delegitimation of terrorism.[58] Already prior to 11 September, Putin had repeatedly explained that Russia's war against Chechen 'terrorists' was also in the West's interests.[59] The fact that Putin and other high-ranking officials established a link between the terrorist attacks against the United States and Russia's fight against Islamic terrorism in Chechnya immediately after 11 September suggests that the idea of using the attacks to change the international perception of Russia's war in Chechnya must have played a crucial role in the Russian leadership's calculations. In Putin's 11 September 2001 television broadcast, he argued: 'What happened today underscores once more the urgency of Russia's proposal that the international community join forces to combat terrorism, the plague of the 21st century. Russia knows firsthand what terrorism is.'[60]

Yet two objections can be raised against this explanation of Russia's far-reaching cooperation in terms of an attempt to achieve international diplomatic delegitimation of terrorism. First, how reasonable was the expectation that the Western perception of Russia's war in Chechnya would change if Russia joined forces with the United States? On 13 September 2001 Golotyuk argued that a revision of the Western perception of Russia's campaign in Chechnya was unlikely due to the inability of both sides to agree on a common definition of terrorism and due to the difference between the nature of international terrorism and the Chechen conflict.[61]

Post-11 September events support this sceptical prediction. From the Russian point of view, the results of the delegitimation strategy were at best mixed. With regard to the United States, Russia was somewhat successful. Although at first the United States hesitated to change its view of Moscow's behaviour in Chechnya,[62] in the mid-term, US criticism was toned down. US President Bush's rhetoric of fighting global 'evil' left him with little room for manoeuvre and resulted in indirect support for Russia's approach to Chechnya at least for a few years after 11 September. With regard to Europe, the situation is different. Directly after 11 September, Russia seems to have succeeded. After President Putin's September 2001 speech in the German Bundestag,[63] German Chancellor Gerhard Schröder argued that the West would need to re-evaluate Russia's war in Chechnya.[64] Yet already in January 2002 in a press conference with French President Jaques Chirac, President Putin began to criticise double standards in the Western media.[65] Thus, shortly after 11 September 2001, the Europeans have returned to their position prior to 11 September and repeatedly called upon Moscow to start negotiations with Chechen rebels.[66]

Second, one might argue that from the Realist perspective, as I have defined it here, perceptions should not matter. Thus, from the Realist point of view, it is striking that Russia's leadership gave so much priority to the need to change international perceptions of Russia's approach to the Chechen conflict at all.

One can conclude that while evidence clearly suggests that the Russian leadership hoped to use 11 September as a means to change international perceptions of Russia's war in Chechnya, such an attempt cannot be explained in terms of the Realist power-maximizing hypothesis. Neither does the expectation to change the international perception of

Russia's operation in Chechnya seem to have been likely, nor can concerns to change perceptions be explained in Realist terms.

Concessions on other contentious issues in Russia's relations with the West. Furthermore, Realists might argue that open-ended instrumental cooperation was a rational strategy aimed at gaining strategic concessions from the West. First, the Anti-Ballistic Missile (ABM) treaty issue loomed large throughout the year 2001. While Washington made clear that it wanted to install a National Missile Defence (NMD), which required changes to the ABM treaty, the terms for doing so were unclear. Until the summer of 2001, the situation was characterized by tension between Russia and the United States. US Defence Secretary Donald Rumsfeld argued in February 2001, 'Russia is an active proliferator. They are part of the problem. They are selling and assisting countries like Iran, North Korea and India and other countries with [WMD] technologies, which are threatening [. . .] the United States'.[67] The Russian leadership denied such allegations and defended its right to sell arms to these countries.[68] As a result, Moscow warned that US withdrawal from the ABM Treaty would trigger a new nuclear arms race, and it threatened to deploy multiple independently targetable nuclear missiles.[69]

Yet by mid 2001, the contours of a possible solution to the ABM issue were already emerging. Due to Russia's weak negotiation position, Russia tried to link the ABM issue to strategic arms cuts. The START II treaty envisaged that both sides would reduce the number of warheads to 3500 by the end of 2007, and plans for START III aimed to reduce the number further to 2500. The Russian leadership was, however, interested in even more far-reaching cuts. At a meeting of the Association of South East Asian Nations (ASEAN) on 25 July 2001 Foreign Minister Igor Ivanov suggested that the question of NMD (National Missile Defence) be linked to a strategic arms reduction to a level of 1500 warheads.[70] President Putin and President Bush discussed such proposals at their Genoa meeting of 22 July 2001.[71] Such a solution to the ABM issue would have been a success for both sides. While the United States would be allowed to build a NMD, Putin could point to a significant achievement of his diplomacy.[72]

These parameters for an agreement were reflected in the developments that unfolded in the following months. At a three-day summit between Bush and Putin in November 2001, Bush announced that the United States was willing to reduce the number of warheads to a level between 1700 and 2200 over the next decade.[73] On 13 December 2001 Bush then announced that Washington would withdraw from the ABM

Treaty,[74] and the Russian leadership's response was more measured than many expected. Putin called the US decision a 'mistake', but he affirmed that the 'US decision does not pose a threat to the national security of the Russian Federation'.[75] Finally, on 24 May 2002, the two sides signed a treaty that called both sides to reduce their strategic weapon arsenals to 1700–2200.[76] While Russian officials described this treaty as a success, it must have been a disappointment for Moscow. On the one hand, the number of warheads was reduced. But on the other hand, contrary to the mid 2001 agreement, the treaty did not require the destruction of warheads and envisioned only marginal verification procedures.

Thus, the question is whether it was reasonable for Moscow to expect that by cooperating with the United States in the 'War on Terrorism', it could soften the US stance on the ABM issue. President Putin seems to have believed so. In an interview on 22 September 2001, he indicated that while he still regarded US withdrawal from the ABM treaty as an 'erroneous step', there would be no 'hysteric reaction on part of Russia'.[77] But how realistic was the expectation that Russia could change the US position on the ABM issue? The above-described developments suggest that the Russian leadership's cooperative approach did not have a significant impact on US policy, since the contours of the final agreement were already discussed before 11 September. Could this result not already have been expected in September 2001? Only under the assumption that Moscow could change the overall 'terms of trade' in East–West relations does an expectation that Moscow could change the US stance on the ABM issue make sense. Yet this expectation does not follow easily from Realism. Would it not have been much more prudential to link cooperation in the US 'War on Terrorism' to *explicit* concessions on the ABM issue?

Second, Realists could argue that close cooperation with the United States was a rational strategy aimed at improving NATO–Russia relations. And indeed one might argue that Moscow was to some extent successful. At a Permanent Joint Council (PJC) meeting on 7 December 2001, the establishment of a new NATO–Russia Council (NRC) was officially announced. This process culminated in the creation of the council at the NATO–Russia Summit of 28 May 2002 in Rome.[78] The timing of this announcement suggests that the NATO member states were partly driven by the desire to reciprocate. Yet, while the council's creation was certainly an achievement for Russian diplomacy, even prior to 11 September there had been efforts to transform NATO–Russia relations. Thus, Russia's cooperation in the 'War on Terrorism' might have catalysed this process, but closer cooperation between NATO and Russia might have been offered to Russia anyway.[79] Again, it is necessary to ask whether it would not have been more prudential from the Realist perspective to make cooperation conditional on *explicit* promises that NATO–Russia relations would improve.

Furthermore, critics of a cooperative foreign policy have pointed out that not only were indirect pay-offs unlikely, but that a too-cooperative response had significant costs. Did Russia not risk losing its standing as an independent great power by cooperating too closely with the United States and also risk undermining other important relationships with countries such as China and Iran?[80] Primakov warned that Russian–Chinese relations might be severely undermined by a Russian–US rapprochement. He said: 'In the course of a meeting with Jian Zemin in Beijing, in early 2002, I could see for myself that the Chinese leadership was seriously concerned' by the presence of US forces in close proximity to Russian and Chinese borders.[81]

In other words, this discussion suggests that while Russia's leadership might have hoped that *open-ended instrumental cooperation* would provide some indirect gains on the ABM issue and NATO–Russia relations, the likelihood of success was at best limited. The underlying reason that made a fundamental reorientation unlikely was the lack of common interests between the United States and Russia. Advisor to the Chairman of the State Duma Foreign Affairs Committee Vladimir Frolov argued: 'Putin has not made a compelling case [...] to the Russian political class in favor of a lasting alliance-type relationship with the United States that would transcend the narrow agenda of the war on terrorism. [...] The war against terror is too narrow a basis for U.S.-Russian alliance to emerge and endure.'[82] In other words, it is surprising from a Realist point of view that Russia's leadership has based its foreign policy on the assumption that it could change the 'terms of trade' in East–West relations, and therefore did not link cooperation to *explicit* concessions on these issues. Would Realism not expect an approach of such linkages rather one basing cooperation on the good will of others? And even more surprisingly, Russia's leadership was in a comparably strong position in this case and did not fully use its leverage.

In summary, in this analysis I have shown that the Russian leadership was certainly interested in gaining some returns by cooperating with the United States in the 'War on Terrorism'. Thus, the Realist power-maximization hypothesis explains why Russia's leadership did not choose a policy of *almost unqualified cooperation*. Yet at the same time, due to the indeterminacy of the Realist power-maximization hypothesis, Realism fails to explain why the Russian leadership chose what

I have called *open-ended instrumental cooperation* instead of *conditional cooperation*. In other words, the Realist power-maximizing hypothesis fails to explain the swiftness of the Russian leadership's reaction, its far-reaching extent, and the fact that Moscow cooperated with Washington without explicitly asking for concessions. The next section therefore analyses whether ideational factors and, in particular, *pragmatic geoeconomic Realism* can help to explain these phenomena.

Collective ideas and Russia's swift and far-reaching reaction

To explain the swiftness of the Russian leadership's response one needs to take into account the importance that *pragmatic geoeconomic Realism* placed on matching means to ends. In contrast to the defence of dogmatic geopolitical positions, which was a characteristic of the previous period of Russian foreign policy thinking, pragmatism required the Russian leadership to carefully assess capabilities and design strategies accordingly in order to avoid wasting scarce resources. This pragmatic view helps to explain why Russia's leadership was willing to go along with developments, rather than lose time in trying to prevent the deployment of Western forces to the region or demanding that the UN should play a leading role. In other words, if *geopolitical Realism* had affected the Russian leadership's foreign policy thinking at that time, it seems probable that the Russian reaction would have been quite different. Yet, while the pragmatism of the foreign policy thinking of that time helps to explain the swiftness with which the Russian leadership reacted to developments, it does not explain why Moscow acquiesced in the deployment of Western troops to Central Asia benevolently, why it cooperated so extensively, and why it did not make cooperation dependent on explicit side-payments.

To explain the benevolent nature of acquiescence, we must take into account the fact that the foreign policy thinking of that time acknowledged that Russia's great power status could not simply be assumed, but had to be *earned* by means of responsible foreign policy action that would gain Western respect. This kind of thinking helps to explain why the question of whether to acquiesce in the deployment of Western troops to Central Asia was not only a question of whether acquiescence would enhance or weaken Russia's power position in Central Asia. Acquiescence was seen in the broader context of Russia's relations with the West. In this sense, acquiescence became a symbol for Russia's constructive behaviour.[83] Yet if acquiescence was to serve as a symbol, then it had to be given voluntarily rather than as the result of coercion.

Thus, the desire to portray Russia as a responsible great power helps to explain why acquiescence was of a benevolent kind and why the rhetoric of that time emphasized the communality of interests between Russia and the West.[84] Russia's leadership compared Russian–US cooperation in the 'War on Terrorism' with the Russian–US alliance of the Second World War.[85] And similarly to Bush's rhetoric that nations had to decide whether they were 'with us or with the terrorists',[86] Putin emphasized that the 11 September attacks were a declaration of war on the entire civilized world, which required a united response.[87]

In addition to Russia's desire to be perceived as a responsible actor, we also need to take into account that while *pragmatic geoeconomic Realism* still perceived the nature of international relations in competitive terms, it was more optimistic about the likelihood of positive-sum cooperation. Thus, Putin might have been concerned about the mid-term impact of the deployment of Western troops in Central Asia, but he was more optimistic than many members of the Russian military that Russia would be able to make some significant security gains.[88] Asked whether he was concerned about the increasing influence of the United States in Central Asia, Putin argued that he was 'more concerned about the existence of bases to train terrorists in northern Afghanistan which then fight in the North Caucasus'.[89] While Lieven's explanation portrays positive-sum cooperation as almost self-evident, my discussion of the impact of foreign policy ideas suggests that this view can only be explained by taking into account the dominant thinking of that time. Thus, it is contingent rather than self-evident.

In other words, benevolent acquiescence in the deployment of Western forces to Central Asia can only be explained if we take into account the foreign policy thinking of the leadership, which hoped to portray Russia as a responsible international actor, and regarded positive-sum gains of cooperation as likely. Rather than trying to increase international status by balancing against developments, Putin seems to have hoped that by cooperating with the United States, he would acquire 'the status of Chief US ally in the southern subregion of the CIS – in which case all subsequent decisions made by the Central Asian countries will be (or appear to be, which is the same thing under the circumstances) merely a consequence of Moscow's decision'.[90] A number of statements by Putin during that period reflect this kind of reasoning. He argued, for example, that '[i]f Russia gains the status of an equal member of the international community, then it should not be afraid of the emergence of closer relations between its allies and other states in general, and between the Central Asian states and the United States in particular'.[91]

Yet, while this discussion suggests that the Russian leadership hoped to change the image of Russia, the desire to create a new image was not an end in itself. The underlying rationale was that a better reputation could be transformed into domestic and foreign policy dividends.[92]

This desire to establish an image of Russia as a responsible international actor is also a significant factor for explaining why the Russian leadership hoped to use the 11 September terrorist attacks to change the international perception of Russia's approach to the Chechen conflict. My analysis of the evolution of the Russian leadership's foreign policy thinking in Chapter 3 suggests that while military security continued to play an important role in the Russian leadership's thinking at that time, the conceptions of threats (hard vs. soft security issues) and of potential means to counter these threats (military vs. political) were broader. In particular, *pragmatic geoeconomic Realism* acknowledged that soft security issues, such as how Russia coped with the problem in Chechnya, had an impact on the international perception of Russia and worked to the disadvantage of Moscow. Consequently, while it is difficult for Realists to explain the Russian leadership's desire to change the international perception of the Chechen conflict, it makes sense if we take into account a broader conception of threats, which was reflected in the Russian leadership's foreign policy thinking.

To explain why the Russian leadership decided to cooperate with the United States in such a far-reaching manner and did not make cooperation conditional on explicit concessions, for example, on the ABM issue or NATO–Russia relations, we need to take into account changes in the perception of the nature of international relations. Rather than attempting to change the rules of international affairs, as *geopolitical Realism* demanded, *pragmatic geoeconomic Realism* argued that the best way to serve Russia's interest was to use existing rules to the country's advantage. This is why Putin defended his decision to support the United States by referring to the fact that a confrontational foreign policy or isolationism was counterproductive[93] and that cooperation was much more prudential.[94]

In addition, the Russian leadership seems to have hoped that by cooperating with the United States, it could change the logic of interaction between Russia and the United States. Consequently, in the aftermath of the attacks, Putin repeatedly expressed the hope that Russia and the United States would establish a new long-term partnership founded on common interests, which would produce mutual gains and best serve Russia's interests, as well as the interests of the world.[95] In an address to Russian diplomats in 2002, Putin argued, 'a new, close partnership between Russia and the United States is not only in the interests of our nations. It also has a positive impact on the entire system of international relations and, therefore, remains one of our unquestionable priorities'.[96] The timing of Moscow's decisions to close Russia's intelligence-gathering station in Cuba (at Lourdes) and its naval base in Vietnam (at Cam Ranh) soon after 11 September and shortly before a meeting between President Putin and President Bush in Shanghai on 18 October 2001 support the claim that the Russian leadership sought a change in the bilateral climate.

In short, the analysis suggests that only by taking into account the impact of the leadership's foreign policy thinking at that time can we explain why the Russian leadership chose *open-ended instrumental cooperation* rather than *conditional cooperation*. First, pragmatism explains the swiftness of the response. Second, the idea that Russia's great power status had to be *earned* by responsible foreign policy behaviour helps explain why the Russian leadership acquiesced in the deployment of Western troops benevolently and why it tried to use the attacks to change the international perception of its war in Chechnya. Finally, to explain why the Russian leadership hoped to be able to change the 'terms-of-trade' in Russia's relations with the West, we need to take into account a change in the perception of the nature of international relations. Rather than trying to oppose international developments, *pragmatic geoeconomic Realism* suggested that Russia should better adapt along with them.

Conclusion

The chapter set out to explain the Russian leadership's response to the 11 September terrorist attacks. The analysis offers three major observations. First, the *external dimension* of Realism explains why the Russian leadership did not choose an *almost confrontational response*. Such an approach would have isolated Russia internationally. Second, the *behavioural dimension* of Realism explains why the Russian leadership did not conduct an *almost unqualified cooperative* foreign policy. Evidence suggests that Moscow was certainly hoping to use the 11 September attacks and the US reaction to bolster its own interests. Yet due to the indeterminacy of the Realist power-maximizing hypothesis, the *behavioural dimension* of Realism does not explain why Russia chose *open-ended instrumental cooperation* instead of *conditional cooperation*. Third, to explain this choice, I suggest that we need to take into account *pragmatic geoeconomic Realism*. In other words, this case study supports my second hypothesis on the extent to which collective ideas mattered in Russian foreign policy. While external constraints and the power-maximizing hypothesis suggest that it was rational for Moscow to react with some kind of cooperation, collective ideas need to be taken into account to explain the nature and extent of that cooperation.

The major implication of the analysis is that Moscow's response would have probably been quite different had the terrorist attacks occurred, for example, in the year 1998. Chapter 3 suggests that the foreign policy thinking at that time was dominated by a *geopolitical* kind of *Realism*. While external constraints would have made an *almost confrontational response* unlikely, *geopolitical Realism* would have pointed to a *conditional cooperative* foreign policy. This counterfactual analysis highlights the contention that collective ideas are an important variable in explaining Russia's foreign policy.

In addition, the in-depth analysis of a wide range of Realist explanations shows that these arguments are often based on implicit assumptions that are not part of the Realist mainstream perspective, as defined in the study. In other words, these Realist explanations are often based on independent variables that are contingent rather than exogenous. As a result, foreign policy outcomes conceived of as unpredictable at the time of decision-making seem to be almost inevitable with hindsight.

Part III Implications

7
Conclusion

This study seeks to shed light on the sources of Russian foreign policy towards the West during the first one-and-a half decades after the dissolution of the Soviet Union. In particular, it tries to answer two major questions: How can we explain change in the Russian leadership's approach towards the West? And how did the Russian leadership adapt the country's foreign policy to the post-Cold War conditions? The following sections summarize the findings of the three case studies, and draw explanatory and theoretical implications from the findings.

Summary of findings

In conclusion, the case studies confirm the first hypothesis on the impact of external constraints on Russian foreign policy in four instances. External constraints are the single most important factor explaining the Russian leadership's decisions to join NATO's Partnership for Peace programme in 1994/95, sign the NATO–Russia Founding Act in 1997, and cooperate with the West in the final conflict resolutions in autumn 1995 in Bosnia and in spring 1999 in Kosovo. All these decision-making situations were characterized by the presence of the Western states' determination to pursue their objectives regardless of Moscow's preferences. In other words, in all these cases, the Russian leadership was confronted with a stark choice between confronting the Western states and cooperating with them. Consistent with the first hypothesis, the Russian leadership reacted in a risk-averse manner and chose cooperation rather than confrontation. It is noteworthy that these decisions contradicted the Russian leadership's perception of Russia's national interests, and they were taken despite strong domestic opposition.

The second hypothesis on the impact of collective ideas is confirmed in ten instances. The analysis of the evolution of the Russian leadership's foreign policy thinking in Chapter 3 suggests that from 1992 to 1993/94, *liberal ideas* shaped the Russian leadership's foreign policy thinking. The case studies show that these *liberal ideas* are vital to explaining why in the period from late 1991 to 1993/94 the Russian leadership indicated that it wanted to join NATO, why it did not oppose the Visegrad countries' intention to join the alliance, and why it supported the West almost without qualifications in its attempts to address the conflict in Bosnia. In all these instances, it would have been conceivable for the extent of Russian cooperation to be more restrained. Such a more restrained approach would have resembled the foreign policies of some other European states. Yet, the Russian leadership's conception of Russia as a *normal* great power and its desire to gain recognition that post-Soviet Russia belonged to the club of Western great powers largely explain why it cooperated with the West so closely. In other words, in this early period of post-Soviet Russian foreign policy *liberal ideas* had a crucial impact not only on foreign policy rhetoric but also on foreign policy action.

In the period from 1993/94 to 2000, *geopolitical Realism* replaced these *liberal ideas*. The case studies suggest that *geopolitical Realist ideas* need to be taken into account to explain why the Russian leadership began to balance cautiously against NATO enlargement post 1993/94, and why Moscow's approaches became increasingly confrontational to the Bosnian conflict from 1994 until September 1995 and to the Kosovo conflict from March 1998 until mid April 1999. The Balkan case study suggests, for example, that Moscow's willingness to side with the Serbs during the conflict in Kosovo made military intervention led by NATO more likely. While military intervention starkly contradicted Russia's interests, Moscow did not pursue a more cooperative foreign policy with the West, which might have made military intervention less likely, since it perceived the conflict in *dogmatic geopolitical terms*. Again, ideational factors not only had an impact on foreign policy rhetoric, but also on policy action.

Yet the extent to which collective ideas mattered in this period was slightly less than in the first period. The fact that Moscow did not welcome NATO enlargement, for example, was not surprising and can be explained without recourse to ideational factors. What was surprising, however, was the degree of Moscow's suspicion about Western intentions and the emphasis on geopolitical rather than geoeconomic threats. As a result, the Russian leadership was preoccupied with the prospect of

NATO enlargement and perceived it not only as a potential but as an imminent threat.

The hypothesis on the impact of collective ideas is further supported if one focuses on foreign policy strategies in this period. Chapter 3 on the evolution of the Russian leadership's foreign policy discourse suggests that the thinking on strategy from 1993/94 to 1996 was still impacted by *liberal ideas*. These liberal ideas explain why in this period the Russian leadership repeatedly used the threat of the rise to power of nationalists and communists as a lever in Russia's relations with the West. The application of such a domestic threat is difficult to reconcile with the Realist approach as defined here. In Chapter 3, I further argue that in the period from 1996 to 2000, *liberal ideas* in the thinking on strategy were replaced by *dogmatic geopolitical ideas*, which emphasized diversification of foreign relations and attempts to establish counteralliances. As shown, these ideas on strategy were also reflected in Russia's actual foreign policy, especially in its rhetoric.

To explain why from 2000 to 2004 the Russian leadership reacted soberly to the second round of NATO enlargement including, inter alia, the Baltic states and why it supported the US 'War on Terrorism' swiftly and substantively, we need to take into account the impact of *pragmatic geoeconomic Realism*. Yet the explanatory role of *pragmatic geoeconomic Realist ideas* was smaller than the role of collective ideas in the previous periods. With regard to the Russian leadership's approach to the second round of NATO enlargement, an increasingly confrontational strategy, like that of the 1990s, was unlikely to be productive. In this sense, given past experience and the small number of reasonable foreign policy alternatives at that time, it was to be expected that the Russian leadership would react more soberly to the second round of enlargement. Similarly, it was likely that Moscow would react with some kind of cooperation to the 11 September 2001 terrorist attacks. While the overall direction of changes in Russian foreign policy in the period from 2000 to 2004 can well be explained by changes in external circumstances, to explain the kind of responses, I suggest, however, that the Russian leadership's foreign policy thinking needs to be taken into account. The impact of *pragmatic geoeconomic Realism* is, for example, vital to explain the extent and kind of Russia's cooperation to the 11 September 2001 terrorist attacks and Moscow's benevolent acquiescence in the deployment of Western forces to Central Asia.

Finally, *cultural geostrategic Realism* with its more negative view of international relations, its acknowledgment that Russia's 'near abroad' represented an arena also for competition about value systems, its emphasis on

Russia's uniqueness, and its more optimistic assessment of the country's capabilities needs to be taken into account to explain Moscow's more ambiguous and assertive approach to NATO post 2004. On the one hand, *cultural geostrategic Realist ideas* explain why Russia continued cooperation in the NATO–Russia Council. Here Russia's unique status was acknowledged and Moscow met NATO members at eye-level. On the other hand, Russia's opposition to a third round of NATO enlargement and Moscow's toughening stance on issues such as the US plans for the construction of a missile defence system in Europe and the CFE Treaty can only be explained by taking into account *cultural geostrategic Realism's* more positive assessment of Russia's capabilities. Given the fact that Moscow had a number of reasonable foreign policy alternatives available, collective ideas played a greater explanatory role in this period compared with the previous period.

In short, the three case studies support the hypotheses of the study overall. In cases where external constraints were formidable, Moscow chose cooperation rather than confrontation. In cases where external constraints were not formidable, collective ideas had an impact both on foreign policy rhetoric and action.

However, two qualifications need to be made. First, especially during the mid and late 1990s, there was a significant discrepancy between the assertive tone of Russian foreign policy rhetoric and more restrained foreign policy action. In this sense, the impact of *geopolitical Realist ideas* seems to have been higher on rhetoric than on action. Yet, it is to re-emphasize that this does not mean that ideational factors had an impact only on rhetoric. As demonstrated in the case studies, foreign policy ideas were consequential and were reflected in Russian foreign policy action. This finding contradicts the arguments of some of the Realists mentioned in the Introduction, who argue that *geopolitical Realist ideas* had an impact only on rhetoric and not on action, if at all.

Second, while major patterns in Russia's approach can be explained by focusing primarily on external constraints and collective ideas, the case studies have highlighted that especially during the early and mid 1990s, domestic legislative factors had an impact on the timing of foreign policy decisions and on the Russian leadership's foreign policy rhetoric. Domestic legislative opposition to the leadership's approach to the Bosnian conflict in 1992/93, for example, explains inconsistencies in the Kremlin's approach. Yet, despite this marginal impact, the study suggests that throughout the period under consideration, when push came to shove, the Russian leadership disregarded domestic legislative criticism. This was the case both with regard to joining the NATO–Russia Founding

Act in 1997 and with regard to Moscow's decisions to join the West during the Bosnian crisis in the autumn of 1995 and during the Kosovo conflict in the spring of 1999. Furthermore, especially post 1999, the impact of domestic politics on Russian foreign policy significantly declined so that Putin never had to face a significant legislative opposition to his foreign policy. The major reasons for this lack of legislative opposition were two changes in the distribution of power between the executive and the legislative. In the 1999 parliamentary elections, a party of power was able to win a substantial share of votes so that Putin was able to rely on a coalition of centrist forces in the lower house, the Russian Duma. Centrist forces again gained a majority in the 2003 parliamentary elections. Furthermore, due to changes in the composition of the upper house, the Federal Council, the creation of federal districts, and the establishment of presidential representatives, the role and influence of governors on foreign policy declined.[1] As a result, post 1999 the executive had support from the legislature for most of its domestic programmes and for its foreign policy.

Implications

Explanatory implications

What are the implications of the study's findings for the two major research questions posed at the outset? On the one hand, the findings suggest that at the macro level the Russian leadership adapted Russian foreign policy fairly consistently and, most importantly, peacefully to the post-Cold War conditions. If we recall that in 1987, Paul Kennedy predicted in his comprehensive study *The Rise and Fall of the Great Powers* that '[t]here is nothing in the character of the tradition of the Russian state to suggest that it could ever accept imperial decline gracefully';[2] post-Cold War Russian foreign policy disproved this expectation. Quite to the contrary, the post-Soviet Russian leadership instantly and consistently acknowledged that it would be counterproductive to try and compensate for the country's decline by conducting an aggressive or expansionist foreign policy.[3] Moscow accepted the country's weak relative power position. In this sense, the Russian leadership acted in accordance with Realist expectations.

On the other hand, at a micro level Moscow's adaptation to the new post-Cold War conditions was not as smooth as some Realists would expect. While external constraints were the decisive factor in some cases, in many cases external constraints did not predetermine Russian foreign policy outputs. This means that in many cases the Russian leadership had some foreign policy options to choose from. As I have argued in Chapter 2, in these cases Realists assume that state leaders are typically able to comprehend an 'objective material reality' instantly and to act rationally to maximize their nation's relative power positions. This study suggests, however, that this hypothesis is not necessarily wrong, but that it has only limited analytical value due to its indeterminacy in many cases. After the end of the Cold War, it was often far from self-evident what kind of foreign policy would maximize Russia's relative power position. With regard to NATO enlargement, for example, Chapter 4 suggests that it was not clear whether careful attempts to balance against NATO enlargement or the acceptance of the unavoidable would have best maximized the Russian relative power position during the 1990s. Consequently, the study confirms the working assumption that Russia's leadership should be viewed not as an actor that could comprehend an 'objective material reality' but rather as a social actor engaged in a cognitive process of adaptation to comprehend the new conditions.

Initially, the Russian leadership embraced a liberal answer. It then replaced this liberal outlook with three different types of Realist conceptualizations of international relations, Russia's identity, its international status and role, and its ideas on strategy. Contrary to the Realist claim that a state's leadership would 'know' what rational power-maximization meant in every situation and that states would adapt to changes in the distribution of power smoothly, the analysis suggests that given the high level of uncertainty in the first post-Cold War decade, this was not the case.

While this finding challenges some Realist, and especially neo-Realist interpretations, this difficult process of adaptation is hardly surprising. In his study of British foreign policy at the turn of the twentieth century, Friedberg concludes that British leaders had great difficulties in adapting the country's foreign policy to Britain's decline. While they aimed to maximize Britain's power position, the high level of uncertainty made it difficult for them to 'read the signs of change' accurately.[4] Similarly, Goldgeier and McFaul show in their study of post-Cold War US foreign policy towards Russia that even the US leadership struggled to come to terms with the post-Cold War situation.[5]

In summary, to explain change in Russian foreign policy towards the West from 1992 to 2007, we need to take into account both changes in external constraints and in collective ideas. This conclusion does not imply that domestic-level factors were irrelevant. It simply suggests that by focusing on external constraints and collective ideas, we can explain major, but by no means not all, facets of Russia's approaches in the country's first one-and-a-half decades.

The case studies also shed some light on the conditions under which collective ideas had the greatest impact on Russian foreign policy in this period. The most important factor that determined the degree to which ideational factors mattered is the level of uncertainty. Two different kinds of uncertainty need to be distinguished: structural and strategic uncertainties. While structural uncertainty characterizes the degree of lack of knowledge about dynamics in international relations and about the major sources of states' conduct, strategic uncertainty characterizes the degree of lack of knowledge about most efficient strategies to achieve objectives.

With regard to structural uncertainty the early and mid 1990s were characterized by a low level of certainty about the dynamic of post-Cold War international relations, both with regard to how states would interact and with regard to the role and shape of major international institutions. In the early 1990s, the West itself did not have a clear vision of how it wanted to approach post-Cold War international affairs. This situation changed to some extent towards the mid 1990s, when it became increasingly clear that the West would not base its approach towards Russia on the assumption of shared values. This position raised the costs of a Russian foreign policy based on liberal assumptions. Yet during the mid 1990s, it was not yet evident whether the West was willing to grant Russia a status as an equal member of the Western club. Only after the West took the decisions to enlarge NATO, to intervene militarily even without a UN mandate, and to shape major European institutions to its liking was structural uncertainty significantly reduced. As a result, by the end of the 1990s, this increased clarity about the shape of post-Cold War international relations narrowed the scope of reasonable foreign policy options for the Russian leadership.

Up until the 2003 US-led Iraq War, the shape of the dynamics of international affairs seemed highly determined. Yet the US inability to not only win the Iraq War but to also win the peace has undermined this certainty again. In addition to this, rapid growth rates of the so-called BRIC countries – Brazil, Russia, India, and China – and their much more self-conscious behaviour on the international arena (as can be witnessed in the context of WTO negotiations) have decreased certainty about the shape of international affairs in the last few years.

The level of strategic uncertainty underwent similar changes. In the early 1990s, the Russian leadership hoped to gain significant concessions from the West by cooperating with the West almost without qualifications. In the mid and late 1990s, it then hoped to gain most by conducting a more assertive foreign policy. Developments throughout the 1990s showed that both strategies were flawed. At the end of the 1990s, the lesson learnt was that Russia had to assert its interests, but in doing so it needed carefully to match ambitions and capabilities. In this sense, in the period from 2000 to 2004 the Russian leadership had a much clearer sense of what kind of foreign policy strategy would not work. However, post 2003/04, strategic uncertainty increased. Rapid economic growth in Russia did not only have a positive impact on the Russian government's ability to pay pensions and wages and thus significantly contribute to political stability in Russia, but it allowed Moscow to manage without additional international loans and to make early repayments of its debts. The positive economic performance increased Russia's international leverage and autonomy. For the first time after the dissolution of the Soviet Union was the Western leverage on Russia fairly limited and Moscow was in a position to engage actively in international affairs, particularly in the CIS area, rather than mainly react to developments.[6]

Changes in the level of structural and strategic uncertainties co-vary with changes in the degree to which collective ideas affect Russian foreign policy outputs throughout the period. The high levels of uncertainties in the early 1990s explain why the impact of collective ideas on Russian foreign policy was high immediately after the dissolution of the Soviet Union. Similarly, the decreasing impact of ideational factors on foreign policy outputs throughout the 1990s and especially from 2000 to 2004 can be explained with the reduction of structural and strategic uncertainties in the course of the 1990s through to 2003/04. While the reduction of structural uncertainty narrowed down the number of reasonable foreign policy objectives, the decrease in strategic uncertainty limited the number of reasonable foreign policy strategies. Thus, Russia's foreign policymakers simply had fewer choices with the result that collective ideas played a smaller role. Finally, rising uncertainties post 2003/04 correlate with the rise of the impact of collective ideas as shown in the analysis of Russia's approach to NATO post 2004 in Chapter 4.

If we assume that the past can help us anticipate the future to some extent, these findings suggest that collective ideas should continue to play an important role in explaining Russian foreign policy when there are high levels of structural and strategic uncertainties. Since structural and strategic uncertainties are higher now than they were from 2000 to 2004, the question is what kind of Russian foreign policy should we expect in the near future?

There is agreement among many foreign policy analysts that contemporary Russia has 'left the West'. Trenin argues, for example, that the United States and Europe 'must recognize that the terms of Western-Russian interaction, conceptualized at the time of the Soviet Union's collapse 15 years ago and more or less unchanged since, have shifted fundamentally' and he concludes 'Russia's leaders have given up on becoming part of the West and have started creating their Moscow-centred system'.[7] Similarly, regarding the question of Russia's integration into Europe, Neumann argues that 'Russia will continue to be *in* Europe, but not *of* Europe: it will be a player, but it will be a player of a different kind'.[8] As a result, it is predicted that Russian foreign policy will become more active and assertive, signal to the world that Russia should not be treated like a second-rate developing or regional great power, US-centrism will decrease, Western criticism will not be taken as seriously by Moscow, and Russia will diversify its relations with non-Western countries to foster its interests. Yet, this more independent approach does not imply that Russia's foreign policy will be anti-West. That means that there is scope for cooperation with Russia on issues of mutual interest.[9]

While I agree with these predictions for the contours of Russian foreign policy in the very near future, I hesitate to make predictions for the mid-term. As this study highlights, Russian foreign policy thinking is far from being settled. While it is unlikely that Russia will return to a policy of unqualified cooperation with the West or that it will confront the West, Moscow is not 'doomed' to pursue a more active and assertive foreign policy outside the Western consensus. Changes in the external environment, in domestic power distribution, or in a process of learning and re-thinking can alter the foreign policy thinking again. Putin enjoyed great popularity in Russia due to high commodity prices and economic recovery after the 1998 financial crisis. In the case of an economic downturn, Putin's successor, Dmitry Medvedev, will lack the legitimacy that Putin enjoyed, which might lead to changes in the foreign policy thinking and thus to changes in Russia's foreign policy conduct.[10]

Finally, the case studies suggest two observations as to the sources of collective ideas. First, changes in the Russian leadership's foreign policy thinking are to some extent explainable in terms of learning.[11] On hindsight, *liberal thinking, geopolitical Realism,* and *pragmatic geoeconomic Realism* were inadequate representations of post-Cold War conditions. The *liberal* conception was flawed, since it paid too little tribute to the competitive nature of international relations and it relinquished interests too easily. *Geopolitical Realism* was also unsound, since attempts to conduct an ambitious and assertive foreign policy undermined Russia's international credibility as long as Moscow lacked the means to back-up its threats in order to sustain such a policy.[12] Furthermore, as argued in the case studies, by conducting increasingly uncooperative foreign policies, in some cases Russian diplomacy seems to have contributed to the creation of undesirable situations of stark choice. This was the case, for example, in autumn 1995 during the Bosnian conflict and after mid April 1999, with regard to the Kosovo conflict. Had Russia's leadership cooperated with the West earlier, or had it simply declared that it disagreed without attempting to get involved more closely in these conflicts – as the Chinese did – Moscow might have fared better. Finally, the cooperative foreign policy towards the West based on *pragmatic geoeconomic Realist ideas* in the period from 2000 to 2004 was increasingly challenged due to a perceived lack of reciprocity. While Moscow believed to have made major concessions to the West, the Western states pushed forward NATO enlargement, initially did not close military bases in Central Asia, and by planning to set up a missile defence system in Europe, they undermined the strategic balance of power. The rise of *geopolitical Realism* can therefore be seen as a response to the flaws of *liberal thinking*, *pragmatic geoeconomic Realism* can be seen as a response to the failure of a foreign policy based on *geopolitical Realism*, and *cultural geostrategic Realism* can be seen as a response to the flaws of *pragmatic geoeconomic Realism*. Thus, changes in the Russian leadership's foreign policy thinking seem to have been partly influenced by feedback.

Second, it is, however, insufficient to explain changes in foreign policy thinking only or mainly in terms of learning. It is one thing to acknowledge a foreign policy failure, but it is a very different thing to draw lessons. Thus, while learning represents an important trigger for change, it in itself does not account for the lessons learnt. Learning does not, for example, explain why throughout the period, the Russian leadership was so preoccupied with gaining international recognition for the country's status as a great power. To explain this desire, one needs to take a longer historical perspective. Neumann argues that 'there are examples from 500 years ago to show that gaining the recognition of the European powers is a theme that runs through Russian history in its entirety'.[13] This historical strand was reinforced by a sense of damaged pride and humiliation, which resulted from the country's decline from superpower to regional great power status after the dissolution of the Soviet Union. Statements such as 'Russia will always be a great power'[14] reflect the extent to which status recognition mattered in Russian foreign policy thinking.

It is also important to emphasize that soft-factors such as status recognition were consequential. The desire for recognition as a great power had, for example, a significant impact on the West's ability to influence Russia. US Deputy Secretary of State Strobe Talbott argues that '[t]his was a pattern [. . .]: Yeltsin's desire for the spotlight at high-prestige international gatherings gave us leverage over him on issues where we had run into an impasse with his government'.[15] Indirectly, Yeltsin supports this assessment in his diaries, where he – not without satisfaction – argues that '[n]o other U.S. president [than Clinton] came to Moscow so many times. [. . .] No other U.S. president engaged in such intensive negotiations with the leaders of our country or provided us with such large-scale aid, both economic and political'.[16]

This finding undermines claims of Realists such as Henry Kissinger or William Odom, who argue that the West should do what is best for its own interests without worrying about the impact of these policies on Russia. During the debate about NATO enlargement Kissinger argued, for example, '[w]hoever heard of a military alliance begging with a weakened adversary? NATO should not be turned into an instrument to conciliate Russia or Russia will undermine it'.[17] Similarly, Odom claims that 'Western magnanimity cannot change Russia's foreign policy behaviour for the better; it is far more likely to make it worse'.[18] Yet engaging Russia and reassuring it that it could still play an important role on the international stage have been prudential Western strategies. An example of the utility of engaging Russia was, for example, Moscow's contribution to the final conflict resolution during the Kosovo conflict in the period after mid April 1999.[19]

Theoretical implications

From a theoretical point of view, the study suggests one way to combine Realism and a 'thin' version of Social Constructivism. In so doing, it seeks to contribute to the body of literature that tries to synthesize different analytical perspectives rather than claiming the dominance of one above the other.[20] Realists normally focus on the context of choice situations and assume that decision-makers can somehow 'objectively' derive the national interest from the relative power position of states and devise most effective strategies to achieve these interests. While I emphasize here the importance of external constraints, I am sceptical about the utility of the Realist power-maximization hypothesis because of its indeterminacy in cases where interests and gains are not immediately obvious. In such cases, the Realist power-maximizing hypothesis can only work if one makes more specific assumptions about how a state defines its national interests and how it calculates the expected utility of foreign policy strategies. Social Constructivists, on the other hand, have in the past focused primarily on demonstrating the impact of ideas on foreign policy, without being sufficiently explicit about the extent to which and the conditions under which these ideas matter. While these theorists tended to neglect the impact of power relations, they stressed the importance of collective ideas for understanding how a state defines its national interest and how it calculates the expected utilities of foreign policy strategies.

The study suggests that by combining a 'thin' version of Social Constructivism and Realism, both can benefit from one another and improve foreign policy analysis. That suggestion does not mean that all sets of collective ideas are compatible with Realism. The *liberal thinking* that dominated the Russian leadership's foreign policy thinking from 1992 until 1993, for example, contradicts Realist assumptions. But the latter three perspectives, *geopolitical Realism*, *pragmatic geoeconomic Realism*, and *cultural geostrategic Realism*, despite their significant differences, all share some fundamental assumptions that qualify them as Realist. In other words, while 'ideal type' Realism creates the impression that there is only one Realist rationale, this study suggests that there are a great variety of Realist interpretations of what it means in concrete terms for states to maximize their power position. To some degree, this distinction between different Realist rationales in Russian foreign policy thinking is akin to the discussion between offensive and defensive Realists. This debate shows that even within the established school of Realism, an agreement about what kind of foreign policy qualifies as Realist is lacking.[21] This study adds to this discourse by describing some specific Russian versions of Realist reasoning.

In addition to establishing a framework for the analysis of the impact of material and ideational factors, what theoretical generalizations can we draw? On the one hand, it is important to refrain from overestimating the implications of this study for International Relations theory. While the framework employed here to analyse Russian foreign policy could be used for other states, its specific findings about the content of collective ideas are not generalizable. On the other hand, there are some points that might have wider theoretical significance.

First, the analysis suggests that the impact of collective ideas on foreign policy outputs positively correlates with the level of structural and strategic uncertainties. The higher the level of structural uncertainty and the less clearly defined national interests are in concrete terms, the more important it is to know how a state's leadership conceives of the nature of international relations and the country's status, role, and primary interests. Furthermore, the higher strategic uncertainty, the more important it is to investigate how a state leadership calculates costs and benefits of foreign policy alternatives.

Second, the impact of collective ideas on a state's foreign policy is positively related to the relative power position of a state. Since the range of foreign policy options of a relatively strong power is less constrained by external factors, collective ideas should play a greater role in the study of relatively strong powers.

Third, while much of the Social Constructivist literature has focused on the impact of international norms and values on a state's foreign policy,[22] the analysis suggests the value of greater attention to domestic norms and values.[23] Despite the fact that this study has not systematically enquired into the origins of foreign policy ideas, it notes that the Russian leadership's foreign policy thinking was significantly affected by domestic rather than international norms.

Finally, and most surprisingly, collective ideas can also play a great role in cases where national security is at stake, that is, in cases of *high politics*. Realists normally claim that national security is mainly a domain of material power considerations and that ideational factors do not matter here. The fact that the hypotheses about the impact of collective ideas was supported in three 'hard cases', that is, in cases where conventional wisdom would expect ideational factors to play at best a marginal role, casts serious doubt on the Realist claim. It seems that collective ideas played such an important role especially in the security sphere, because issues such as NATO enlargement or military interventions in the Balkans (a region that was considered a traditional Russian sphere of influence) posed a significant challenge to the Russian leadership's understanding of the country's status and role in the world. NATO enlargement and these military interventions contradicted the Russian leadership's view of Russia. While this sense of humiliation did not lead to a reckless response, damaged pride is an important factor in explaining the Russian leadership's preoccupation with NATO enlargement and Moscow's desperate and sometimes counterproductive attempts to balance against the West. Thus, the study suggests that collective ideas can play an important role even in issues of *high politics* when the behaviour of external actors significantly contradicts the leadership's perception of the own country. While this finding might be compatible with classical Realism, it poses a significant challenge to structural Realism.

Due to its focus on questions of high politics, the study is incomplete, and it raises a number of questions for further research. First, more systematic research needs to be done on cases where economic interests were at stake. Second, the impact of collective ideas on Russia's approach towards the countries of the former Soviet Union could be examined in order to assess whether and what kind of collective ideas played a role in this sphere.[24] It would be of interest to compare the extent to which collective ideas mattered and whether they were of a similar or different kind than the ideas analysed here.

Third, the sources of Russia's conduct towards states that neither belong to the West nor to the former Soviet Union, such as China, India, Iran, Iraq, or Syria, should be examined and integrated into this model.[25] Such an analysis would help better to delineate the impact of collective ideas.

Furthermore, while the study demonstrates the impact of collective ideas on Russian foreign policy outputs, it does not offer a systematic treatment of the sources of change in the Russian leadership's foreign policy thinking. Far more could be said about the degree to which the sets of collective ideas identified here were affected by material or non-material factors. It might be the case, for example, that Russian foreign policy thinking was shaped primarily by material factors. This conclusion would imply that collective ideas served only as an intervening variable. In this case, ideational factors would still be important, but their relative impact (vis-à-vis material factors) would be much less significant. Some Realist scholars have pursued this line of argument. In analysing the end of the Cold War, Brooks and Wohlforth accept the Social Constructivist critique of the assumption of exogenous and uniform interests and agree that states might have variously defined interests. Yet they challenge the Social Constructivist claim that these interests are the result of social processes. They suggest that the variance in states' interests can often be explained by material factors.[26]

In other words, to answer comprehensively the question to what degree non-material factors matter, it is imperative for Social Constructivists to offer an answer to the question of what mix of factors impacts a country's leadership's foreign policy thinking.[27] To assess the sources of the foreign policy thinking, the impact of five potential factors should be assessed:[28] (1) concerns about external constraints; (2) concerns about state power-maximization (both are Realist concerns); (3) the leadership's concern to stay in power; (4) concerns about the interests of domestic lobby groups (both are Liberal concerns);[29] and (5) concerns about appropriate action, that is, foreign policy action that is motivated by the desire to embed such action into a historical and cultural narrative.[30] Figure 7.1 illustrates how these concerns impact collective ideas and, as a result, also foreign policy outputs.

In conclusion, in this study I offer a systematic analysis of the major determinants of Russian foreign policy towards the West from 1992 to

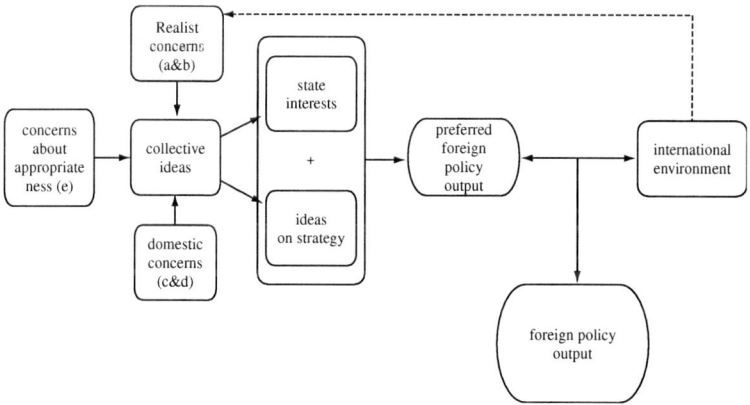

Figure 7.1 Collective ideas as the dependent variable.

2007. I show that both external constraints and collective ideas played major roles in shaping Russian foreign policy outputs and need to be taken into account to explain change in Russian foreign policy. Furthermore, the study demonstrates that while Realists correctly predict that Moscow would not react with an aggressive or expansionist foreign policy to the dissolution of the Soviet Union, the Russian leadership did not adapt the county's foreign policy as smoothly to post-Cold War conditions as Realists would expect. The Russian leadership was engaged in a cognitive process to comprehend the post-Cold War situation. Most surprisingly from the theoretical viewpoint, ideational factors were consequential even in cases where conventional wisdom would expect little impact of this variable. The reason why collective ideas played a crucial role even in issues relating to *high politics* was that the West's determination to enlarge NATO contradicted the Russian leadership's conception of Russia's international status and role. In short, this study demonstrates the merits of combining different analytical approaches to increase explanatory power.

Notes and References

Chapter 1: Introduction

1. I use the term West here to refer narrowly to the United States and the Western, Central, and Eastern European countries. It does not include countries such as Japan, Australia, and New Zealand.
2. In the study, Russian names and titles of articles are generally transliterated in accordance with the Library of Congress Transliteration Table. Two exceptions occur. First, in the text, names of Russian officials and academics are rendered in familiar spellings commonly used in the academic\ literature. Second, references reproduce the transliteration used by the publisher.
3. P. Shearman, 'Defining the National Interest: Russian Foreign Policy and Domestic Politics', in Roger E. Kanet, et al., eds, *The Foreign Policy of the Russian Federation* (New York: St. Martin's Press, Inc., 1997), 1–27. W. E. Ferry and R. E. Kanet, 'Towards the Future: Emerging Trends in Russian Foreign Policy', in Roger E. Kanet, et al., eds, *The Foreign Policy of the Russian Federation* (New York: St. Martin's Press, Inc., 1997), 192–201. A. C. Lynch, 'The Evolution of Russian Foreign Policy in the 1990s', in Rick Fawn, et al., eds, *Russia after Communism* (London: Frank Cass, 2002), 161–82. L. Buszynski, 'Russia and the West: Towards Renewed Geopolitical Rivalry?' *Survival*, vol. 37, no. 3 (Autumn 1995), 104–25.
4. M. Bowker, 'The Place of Europe in Russian Foreign Policy', in Mark Webber, ed., *Russia and Europe: Conflict or Cooperation?* (Basingstoke: Macmillan Press, 2000), 22–45, p. 39.
5. L. Aron, 'The Foreign Policy Doctrine of Postcommunist Russia and its Domestic Context', in Michael Mandelbaum, ed., *The New Russian Foreign Policy* (New York: Council on Foreign Relations, 1998), 23–63, p. 31.
6. Y. Primakov, 'Russia in World Politics – A Lecture in Honor of Chancellor Gorchakov', *International Affairs (Moscow)*, vol. 4, no. 3 (1998) 7–12. For an analysis of Gorchakov's foreign policy and the impact of his thinking on contemporary Russia, see F. Splidsboel-Hansen, 'Past and Future: Aleksandr Gorchakov and Russian Foreign Policy', *Europe-Asia Studies*, vol. 54, no. 3 (May 2002) 377–96.
7. The terms 'international relations', 'realism'/'realist', 'social constructivism'/ 'social constructivist', and 'liberalism'/'liberal' are capitalized when they refer to the academic discipline of international relations and its theories.
8. P. J. Marantz, 'Neither Adversaries Nor Partners: Russia and the West Search for a New Relationship', in Roger E. Kanet, et al., eds, *The Foreign Policy of the Russian Federation* (New York: St. Martin's Press, Inc., 1997), 78–101, p. 79. A. C. Lynch, 'The Realism of Russia's Foreign Policy', *Europe-Asia Studies*, vol. 53, no. 1 (2001) 7–31, p. 25.
9. P. Kubicek, 'Russian Foreign Policy and the West', *Political Science Quarterly*, vol. 114, no. 4 (1999–2000) 547–68, pp. 567–8.

10. M. Bowker, *Russian Foreign Policy and the End of the Cold War* (Aldershot: Dartmouth Publishing Company Limited, 1997), p. 206.
11. M. Mandelbaum, ed., *The New Russian Foreign Policy* (New York: Council on Foreign Relations, 1998), p. 21.
12. Kubicek, 'Russian Foreign Policy and the West', p. 25.
13. R. Legvold, 'Russia's Unformed Foreign Policy', *Foreign Affairs,* vol. 80, no. 5 (Sep/Oct 2001) 62–75.
14. R. Legvold, ed., *Russian Foreign Policy in the Twenty-First Century & The Shadow of the Past* (New York: Columbia University Press, 2007), p. 65.
15. B. Lo, *Russian Foreign Policy in the Post-Soviet Era: Reality, Illusion and Mythmaking* (Basingstoke: Palgrave Macmillan, 2002), pp. 5–6. For a similar conclusion, see P. Shearman, 'The Sources of Russian Conduct: Understanding Russian Foreign Policy', *Review of International Studies,* vol. 27, no. 2 (April 2001) 249–63, p. 254.
16. While Andrei Tsygankov puts forward a comprehensive argument, linking identity to Russian foreign policy outputs, he does not specify the extent to which foreign policy ideas mattered. A. P. Tsygankov, *Russia's Foreign Policy: Change and Continuity in National Identity* (Oxford: Rowman & Littlefield, 2006).
17. For other Social Constructivist analyses of Russian foreign policy, see T. Hopf, *Social Construction of International Politics: Identities & Foreign Policies, Moscow, 1995 and 1999* (Ithaca, N.Y.: Cornell University Press, 2002). T. Hopf, 'Identities, Institutions, and Interest: Moscow's Foreign Policy from 1945–2000', September 2003, available at: http://psweb.sbs.ohio-state.edu/faculty/thopf/IdentitiesInstitutionsInterestsNov03.pdf (accessed: 7 July 2007). J. Richter, 'Russian Foreign Policy and the Politics of National Identity', in Celeste A. Wallander, ed., *The Sources of Russian Foreign Policy After the Cold War* (Boulder, Colo.: Westview, 1996), 69–93. Sakwa is difficult to label. While he emphasizes the 'new Realism' in Putin's foreign policy, he also acknowledges that a rethinking has happened after 1999 and that Russian foreign policy under Putin is guided by 'cooperative pragmatism', which is distinct from Primakovian 'confrontative pragmatism'. R. Sakwa, *Putin: Russia's Choice* (London: Routledge, 2004), pp. 209–10.
18. M. McFaul, 'A Precarious Peace – Domestic Politics in the Making of Russian Foreign Policy', *International Security,* vol. 22, no. 3 (Winter 1997/98) 5–35, p. 21. J. Checkel, 'Structure, Institutions, and Process – Russia's Changing Foreign Policy', in Adeed Dawisha, et al., eds, *The Making of Foreign Policy in Russia and the New States of Eurasia* (Armonk, N.Y.: M.E. Sharpe, Inc., 1995), 42–65, pp. 45–6.
19. A. V. Kozhemiakin, 'Democratization and Foreign Policy Change: The Case of the Russian Federation', *Review of International Studies,* vol. 23, no. 1 (1997) 49–74, p. 64 and 73. A. V. Kozhemiakin, *Expanding the Zone of Peace? Democratization and International Security* (Basingstoke: Macmillan Press, 1998), pp. 65–6. R. E. Kanet and S. M. Birgerson, 'The Domestic-Foreign Policy Linkage in Russian Politics: Nationalist Influences on Russian Foreign Policy', *Communist and Post-Communist Studies,* vol. 30, no. 4 (1997) 335–44, pp. 340 and 343. P. Marantz, 'Russian Foreign Policy During Yeltsin's Second Term', *Communist and Post-Communist Studies,* vol. 30, no. 4 (1997) 345–51, p. 350. G. Kennan, 'A Fateful Error', *The New York Times,* 5 February 1997.

154 Notes and References

20. McFaul, 'A Precarious Peace', p. 21.
21. P. J. Dobriansky, 'Russian Foreign Policy: Promise or Peril?' *The Washington Quarterly*, vol. 23, no. 1 (Winter 2000) 135–44, p. 136.
22. Good example for works that delineate the extent to which domestic factors impacted Russian foreign policy, see N. Malcolm; A. Pravda; R. Allison and M. Light, *Internal Factors in Russian Foreign Policy* (Oxford: Oxford University Press, 1996). N. Malcolm and A. Pravda, 'Democratization and Russian Foreign Policy', *International Affairs*, vol. 72, no. 3 (1996) 537–52.
23. A similar argument is put forward by Kubicek and MacFarlane, see Kubicek, 'Russian Foreign Policy and the West', pp. 567–8 and N. MacFarlane, 'The "R" in BRICs: Is Russia an Emerging Power?' *International Affairs*, vol. 81, no. 1 (2006) 41–57, pp. 42 and 53.
24. While Russia had significant nuclear capabilities, this factor played only a limited role, since nuclear weapons can only to a limited degree be transformed into political influence.
25. M. Cox, ed., *Rethinking the Soviet Collapse: Sovietology, the Death of Communism and the New Russia* (London: Pinter, 1998). C. Pursiainen, *Russian Foreign Policy and International Relations Theory* (Aldershot: Ashgate, 2000). D. Trenin and B. Lo, *The Landscape of Russian Foreign Policy Decision-Making* (Moscow: Carnegie Endowment for International Peace, 2005).
26. Good examples for such theory-driven analyses are Malcolm, Pravda, Allison and Light, *Internal Factors*. C. A. Wallander, ed., *The Sources of Russian Foreign Policy After the Cold War* (Boulder, Colo.: Westview, 1996). Bowker, *Russian Foreign Policy*. T. Hopf, ed., *Understandings of Russian Foreign Policy* (Pennsylvania: Pennsylvania State University Press, 1999). Legvold, ed., *Russian Foreign Policy*. Tsygankov, *Russia's Foreign Policy: Change and Continuity in National Identity*. T. Ambrosio, 'The Russio-American Dispute over the Invasion of Iraq: International Status and the Role of Positional Goods', *Europe-Asia Studies*, vol. 57, no. 8 (December 2005) 1189–210.

Chapter 2: Framework for Analysis

1. K. N. Waltz, *Theory of International Politics* (Reading, Mass.: Addison-Wesley, 1979), p. 8.
2. G. King, R. O. Keohane and S. Verba, *Designing Social Inquiry: Scientific Inference in Qualitative Research* (Princeton, N.J.: Princeton University Press, 1994), p. 20.
3. For the sake of simplicity, I speak of Realism without making any distinctions between various strands. This simplification seems to be justified when the approach is contrasted with other major schools of International Relations, such as Social Constructivism or Liberalism. I acknowledge, however, that at least two major strands of Realism can be distinguished. One is classical Realism, which is associated with E. H. Carr and Hans Morgenthau. The other is neo-Realism, represented by Kenneth Waltz. For classical Realism, see E. H. Carr, *The Twenty Years' Crisis, 1919–1939: An Introduction to the Study of International Relations* (Basingstoke: Macmillan, 1939). H. J. Morgenthau, *Politics Among Nations: The Struggle for Power and Peace*, 5 ed. (New York: Knopf, 1949). For neo-Realism, see Waltz, *Theory of International Politics*. For

a recent critique of the lack of distinctiveness of Realism, see J. W. Legro and A. Moravcsik, 'Is Anybody Still a Realist', *International Security*, vol. 24, no. 2 (Fall 1999) 5–55. For a response to this article, see 'Correspondence – Brother, Can You Spare a Paradigm? (Or Was Anybody Ever a Realist?)', *International Security*, vol. 25, no. 1 (Summer 2000) 165–93. For a contribution that emphasizes the breadth and historical roots of Realism, see J. Haslam, *No Virtue Like Necessity: Realist Thought in International Relations since Machiavelli* (New Haven, Conn.: Yale University Press, 2002). For a discussion of the differences between Realism and neo-Realism, see J. Donnelly, *Realism and International Relations* (Cambridge: Cambridge University Press, 2000).
4. The following core assumptions are summarized and discussed in P. J. Katzenstein, R. O. Keohane and S. D. Krasner, 'International Organization and the Study of World Politics', *International Organization*, vol. 52, no. 4 (Autumn 1998) 645–85, pp. 658–63.
5. A. S. Yee, 'Thick Rationality and the Missing "Brute Fact": The Limits of Rationalist Incorporations of Norms and Ideas', *The Journal of Politics*, vol. 59, no. 4 (November 1997) 1001–39, p. 1003.
6. P. Gourevitch, 'The Second Image Reversed: The International Sources of Domestic Politics', *International Organization*, vol. 32, no. 4 (Autumn 1978) 881–911, p. 911.
7. P. Gourevitch, 'Domestic Politics and International Relations', in Walter Carlsnaes, et al., eds, *Handbook of International Relations* (London: SAGE Publications, 2002), 309–28, p. 310.
8. Rosecrance distinguishes between 'specific' and 'generalist' Realism. R. Rosecrance, 'Has Realism Become Cost-Benefit Analysis? A Review Essay', *International Security*, vol. 26, no. 2 (Fall 2001) 132–54, p. 134.
9. Waltz, *Theory of International Politics*, Chapter 6.
10. R. L. Schweller, *Deadly Imbalances: Tripolarity and Hitler's Strategy of World Conquest* (New York: Columbia University Press, 1998) or S. M. Walt, *The Origins of Alliances* (Ithaca, N.Y.: Cornell University Press, 1987).
11. For defences of this kind of 'specific' Realism in the post–Cold War period, see W. C. Wohlforth, 'The Stability of a Unipolar World', *International Security*, vol. 24, no. 1 (Summer 1999) 5–41. E. B. Kapstein and M. Mastanduno, *Unipolar Politics – Realism and State Strategies After the Cold War* (New York: Columbia University Press, 1999). For a discussion on soft balancing, see R. A. Pape, 'Soft Balancing against the United States', *International Security*, vol. 30, no. 1 (Summer 2005) 7–45. S. G. Brooks and W. C. Wohlforth, 'Hard Times for Soft Balancing', *International Security*, vol. 30, no. 1 (Summer 2005) 72–108.
12. Rosecrance, 'Has Realism Become Cost-Benefit Analysis?' p. 136.
13. On the distinction between offensive and defensive Realism, see R. Jervis, 'Realism, Neoliberalism, and Cooperation – Understanding the Debate', *International Security*, vol. 24, no. 1 (Summer 1999) 42–63. S. G. Brooks, 'Dueling Realisms', *International Organization*, vol. 51, no. 3 (Summer 1997) 445–77. On offensive Realism, see J. J. Mearsheimer, *The Tragedy of Great Power Politics* (New York: W. W. Norton & Company, 2001). J. J. Mearsheimer, 'The False Promise of International Institutions', *International Security*, vol. 19, no. 3 (Winter 1994/95) 5–49. On defensive Realism, see Walt, *The Origins of Alliances*. C. L. Glaser, 'Realists as Optimists: Cooperation as Self-Help', *International

Security, vol. 19, no. 3 (Winter 1994/95) 50–90. S. v. Evera, *Causes of War: Power and the Roots of Conflict* (Ithaca, N.Y.: Cornell University Press, 1999). J. Snyder, *Myths of Empire: Domestic Politics and International Ambition* (Ithaca, N.Y.: Cornell University Press, 1991).

14. Wohlforth challenges the 'objectivity' of power in the context of Soviet-American relations during the Cold War, see W. C. Wohlforth, *The Elusive Balance: Power and Perceptions during the Cold War* (Ithaca, N.Y.: Cornell University Press, 1993).
15. In Vasquez's view, this indeterminacy indicates that Realism is a degenerating research programme. J. A. Vasquez, *The Power of Power Politics: From Classical Realism to Neotraditionalism* (Cambridge: Cambridge University Press, 1998), Chapter 11.
16. R. Jervis, *Perception and Misperception in International Politics* (Princeton, N.J.: Princeton University Press, 1976), p. 16.
17. R. Jervis, 'Realism in the Study of World Politics', *International Organization*, vol. 52, no. 4 (Autumn 1998) 971–91, p. 982.
18. R. N. Lebow, 'What's so Different About a Counterfactual?' *World Politics*, vol. 52, no. 4 (July 2000) 550–85, pp. 558–9. For a similar argument, see R. L. Doty, 'Foreign Policy as Social Construction: A Post-Positivist Analysis of U.S. Counterinsurgency Policy in the Philippines', *International Studies Quarterly*, vol. 37, no. 3 (September 1993) 297–320, p. 298.
19. Here I focus only on so-called modernist or thin versions of Social Constructivism. Post-modern versions are neglected, since they cannot be combined with the Realist approach. For discussions of the differences between various kinds of Social Constructivisms, see J. G. Ruggie, *Constructing the World Polity – Essays on International Institutionalization* (London: Routledge, 1998). A. Hasenclever, P. Mayer and V. Rittberger, 'Integrating Theories of International Regimes', *Review of International Studies*, vol. 26 (2000) 3–33, pp. 10–1.
20. J. G. Ruggie, 'What Makes the World Hang Together? Neo-utilitarianism and the Social Constructivist Challenge', *International Organization*, vol. 52, no. 4 (Autumn 1998) 855–85, p. 879.
21. J. T. Checkel, 'The Constructivist Turn in International Relations Theory', *World Politics*, vol. 50, no. 2 (January 1998) 324–48, p. 325. T. Hopf, *Social Construction of International Politics: Identities & Foreign Policies, Moscow, 1995 and 1999* (Ithaca, N.Y.: Cornell University Press, 2002), pp. 16–20.
22. A. Wendt, *Social Theory of International Politics* (Cambridge: Cambridge University Press, 1999), p. 372.
23. For a summary of different ways in which ideational factors can potentially impact foreign policy, see S. Telhami and M. Barnett, eds, *Identity and Foreign Policy in the Middle East* (Ithaca, N.Y.: Cornell University Press, 2002), p. 7.
24. O. R. Holsti, 'The Belief System and National Images: A Case Study', in James N. Rosenau, ed., *International Politics and Foreign Policy: A Reader in Research and Theory* (New York: The Free Press, 1969), 543–50, p. 544.
25. J. Goldstein and R. O. Keohane, eds, *Ideas and Foreign Policy: Beliefs, Institutions, and Political Change* (Ithaca, N.Y.: Cornell University Press, 1993), pp. 13–14.
26. N. C. Crawford, *Argument and Change in World Politics: Ethics, Decolonization, and Humanitarian Intervention* (Cambridge: Cambridge University Press, 2002), p. 343. For a similar argument, see E. Laclau and C. Mouffe,

Hegemony & Socialist Strategy: Towards a Radical Democratic Politics (London: Verso, 1985), p. 108.
27. Wendt makes a similar point when he argues that British missiles had a different significance for the United States than Soviet ones. This difference was the result not only of the distribution of power, but of the fact that the United States regarded Britain as a friend and the Soviet Union as a foe. A. Wendt, 'Anarchy is What States Make of it: The Social Construction of Power Politics', *International Organization,* vol. 46, no. 2 (Spring 1992) 391–425, p. 397. Even Morgenthau acknowledged in parts of his writing that states might have variously defined interests, and that rather than assuming those interests as uniform, scholars must see them as part of the sphere of politics. For an elaboration of this argument, see M. C. Williams, 'Why Ideas Matter in International Relations: Hans Morgenthau, Classical Realism, and the Moral Construction of Power Politics', *International Organization,* vol. 58 (Fall 2004) 633–65.
28. M. Finnemore and K. Sikkink, 'Taking Stock: The Constructivist Research Program in International Relations and Comparative Politics', *Annual Review of Political Science,* vol. 4 (2001) 391–416, p. 402.
29. J. Milliken, 'The Study of Discourse in International Relations: A Critique of Research and Methods', *European Journal of International Relations,* vol. 5, no. 2 (June 1999) 225–54, p. 232.
30. A. L. George, *Propaganda Analysis: A Study of Inferences Made from Nazi Propaganda in World War II* (Evanston, Ill.: Row, Peterson and Company, 1959), p. 107.
31. H. Eckstein, 'Case Study and Theory in Political Science', in Fred I. Greenstein, et al., eds, *Handbook of Political Science – Volume 7* (Reading, Mass.: Wesley Publishing Company, 1975), 79–137, pp. 118–20. S. v. Evera, *Guide to Methods for Students of Political Science* (Ithaca, N.Y.: Cornell University Press, 1997), pp. 30 ff. and 75.
32. Morgenthau, *Politics Among Nations.* Waltz, *Theory of International Politics.*
33. A. L. George and T. J. McKeown, 'Case Studies and Theories of Organizational Decision Making', in R. F. Coulam, et al., eds, *Advances in Information Processing in Organizations* (Greenwich: JAI Press, 1985), 21–58.
34. This method should not be confused with process-tracing since process-tracing would require much more knowledge about the Russian foreign policy decision-making process. For a discussion of process-tracing, see A. L. George and A. Bennett, *Case Studies and Theory Development in the Social Sciences* (Cambridge, Mass.: MIT Press, 2005), Chapter 10.
35. J. D. Fearon, 'Counterfactuals and Hypothesis Testing in Political Science', *World Politics,* vol. 43, no. 2 (January 1991) 169–95, p. 178.
36. Lebow, 'What's so Different About a Counterfactual?' p. 568.

Chapter 3: Evolution of the Russian Leadership's Foreign Policy Thinking

1. Such a systematic analysis that comprehensively covers the Russian leadership's foreign policy thinking from 1992 to 2007 does not yet exist. For an analysis of the evolution of the Russian leadership's foreign policy thinking

based primarily on official concepts, blueprints and doctrines, see M. Light, 'In Search of an Identity: Russian Foreign Policy and the End of Ideology', *Journal of Communist Studies and Transition Politics*, vol. 19, no. 3 (September 2003) 42–59. For an analysis of the 1993 and 2000 Foreign Policy Concepts and of the 1997 and 2000 National Security Concepts, see A. Kassianova, 'Russia: Still Open to the West? Evolution of the State Identity in the Foreign Policy and Security Discourse', *Europe-Asia Studies*, vol. 53, no. 6 (2001) 821–39. For an analysis of Putin's foreign policy thinking, see A. P. Tsygankov, 'Vladimir Putin's Vision of Russia as a Normal Great Power', *Post-Soviet Affairs*, vol. 21, no. 2 (2005) 132–58.

2. For analyses that focus on the foreign policy discourse of a wider range of foreign policy actors, see H. Adomeit, 'Russia as a "Great Power" in World Affairs: Images and Reality', *International Affairs*, vol. 71, no. 1 (1995) 35–68. A. G. Arbatov, 'Russia's Foreign Policy Alternatives', *International Security*, vol. 18, no. 2 (Fall 1993) 5–43. N. Malcolm, A. Pravda, R. Allison and M. Light, *Internal Factors in Russian Foreign Policy* (Oxford: Oxford University Press, 1996). A. Pravda, 'The Politics of Foreign Policy', in Stephen White, et al., eds, *Developments in Russian Politics 4* (Basingstoke: Macmillan Press, 1997), 208–22. G. Chafetz, 'The Struggle for a National Identity in Post-Soviet Russia', *Political Science Quarterly*, vol. 111, no. 4 (Winter 1996/97) 661–88. A. Ignatow, *Ideologie, Rhetorik und Realpolitik*, vol. 20, *Bericht des Bundesinstituts für ostwissenschaftliche und internationale Studien* (Köln: Bundesinstitut für ostwissenschaftliche und internationale Studien, 1999). I. Prizel, *National Identity and Foreign Policy: Nationalism and Leadership in Poland, Russia and Ukraine* (Cambridge: Cambridge University Press, 1998), pp. 241–64. G. Simon, 'Auf der Suche nach der "Idee für Rußland"', *Osteuropa*, vol. 47, no. 12 (1997) 1169–90. A. P. Tsygankov, 'From International Institutionalism to Revolutionary Expansionism: The Foreign Policy Discourse of Contemporary Russia', *Mershon International Studies Review*, vol. 41, no. 2 (November 1997) 247–68. For a discussion of Eurasianism in particular, see A. P. Tsygankov, 'Mastering Space in Eurasia: Russia's Geopolitical Thinking after the Soviet Break-up', *Communist and Post-Communist Studies*, vol. 36, no. 1 (2003) 101–27. For a historical discussion of the Russian identity discourse going back to the 18th century, see I. B. Neumann, *Russia and the Idea of Europe: A Study in Identity and International Relations* (London: Routledge, 1996). For a discussion of the Russian identity discourse during the 1990s, see J. H. Billington, *Russia in Search of Itself* (Baltimore, Md.: The Johns Hopkins University Press, 2004). For an analysis of the Russian foreign policy discourse on Russia and Europe, see V. Morozov, 'Inside/Outside: Europe and the Boundaries of Russian Political Community', *CSIS Working Paper*, October 2004, available at: http://www.csis.org/media/csis/pubs/ruseur_wp_023.pdf (accessed: 7 July 2007).

3. A. Kozyrev, 'A Transformed Russia in a New World', *International Affairs (Moscow)*, vol. 39, no. 4 (1992) 81–104, p. 87. This view was also expressed in the first post-Soviet Military Doctrine of 1993, see 'Osnovnye polozheniia voennoi doktriny Rossiiskoi Federatsii – 1993', *Diplomaticheskii vestnik*, no. 23–24 (December 1993) 6–16, p. 7.

4. A. Kozyrev, 'The Ministry of Foreign Affairs Proposes and Defends a Foreign Policy for Russia, published in: *Rossiiskie vesti*, 3 December 1992, p. 2',

CDPSP, vol. XLIV, no. 48 (1992) 14–16, p. 15. For similar arguments, see A. Kozyrev, 'Russian Foreign Minister Outlines Views, published in: Izvestiia, 2 January 1992', CDPSP, vol. XLIV, no. 1 (1992) 22–3, p. 22. A. Kozyrev, 'Kozyrev on Domestic, Foreign Expectations', FBIS-SOV, no. 129 (6 July 1992) 35–42, p. 36.
5. A. Kozyrev, 'Russia and Human Rights', *Slavic Review*, vol. 51, no. 2 (Summer 1992) 287–93, p. 289. For similar arguments, see A. Kozyrev, *Preobrazhenie* (Moscow: Mezhdunarodnye otnosheniia, 1994), p. 47. 'Kontseptsiia vneshnei politiki Rossiiskoi Federatsii – 1993', *reprinted in: Vneshniaia politika i bezopasnost' sovremennoi Rossii 1991–2002 (Volume IV)* (Moscow: Rosspen, 2002), 19–50, pp. 20–1.
6. Kozyrev, 'Russian Foreign Minister Outlines View', p. 22.
7. B. Yeltsin, 'Vystuplenie B.N. El'tsina: zasedanie SB OON vysshem urovne 31 ianvaria', *Diplomaticheskii vestnik*, no. 4–5 (February/March 1992) 48–50, p. 49. B. Yeltsin, 'Summit in Washington: Excerpts from Yeltsin's Speech', *The New York Times*, 18 June 1992, p. 18A. J. A. Baker, *The Politics of Diplomacy: Revolution, War and Peace, 1989–1992* (New York: G.P. Putnam's Sons, 1995).
8. B. Yeltsin, 'Iz poslaniia Prezidenta Rossiiskoi Federatsii Federal'nomu Sobraniiu – 1996', *Diplomaticheskii vestnik*, no. 3 (March 1996) 3, p. 3. B. Yeltsin, 'Rossiia: chelovek, sem'ia, obshchestvo, gosudarstvo', *Diplomaticheskii vestnik*, no. 7 (July 1996) 3–5, p. 3. For a similar point, see 'Kontseptsiia natsional'noi bezopasnosti Rossiiskoi Federatsii – 1997', *Diplomaticheskii vestnik*, vol. 2, no. 2 (1998) 5–18, p. 9.
9. B. Yeltsin, 'Vystuplenie Prezidenta Rossiiskoi Federatsii B.N. El'tsina na 49-i sessii GA OON 26 sentiabria', *Diplomaticheskii vestnik*, no. 19–20 (October 1994) 7–10, p. 8. B. Yeltsin, 'The Russian Federation President's Message to the Federal Assembly, published in: Rossiiskie vesti, 17 February 1995, pp. 1, 3–7', *CDPSP*, vol. XLVII, no. 7 and 8 (1995) 1–6 (no. 7) and 13–5, 28 (no. 8), p. 13. For similar arguments by Kozyrev, see A. Kozyrev, 'The Lagging Partnership', *Foreign Affairs*, vol. 73, no. 3 (May/June 1994) 59–70, p. 63.
10. Yeltsin, 'The Russian Federation President's Message to the Federal Assembly – 1995', p. 14. Also, see Chapter 4 with the case study *Russia's Approaches towards NATO*.
11. Yeltsin, 'Iz poslaniia Prezidenta Rossiiskoi Federatsii Federal'nomu Sobraniiu – 1996', p. 3. B. Yeltsin, 'O natsional'noi bezopasnosti: poslanie Prezidenta Rossiiskoi Federatsii Federal'nomu Sobraniiu', *Diplomaticheskii vestnik*, no. 7 (July 1996) 24–35, p. 25. For similar points by Kozyrev and Primakov, see Kozyrev, 'The Lagging Partnership', p. 63 and Y. Primakov, 'Vystuplenie E. M. Primakova na 51-i sessii GA OON', *Diplomaticheskii vestnik*, no. 10 (October 1996) 33–6, p. 33.
12. B. Yeltsin, 'Vystuplenie B.N. El'tsina (Strasburg, 10 oktabria)', *Diplomaticheskii vestnik*, no. 11 (November 1997) 8–9, p. 9.
13. I. Rybkin, 'Domestic Challenges to Russia's Security', *International Affairs (Moscow)*, vol. 43, no. 4 (1997) 132–43, p. 135.
14. A. Kozyrev, 'Partnership is not Premature, it is Overdue, published in: Izvestiia, 11 March 1994', *CDPSP*, vol. XLVI, no. 10 (1994) 1–3, p. 2. For similar arguments, see Kozyrev, 'The Lagging Partnership', p. 63. A. Kozyrev, 'Nonfestive Reflections on the UN Jubilee', *International Affairs (Moscow)*, no. 3 (Spring 1995) 7–14, p. 8.

160 Notes and References

15. Yeltsin, 'The Russian Federation President's Message to the Federal Assembly – 1995', p. 13. For a similar argument by Kozyrev, see A. Kozyrev, 'The New Russia and the Atlantic Alliance', *NATO Review*, no. 1 (February 1993) 3–6, p. 4.
16. 'The Foreign Policy Concept of the Russian Federation – 2000', available at: http://www.fas.org/nuke/guide/russia/doctrine/econcept.htm (accessed: 7 July 2007). The 2000 Military Doctrine repeated this assessment: 'Voennaia doktrina Rossiiskoi Federatsii – 2000', *Nezavisimaia gazeta*, 22 April 2000, p. 4.
17. 'The Foreign Policy Concept – 2000' For similar arguments by Foreign Minister Ivanov, see I. Ivanov, 'Rossiia i sovremennyi mir', *Nezavisimaia gazeta dipkur'er*, 20 January 2000. I. Ivanov, *The New Russian Diplomacy* (Washington, D.C.: Brookings Institute Press, 2002), pp. 44–5.
18. V. V. Putin, 'State of the Nation – 2002: President Putin's Annual Address to the RF Federal Assembly', *International Affairs (Moscow)*, vol. 48, no. 3 (2002) 1–16, p. 3. For similar arguments, see V. V. Putin, 'Annual Address to the Federal Assembly – 2000', *President of Russia: Official Web Portal*, 8 July 2000, available at: http://kremlin.ru/eng/speeches/2000/07/08/0000_type70029type 82912_70658.shtml (accessed: 7 July 2007). V. V. Putin, 'A State of the Nation Address to the Federal Assembly of the Russian Federation (Moscow, May 16, 2003)', *International Affairs (Moscow)*, vol. 49, no. 4 (2003) 1–17, p. 12.
19. V. V. Putin, "President V. Putin on Priorities for Russian Diplomacy', *International Affairs (Moscow)*, vol. 47, no. 2 (2001) 1–5, p. 4.
20. Putin, 'State of the Nation – 2002', p. 2. For a similar argument, see Putin, 'A State of the Nation Address – 2003', p. 2.
21. Kozyrev, 'The Ministry of Foreign Affairs Proposes'. 'Summary of Draft of Foreign Policy Concept – 1992', *International Affairs (Moscow)*, no. 1 (January 1993) 14–16, p. 15. Yeltsin, 'The Russian Federation President's Message to the Federal Assembly – 1995', p. 13.
22. V. V. Putin, 'Annual Address to the Federal Assembly of the Russian Federation', *President of Russia: Official Web Portal*, 10 May 2006, available at: http://www.kremlin.ru/eng/speeches/2006/05/10/1823_type70029type8291 2_105566.shtml (accessed: 7 July 2007).
23. Ibid. V. V. Putin, 'Speech at Meeting with the Ambassadors and Permanent Representatives of the Russian Federation', *President of Russia: Official Web Portal*, 27 June 2006, available at: http://www.kremlin.ru/eng/speeches/2006/ 06/27/2040_type82912type82913type82914_107818.shtml (accessed: 7 July 2007).
24. Putin, 'State of the Nation – 2006'.
25. V. V. Putin, 'Press Conference following Talks with German Chancellor Angela Merkel', *President of Russia: Official Web Portal*, 21 January 2007, available at: http://www.kremlin.ru/eng/speeches/2007/01/21/1910_type82914 type82915_116974.shtml (accessed: 7 July 2007). V. V. Putin, 'Speech and the Following Discussion at the Munich Conference on Security Policy', *President of Russia: Official Web Portal*, 10 February 2007, available at: http://www.kremlin.ru/eng/speeches/2007/02/10/0138_type82912type8291 4type82917type84779_118135.shtml (accessed: 7 July 2007).
26. V. V. Putin, 'Annual Address to the Federal Assembly – 2007', *President of Russia: Official Web Portal*, 26 April 2007, available at: http://www.kremlin. ru/eng/speeches/2007/04/26/1209_type70029type82912_125494.shtml (accessed: 7 July 2007).

27. V. V. Putin, 'Address by President Vladimir Putin', *President of Russia: Official Web Portal*, 4 September 2004, available at: http://www.kremlin.ru/eng/speeches/2004/09/04/1958_type82912_76332.shtml (accessed: 7 July 2007).
28. V. V. Putin, 'Address to the Federal Assembly of the Russian Federation – 2004', *President of Russia: Official Web Portal*, 26 May 2004, available at: http://www.kremlin.ru/eng/speeches/2004/05/26/1309_type70029type8291 2_71650.shtml (accessed: 7 July 2007). Putin, 'State of the Nation – 2006'.
29. S. Lavrov, 'The Present and the Future of Global Politics', *Russia in Global Affairs*, vol. 5, no. 2 (April–June 2007) 8–21, p. 10.
30. V. V. Putin, 'Interview with Radio Slovensko and Slovakian Television Channel STV', *President of Russia: Official Web Portal*, 22 February 2005, available at: http://www.kremlin.ru/eng/speeches/2005/02/22/2038_type82916_ 84445.shtml (accessed: 7 July 2007).
31. V. V. Putin, 'Transcript of the Press Conference for Russian and Foreign Media – 2006', *President of Russia: Official Web Portal*, 31 January 2006, available at: http://www.kremlin.ru/eng/speeches/2006/01/31/0953_type82915type8291 7_100901.shtml (accessed: 7 July 2007).
32. Putin, 'Address to the Federal Assembly of the Russian Federation – 2004'.
33. Putin, 'State of the Nation – 2007'.
34. S. Lavrov, 'Democracy, International Governance, and the Future World Order', *Russia in Global Affairs*, vol. 3, no. 1 (January–March 2005) 146–56, p. 147. For a similar argument, see 'Obzor vneshnej politiki Rossijskoj Federatsii', 27 March 2007, available at: http://www.mid.ru/brp_4.nsf/sps/ 3647DA97748A106BC32572AB002AC4DD (accessed: 7 July 2007).
35. Lavrov, 'Democracy', p. 155.
36. Kozyrev, 'Russian Foreign Minister Outlines View', p. 22.
37. B. Yeltsin, *The View from the Kremlin* (London: HarperCollins, 1994), p. 138.
38. 'A Transformed Russia', p. 86. Kozyrev, 'The New Russia', p. 3. For a similar argument by Yeltsin, see B. Yeltsin, 'Iz vystupleniia Prezidenta Rossii B.N. El'tsina na zasedanii Verkhovnogo Soveta Rossiiskoi Federatsii – 6 oktiabria 1992', *Diplomaticheskii vestnik*, no. 19–20 (October 1992) 3–4, p. 4.
39. Kozyrev, 'Russian Foreign Minister Outlines View', p. 22. For similar arguments, see A. Kozyrev, 'Vystuplenie Rossii v mezhdunarodnyi valiutnyi fond', *Izvestiia*, 31 March 1992. A. Kozyrev, 'Vystuplenie A. V. Kozyreva: VI s'ezd narodnykh deputatov RF', *Diplomaticheskii vestnik*, no. 9–10 (Mai 1992) 3–7, pp. 4–5. Kozyrev, 'Kozyrev on Domestic, Foreign Expectations', p. 38. For a similar argument by Yeltsin, see Yeltsin, 'Iz Vystupleniia Prezidenta Rossii', p. 4.
40. For usage of this term, see Kozyrev, 'Russian Foreign Minister Outlines View', p. 22. 'A Transformed Russia', p. 86.
41. A. Kozyrev, 'Washington Summit: An End to Nuclear Confrontation', *International Affairs (Moscow)* (August 1992) 3–9, p. 3. For a similar argument, see A. Kozyrev, 'The Union Left Russia a Poor Foreign-Policy Legacy, published in: Nezavisimaia gazeta, 1 April 1992', *CDPSP*, vol. XLIV, no. 13 (1992) 4–6, p. 4. For a similar argument, see Yeltsin, 'Iz Vystupleniia Prezidenta Rossii', p. 4.
42. Yeltsin, *The View from the Kremlin*, pp. 7–8.
43. B. Yeltsin, 'What Yeltsin Told Russian Diplomats, published in: Rossiiskie vesti, 29 October 1992', *CDPSP*, vol. XLIV, no. 43 (1992) 19, p. 19.

162 *Notes and References*

44. Kozyrev, 'Washington Summit', p. 3. A. Kozyrev, 'What Foreign Policy Russia should Pursue', *International Affairs (Moscow)* (February 1993) 3–6, p. 5. Kozyrev, 'The Ministry of Foreign Affairs Proposes'. 'A Transformed Russia', p. 90. For a similar argument by Yeltsin, see Yeltsin, 'Vystuplenie B.N. El'tsina: zasedanie SB OON vysshem urovne 31 ianvaria', p. 49. Yeltsin, 'Summit in Washington', p. 18A.
45. 'A Transformed Russia', p. 86.
46. Kozyrev, 'Russian Foreign Minister Outlines View', p. 22.
47. 'A Transformed Russia', p. 86.
48. These liberal ideas also impacted the thinking on economic reforms in the early 1990s, see Y. Gaidar, *Gosudarstvo i evoliutsiia* (Moscow: Evrasiia, 1995), p. 202. Y. Gaidar, *Days of Defeat and Victory* (Seattle: University of Washington Press, 1999). A. Chubais, ed., *Privatizatsiia po-Rossiiski* (Moscow: Vagrius, 1999). G. W. Breslauer, *Gorbachev and Yeltsin as Leaders* (Cambridge: Cambridge University Press, 2002), p. 250.
49. B. Yeltsin, 'The President of Russia's Speech to the Federal Assembly, published in: Rossiiskaia gazeta, 25 February 1994, pp. 1–2', *CDPSP*, vol. XLVI, no. 8 (1994) 5–8, pp. 6, 8. Kozyrev made similar arguments, see Kozyrev, 'The Lagging Partnership', p. 65.
50. Yeltsin, 'O natsional'noi bezopasnosti', p. 24.
51. B. Yeltsin, 'President Yeltsin's Address to Russian Diplomats', *International Affairs (Moscow)*, vol. 44, no. 3 (1998) 1–6, p. 4. For a similar argument, see B. Yeltsin, 'Iz poslaniia Prezidenta Rossiiskoi Federatsii Federal'nomu Sobraniiu – 1998', *Diplomaticheskii vestnik*, no. 3 (March 1998) 3–4, p. 4.
52. Kozyrev, 'Partnership is not Premature', p. 1. For similar arguments, see Yeltsin, 'The President of Russia's Speech to the Federal Assembly – 1994', p. 8. Kozyrev, 'The Lagging Partnership', p. 62.
53. Y. Primakov, 'A Minister the Opposition Doesn't Curse, published in: Obshchaia gazeta, No. 37, 19–25 September 1996, p. 4', *CDPSP*, vol. XLVIII, no. 39 (1996) 22–3, p. 22. For similar arguments, see Yeltsin, 'O natsional'noi bezopasnosti', p. 25. Yeltsin, 'Rossiia: chelovek', p. 4. For a similar argument expressed by the then Prime Minister, see V. Chernomyrdin, 'Vystuplenie V. S. Chernomyrdina v Gosudarstvennoi Dume Federal'nogo Sobrania Rossiiskoi Federatsii', *Diplomaticheskii vestnik*, no. 9 (September 1996) 3–10, p. 9. For a similar view expressed by Foreign Minister Kozyrev, see Kozyrev, 'The Lagging Partnership', p. 63. Kozyrev, 'Partnership is not Premature', p. 2. For a similar view expressed by then Defence Minister Rodionov, see I. Rodionov, 'What Sort of Defense Does Russia Need?' *Nezavisimoe voennoe obozrenie*, 28 November 1996.
54. Yeltsin, 'President Yeltsin's Address to Russian Diplomats', p. 1. B. Yeltsin, 'Russia at the Turn of a New Era: Annual State of the Nation Address – 1999', *International Affairs (Moscow)*, vol. 45, no. 3 (1999) 1–3, p. 2.
55. Y. Primakov, 'Press konferentsiia Ministra Inostranykh Del Rossii', *Diplomaticheskii vestnik*, no. 2 (February 1996) 3–6, p. 3. For similar arguments, see Kozyrev, 'Partnership is not Premature', p. 2. For similar arguments, see Yeltsin, 'The President of Russia's Speech to the Federal Assembly – 1994', p. 8. Yeltsin, 'The Russian Federation President's Message to the Federal Assembly – 1995', p. 14. Kozyrev, 'The Lagging Partnership', p. 65. Kozyrev, 'Nonfestive Reflections', pp. 10–1.

56. Y. Primakov, *Gody v bol'shoi politike* (Moscow: Sovershenno sekretno, 1999), p. 213. Also, see Kozyrev, 'The Lagging Partnership', p. 69. Primakov, 'Press konferentsiia Ministra Inostranykh Del Rossii', p. 3. Y. Primakov, 'Russia in World Politics – A Lecture in Honor of Chancellor Gorchakov', *International Affairs (Moscow)*, vol. 4, no. 3 (1998) 7–12, p. 10. I. Ivanov, 'A. M. Gorchakov: A Diplomat Serves his Country, Not a Regime', *International Affairs (Moscow)*, vol. 42, no. 2 (1996) 178–87, pp. 183, 4. Rybkin, 'Domestic Challenges', p. 136.
57. Yeltsin, 'President Yeltsin's Address to Russian Diplomats', p. 2. Also, see Yeltsin, 'The Russian Federation President's Message to the Federal Assembly – 1995', p. 13.
58. I. Ivanov, 'The New Russian Identity: Innovation and Continuity in Russian Foreign Policy', *The Washington Quarterly*, vol. 24, no. 3 (Summer 2001) 7–13, p. 10. For a similar argument, see Ivanov, *The New Russian Diplomacy*, p. 15.
59. Putin, 'Annual Address to the Federal Assembly – 2000'.
60. Yeltsin, 'The President of Russia's Speech to the Federal Assembly – 1994', p. 7. Yeltsin, 'The Russian Federation President's Message to the Federal Assembly – 1995', p. 2. Yeltsin, 'President Yeltsin's Address to Russian Diplomats', pp. 1, 4. Yeltsin, 'Iz poslaniia Prezidenta Rossiiskoi Federatsii Federal'nomu Sobraniiu – 1998', pp. 2, 3.
61. Putin, 'Annual Address to the Federal Assembly – 2000'. For similar arguments, see V. V. Putin, 'Rossiia na rubezhe tysiacheletiia', *Rossiiskaia gazeta*, 31 December 1999. 'The Foreign Policy Concept – 2000'. Putin, 'President V. Putin on Priorities', p. 1. Putin, 'A State of the Nation Address – 2003', p. 2.
62. Putin, 'State of the Nation – 2002', pp. 15 and 16. For a similar point, see Putin, 'Rossiia na rubezhe tysiacheletiia'.
63. I. Ivanov, 'Vstrecha v redaktsii – Igor Ivanov: my stali myslit' bolee pragmatichno', *Trud*, 23 January 2003.
64. The 2000 Foreign Policy Concept argues that '[w]hile the military power still retains significant in relations among states, an ever greater role is being placed by economic, political, scientific and technological, ecological, and informational factors.' see 'The Foreign Policy Concept – 2000'. For similar arguments, see Putin, 'Annual Address to the Federal Assembly – 2000'. Putin, 'A State of the Nation Address – 2003', pp. 1, 2.
65. [Emphasis added] V. V. Putin, 'Key Tasks of Russian Diplomacy: Statement by RF President V. V. Putin at an Enlarged Conference with the Participation of RF Ambassadors, at the Ministry of Foreign Affairs of Russia', *International Affairs (Moscow)*, vol. 48, no. 4 (2002) 1–7, p. 2.
66. Ibid. For similar arguments, see Putin, 'President V. Putin on Priorities'. Putin, 'Address to the Federal Assembly of the Russian Federation – 2004'.
67. I. Ivanov, 'Glavnoe – chtoby vneshniaia politika ne privodila k raskolu vnutri strany', *Izvestiia*, 10 July 2002. For a similar argument, see I. Ivanov, 'Tret"i Gorchakovskie chteniia '200 let MID Rossii', *Diplomaticheskii vestnik*, no. 5 (May 2002) 158–62, pp. 159–60.
68. S. Lavrov, 'The Rise of Asia, and the Eastern Vector of Russia's Foreign Policy', *Russia in Global Affairs*, vol. 4, no. 3 (July–September 2006) 68–80, p. 69.
69. Putin, 'State of the Nation – 2007'. For a similar argument, see Putin, 'Interview with Radio Slovensko'.
70. Putin, 'Address to the Federal Assembly of the Russian Federation – 2004'. For similar statements, see Putin, 'Transcript of the Press Conference for Russian

and Foreign Media – 2006'. V. V. Putin, 'Transcript of Press Conference with the Russian Foreign Media – 2007', *President of Russia: Official Web Portal*, 1 February 2007, available at: http://www.kremlin.ru/eng/speeches/2007/02/01/1309_type82915type82917_117609.shtml (accessed: 7 July 2007). S. Lavrov, 'Drugaia Rossiia: vyzov ili novye vozmozhnosti partnerstva?' *Kommersant-Daily*, 1 April 2004. Lavrov, 'The Present and the Future of Global Politics'.
71. 'Urgent Tasks of the Development of the Russian Federation Armed Forces', *Ria-Novosti*, 3 October 2003.
72. Putin, 'Interview with Radio Slovensko'. Putin, 'State of the Nation – 2006'.
73. Putin, 'Speech and the Following Discussion at the Munich Conference on Security Policy'. Putin, 'Transcript of the Press Conference for Russian and Foreign Media – 2006'.
74. Putin, 'Speech at Meeting'. For a similar argument, see V. V. Putin, 'Address at the Plenary Session of the Russian Federation Ambassadors and Permanent Representatives Meeting', *President of Russia: Official Web Portal*, 12 July 2004, available at: http://kremlin.ru/eng/text/speeches/2004/07/12/1323_74425.shtml (accessed: 7 July 2007).
75. Putin, 'Speech at Meeting'.
76. Kozyrev, 'The Ministry of Foreign Affairs Proposes', p. 15. Already in 1992, Kozyrev argued that the US willingness to sign the Joint Understanding on strategic missiles in Camp David in early 1992 would not have been possible had Russia not established relations with the West on the basis of partnership. Kozyrev, 'Washington Summit', p. 8. For a similar argument, see Kozyrev, *Preobrazhenie*, p. 203.
77. [Emphasis added] Kozyrev, 'Russian Foreign Minister Outlines View', p. 22. For a similar point, see Kozyrev, *Preobrazhenie*, p. 51.
78. A. Kozyrev, 'The War Party is on the Offensive, published in: Izvestiia, 30 June 1992', *CDPSP*, vol. XLIV, no. 26 (1992) 3–5, p. 5.
79. Kozyrev, 'The New Russia', p. 3. Yeltsin's press secretary and aide Viacheslav Kostikov argues that Yeltsin believed that the West 'simply had a responsibility to help Russia on its way to democracy'. V. Kostikov, *Roman s prezidentom: zapiski press-sekretaria* (Moscow: Vagrius, 1997), pp. 51, 70.
80. For examples, see Kozyrev, 'The War Party', pp. 4, 5. Kozyrev, 'The New Russia', p. 4, or his speech to the CSCE in December 1992, see W. Safire, 'Kozyrev's Wake-up Slap', *New York Times*, 17 Dec 1992.
81. Yeltsin, 'What Yeltsin Told Russian Diplomats', p. 9. This criticism was shared by other high profile politicians such as Vladimir Lukin, then chairman of the committee on International Affairs of the Supreme Soviet, or Primakov, then general director of Russia's External Intelligence. See 'A Transformed Russia', pp. 93 and 95.
82. A. Kozyrev, 'Rossiia: God minuvshii i god nastupivshii', *Diplomaticheskii vestnik*, no. 1–2 (January 1993) 3–5, p. 4. Kozyrev, 'What Foreign Policy Russia should Pursue', p. 4. 'Kontseptsiia vneshnei politiki Rossiiskoi Federatsii – 1993'.
83. Kozyrev, 'Partnership is not Premature', p. 2.
84. Y. Primakov, 'Vstrecha E.M. Primakova s kollektivom MGIMO', *Diplomaticheskii vestnik*, no. 7 (July 1996) 64–8, p. 64. Primakov, *Gody v bol'shoi politike*, pp. 207–8 and 213.
85. For speeches on Gorchakov, see Ivanov, 'A. M. Gorchakov'. I. Ivanov, 'Vystuplenie I.S. Ivanova na torzhestvennom zasedanii po sluchaiiu 200-letnego iubileia A. M. Gorchakova', *Diplomaticheskii vestnik*, no. 11 (November 1998)

75–7. I. Ivanov, 'Gorchakov: an Epoch in Russian Diplomacy', *International Affairs (Moscow)*, vol. 45, no. 1 (1999) 154–7. Primakov, 'Russia in World Politics'. For a comprehensive analysis of the discourse on Gorchakov, see F. Splidsboel-Hansen, 'Past and Future: Aleksandr Gorchakov and Russian Foreign Policy', *Europe-Asia Studies*, vol. 54, no. 3 (May 2002) 377–96.
86. Primakov, 'Russia in World Politics', p. 8. Also, see Ivanov, 'A. M. Gorchakov', p. 183.
87. Yeltsin, 'President Yeltsin's Address to Russian Diplomats', p. 5.
88. Y. Primakov, 'Izvestia Political Commentator Stanislav Kondrashov interviews Foreign Minister Yevgeny Primakov, published in: Izvestiia, 6 March 1996, p. 3', *CDPSP*, vol. XLVIII, no. 10 (1996) 12–14, p. 13. For a similar argument by Defence Minister Rodionov, see Rodionov, 'What Sort of Defense'.
89. Y. Primakov, 'Yevgeny Primakov Finds Common Diplomatic Language with Duma's International Committee, published in: Izvestiia, 19 February 1996, p. 3', *CDPSP*, vol. XLVIII, no. 6 (1996) 22–3, p. 22. Primakov, 'A Minister the Opposition Doesn't Curse', p. 22. For a similar argument by the then prime minister, see Chernomyrdin, 'Vystuplenie V. S. Chernomyrdina', p. 9. Similar to the emphasis on distinct national interests, the argument was also made that domestically Russia had to find its own approaches rather than copy Western models. See, for example B. Yeltsin, 'Otvety Prezidenta Rossiiskoi Federatsii B.N. El'tsina na voprosy telegrafnogo agentstva "Sin'khua"', *Diplomaticheskii vestnik*, no. 11 (November 1999) 3–4, p. 3.
90. I. Ivanov, 'Ministra Inostrannykh Del Rossiiskoi Federatsii I.S. Ivanova na 53-i sessii General'noi Assamblei OON', *Diplomaticheskii vestnik*, no. 10 (October 1998) 35–8, p. 35. For similar arguments, see Ivanov, 'Gorchakov: an Epoch', p. 155. I. Ivanov, 'Concept of the World in the 21st Century', *International Affairs (Moscow)*, vol. 45, no. 6 (1999) 1–6, p. 2. Yeltsin, 'Russia at the Turn of a New Era: Annual State of the Nation Address – 1999', p. 1. Primakov, 'Vystuplenie E.M. Primakova na 51-i sessii GA OON', p. 35.
91. Kozyrev, 'The Lagging Partnership', p. 61. For a similar argument, see Kozyrev, 'Partnership is not Premature', p. 1.
92. Primakov, 'Izvestia Political Commentator', p. 14. For similar arguments, see Y. Primakov, 'The World on the Eve of the 21st Century', *International Affairs (Moscow)*, vol. 42, no. 5/6 (1996) 2–14, p. 4. Primakov, 'Vystuplenie E.M. Primakova na 51-i sessii GA OON', p. 33. Y. Primakov, *Vosem' mesiatsev plius* . . . (Moscow: Mysl', 2001), p. 239. Ivanov, 'Ministra Inostrannykh Del Rossiiskoi Federatsii I.S. Ivanova na 53-i sessii General'noi Assamblei OON', p. 35.
93. I. Ivanov, 'Interview with Ivanov, published in: Izvestiia, 28 October 1998, pp. 1, 6', *CDPSP*, vol. 50, no. 43 (1998) 13 and 24, p. 13.
94. Y. Primakov, 'Press-konferentsiia, 23 dekabria 1997g', *Diplomaticheskii vestnik*, no. 1 (January 1998) 3–5, p. 3. Primakov, 'Vstrecha E. M. Primakova s kollektivom MGIMO', p. 65. Yeltsin, 'The President of Russia's Speech to the Federal Assembly – 1994', p. 8. Yeltsin, 'Iz poslaniia Prezidenta Rossiiskoi Federatsii Federal'nomu Sobraniiu – 1998', pp. 3–4. Kozyrev, 'Partnership is not Premature', p. 1. Kozyrev, 'The Lagging Partnership', p. 62.
95. Yeltsin, 'President Yeltsin's Address to Russian Diplomats', p. 1. Also, see Yeltsin, 'Russia at the Turn of a New Era: Annual State of the Nation Address – 1999', p. 2.

96. Putin, 'Key Tasks of Russian Diplomacy', p. 3. For a similar argument, see Ivanov, *The New Russian Diplomacy*, pp. 13–14.
97. Putin, 'A State of the Nation Address – 2003', p. 12.
98. I. Ivanov, 'Mezhdunarodnaia bezopasnost' v epokhu globalizatsii', *Global'noi politike*, vol. 1, no. 1 (January–March 2003) 36–47, p. 36. Putin, 'A State of the Nation Address – 2003', pp. 12–13.
99. 'Vystuplenie na press-konferentsii v natsional'nom press-klube Ssha (20 Sept 2002), reprinted in: I. Ivanov, *Rossiia v sovremennom mire – otvety na vyzovy XXI veka* (Moscow: Olma-Press, 2004), p. 427. For similar comments, see I. Ivanov, 'Kakoi mir nam nuzhen', *Kommersant-Daily*, 20 November 2002. I. Ivanov, 'Nel'zia siloi naviazyvat' demokraticheskie tsennosti', *Kommersant-Daily*, 5 Mar 2003, p. 10.
100. I. Ivanov, 'New Prospects for Diplomacy', *International Affairs (Moscow)*, vol. 48, no. 6 (2002) 1–14, p. 10.
101. D. Lynch, *Russia Faces Europe* (Paris: Institute for Security Studies, 2003), p. 94.
102. Putin, 'State of the Nation – 2002', p. 2. For a similar argument, see I. Ivanov, 'Formation of New Russian Foreign Policy Completed', *International Affairs (Moscow)*, vol. 47, no. 4 (2001) 1–7, p. 2.
103. Putin, 'President V. Putin on Priorities', p. 2. For similar arguments, see Putin, 'Annual Address to the Federal Assembly – 2000'. Putin, 'State of the Nation – 2002', p. 3.
104. V. V. Putin, 'Annual Address to the Federal Assembly – 2001', *President of Russia: Official Web Portal*, 3 April 2001, available at: http://kremlin.ru/eng/speeches/2001/04/03/0000_type70029type82912_70660.shtml (accessed: 7 July 2007). For similar arguments, see Putin, 'State of the Nation – 2002', p. 15. I. Ivanov, 'Vystuplenie I.S. Ivanova na prezentatsii knigi "Novaia rossiiskaia diplomatiia. 10 let vneshnei politiki Rossii"', *Diplomaticheskii vestnik*, no. 6 (June 2002) 15–16, p. 15.
105. While not similarly vehemently, already in 1995 Yeltsin called upon the Russian diplomatic corps to 'make sure that our actions and intentions are understood correctly' abroad. Yeltsin, 'The Russian Federation President's Message to the Federal Assembly – 1995', p. 13.
106. Putin, 'Annual Address to the Federal Assembly – 2000'.
107. Putin, 'President V. Putin on Priorities', p. 4. For a similar argument, see Putin, 'Rossiia na rubezhe tysiacheletiia'.
108. Putin, 'Address to the Federal Assembly of the Russian Federation – 2004'.
109. Putin, 'Speech at Meeting'. See also Putin, 'Transcript of the Press Conference for Russian and Foreign Media – 2006'. Putin, 'Speech and the Following Discussion at the Munich Conference on Security Policy'. Lavrov, 'The Rise of Asia'.
110. V. V. Putin, 'Responses to Questions from Russian Journalists following the Russia-EU Summit and Press Conference', *President of Russia: Official Web Portal*, 25 May 2006, available at: http://www.kremlin.ru/eng/speeches/2006/05/25/2359_type82915_106123.shtml (accessed: 7 July 2007).
111. Lavrov, 'The Rise of Asia'.
112. Ibid.
113. Putin, 'Speech at Meeting'.
114. Putin, 'State of the Nation – 2006'. For a similar argument, see Lavrov, 'Democracy'.

115. This conclusion supports Light's assessment, see Light, 'In Search of an Identity', p. 53.
116. Kozyrev, 'Russian Foreign Minister Outlines View', p. 22. For a similar argument, see Kozyrev, *Preobrazhenie*, pp. 41–6 and 211–2.
117. For a similar argument, see Tsygankov, 'Vladimir Putin's Vision of Russia as a Normal Great Power'.

Chapter 4: Russia's Approaches towards NATO

1. P. Kubicek, 'Russian Foreign Policy and the West', *Political Science Quarterly*, vol. 114, no. 4 (1999–2000) 547–68, p. 556. For a similar argument, see S. Croft, 'Guaranteeing Europe's Security? Enlarging NATO Again', *International Affairs*, vol. 78, no. 1 (2002) 97–114, p. 110.
2. More balanced accounts are to be found in: M. A. Smith and G. Timmins, 'Russia, NATO and the EU in an Era of Enlargement: Vulnerability or Opportunity?' *Geopolitics*, vol. 6, no. 1 (Summer 2001) 69–90. V. G. Baranovsky, *Russia's Attitudes Towards the EU: Political Aspects* (Helsinki: The Finnish Institute of International Affairs, 2002).
3. In 1997, the NACC was replaced by the Euro–Atlantic Partnership Council.
4. 'Partnership for Peace: Invitation', *NATO Press Communiqué M-1(94)2*, 10–11 January 1994, available at: http://www.nato.int/docu/comm/49–95/c940110a.htm (accessed: 7 July 2007). 'Remarks by the Secretary General at the Acceptance of the Russian Partnership for Peace', *NATO Speeches*, 31 May 1995, available at: http://www.nato.int/docu/speech/1995/s950531a.htm (accessed: 7 July 2007).
5. W. Christopher, *In the Stream of History: Shaping Foreign Policy for a New Era* (Stanford: Stanford University Press, 1998), p. 130. J. M. Goldgeier and M. McFaul, *Power and Purpose: U.S. Policy Towards Russia after the End of the Cold War* (Washington, D.C.: The Brookings Institution Press, 2003), p. 193. H. Gardner, *Dangerous Crossroads* (London: Praeger, 1997), p. 12.
6. B. Kazantsev, 'Pervye shagi k partnerstvu Rossii s NATO', *Mezhdunarodnaia zhisn*, no. 10 (1994) 22–9, p. 24.
7. S. Talbott, *The Russia Hand* (New York: Random House, 2002), p. 136.
8. Transcript of the conversation between US President Clinton and Russian President Yeltsin, Moscow, 10 May 1995, cited in: R. D. Asmus, *Opening NATO's Door: How the Alliance Remade Itself for a New Era* (New York: Columbia University Press, 2002), pp. 116–17. Also, see B. Clinton, *My Life* (New York: Alfred A. Knopf, 2004), p. 655.
9. Asmus, *Opening NATO's Door*, p. 170.
10. 'Yeltsin's Head of Administration Calls on NATO to Sign Treaty with Russia', *BBC Summary of World Broadcasts*, 5 February 1997.
11. 'Founding Act on Mutual Relations, Cooperation and Security between NATO and the Russian Federation', *NATO*, 27 May 1997, available at: http://www.nato.int/docu/basictxt/fndact-a.htm (accessed: 7 July 2007).
12. 'Details of Foreign Minister's Address to MPs on NATO–Russia Act', *BBC Summary of World Broadcasts*, 24 May 1997. B. Yeltsin, 'Radio Address', *Itar-Tass*, 30 May 1997.
13. A. Pravda, 'Foreign Policy', in Stephen White, et al., eds, *Developments in Russian Politics 5* (Basingstoke: Palgrave, 2001), 215–35, p. 229.

14. R. Hunter and S. M. Rogov, *Engaging Russia as Partner and Participant: The Next Stage of NATO-Russia Relations* (Santa Monica: RAND Corporation, 2004), p. 2.
15. See Chapter 5 on Russia's responses to the Balkan crises for an in-depth analysis.
16. N. MacFarlane, 'NATO in Russia's Relations with the West', *Security Dialogue*, vol. 32, no. 3 (September 2001) 281–96, p. 286. This assessment is shared by Baranovsky; see V. G. Baranovsky, 'Russia: A Part of Europe or Apart from Europe?' *International Affairs*, vol. 76, no. 3 (2000) 443–58, p. 446.
17. J. Perlez, 'Trying to Make the Twain of East and West Meet', *The New York Times*, 17 April 1998.
18. [Emphasis added] Memcon entitled: "Morning Meeting with Russian President Yeltsin: NATO-Russia, START, ABM/TMD" of 21 March 1997, cited in: Asmus, *Opening NATO's Door*, p. 200.
19. B. N. Yeltsin, *Midnight Diaries* (London: Weidenfeld & Nicolson, 2000), p. 131.
20. V. Nikonov, 'Partnerstvo vo Imia Mira', *Nezavisimaia gazeta*, 7 April 1994. For a similar critical assessment by the Chairman of the Duma's Foreign Affairs Committee Lukin, see I. Rodin, 'NATO's Program is not Entirely to the Liking of the State Duma', *CDPSP*, vol. XLVI, no. 11 (1994) 7–8.
21. S. Parkhomenko, 'Minister Kozyrev as a Man, published in: Izvestiia, 30 June 1994, p. 2', *CDPSP*, vol. XLVI, no. 26 (1994) 21–2.
22. 'Duma Deputies Call for Missile Production to Counter NATO Expansion Plans', *BBC Summary of World Broadcasts*, 30 January 1997. 'Anti-NATO Organisation Holds News Conference', *BBC Summary of World Broadcasts*, 24 February 1997.'State Duma Sets Up anti-NATO Commission', *BBC Summary of World Broadcasts*, 4 April 1997.
23. I. Rodin, 'Kommunisty ne iskliuchaiut razona Dumy', *Nezavisimaia gazeta*, 30 May 1997.
24. A. A. Sergounin, 'Russian Domestic Debate on NATO Enlargement: From Phobia to Damage Limitation', *European Security*, vol. 6, no. 4 (Winter 1997) 55–71, p. 55. For overviews of the domestic debate, see J. L. Black, *Russia Faces NATO Expansion: Bearing Gifts or Bearing Arms?* (Oxford: Rowman & Littlefield Publishers, Inc., 2000). R. Dannreuther, 'Russian Perceptions of the Atlantic Alliance', *Final Report for the NATO Fellowship 1995–1997*. V. Gorskii, 'Problems and Prospects of NATO-Russia Relationship: The Russian Debate', *NATO*, http://www.nato.int/acad/fellow/99–01/gorskii.pdf (accessed: 7 July 2007).
25. 'The Rome Declaration', *NATO*, 8 November 1991, available at: http://www.nato.int/docu/basictxt/b911108b.htm (accessed: 7 July 2007).
26. B. Yeltsin, 'Russian President Says Russia Wants to Join NATO', *Tass*, 20 December 1991.
27. A. Karpychev, 'Russia Wants to Join NATO, published in: Pravda, 25 December 1991, p.1', *CDPSP*, vol. XLIII, no. 52 (1991) p. 19
28. 'A Transformed Russia in a New World', *International Affairs (Moscow)*, vol. 39, no. 4 (1992) 81–104, p. 86.
29. A. Kozyrev, 'The New Russia and the Atlantic Alliance', *NATO Review*, no. 1 (February 1993) 3–6, p. 5.
30. B. Yeltsin, 'Russian and Polish President Sign Joint Declaration', *Itar–Tass*, 25 August 1993.
31. J. Perlez, 'Yeltsin "Understands" Polish Bid for a Role in NATO', *The New York Times*, 26 August 1993.

32. V. Yelagin, 'What Wasn't understood in Warsaw?' published in: Segodnia, 14 September 1993, p. 9', *CDPSP*, vol. XLV, no. 37 (1993) 16–17.
33. The letter was reprinted in: *SIPRI Yearbook 1994*, Stockholm International Peace Research Institute (Oxford: Oxford University Press, 1994), pp. 249–50.
34. Interviews with J. F. Collins, *1990–93 Deputy Chief of Mission and Charge d'affaires at the US Embassy in Moscow; 1993–97 Ambassador-at-large and Special Advisor to the US Secretary of State for the Newly Independent States; 1997 until 2001 Ambassador to the Russian Federation*, interviewed in Washington, D.C. on 11 May 2005. T. Parkhalina, *Director of the Centre for European Security and Deputy Director of the Institute of Scientific Information for Social Science of the Russian Academy of Sciences (INION RAN)*, interviewed in Moscow on 3 June 2005.
35. Asmus, *Opening NATO's Door*, pp. 46–7.
36. B. Yeltsin, 'Russian and Polish Presidents Hold News Conference', *Itar–Tass*, 25 August 1993. For similar statements by Kozyrev, see Perlez, 'Yeltsin "Understands"'. A. Kozyrev, 'Vostochnaia Evropa v novykh usloviiakh i vneshniaia politika Rossii', *Diplomaticheskii vestnik*, no. 23–24 (1993) 59–61.
37. B. Yeltsin, *Rossiiskaia gazeta*, 30 May 1994. For a similar argument, see B. Yeltsin, 'The President of Russia's Speech to the Federal Assembly, published in: Rossiiskaia gazeta, 25 February 1994, pp. 1–2', *CDPSP*, vol. XLVI, no. 8 (1994) 5–8, p. 8.
38. 'Final Communique', *NATO Communiqué M-NAC-2(94)116*, 1 December 1994, available at: http://www.nato.int/docu/comm/49–95/c941201a.htm (accessed: 7 July 2007).
39. D. Williams, 'Yeltsin, Clinton Clash Over NATO's Role', *The Washington Post*, 6 December 1994.
40. B. Yeltsin, 'The Russian Federation President's Message to the Federal Assembly, published in: Rossiiskie vesti, 17 February 1995, pp. 1, 3–7', *CDPSP*, vol. XLVII, no. 7 and 8 (1995) 1–6 (no. 7) and 13–15, 28 (no. 8), p. 14.
41. B. Yeltsin, 'Yeltsin at Press Conference', *Rossiiskie vesti*, 9 September 1995.
42. B. Yeltsin, 'Vystuplenie Presidenta Rossiiskoi Federatsii Borisa El'tsina pri predstavlenii poslaniia Federal'nomu Sobraniiu RF – 1997', *Rossiiskie vesti*, 11 March 1997.
43. 'NATO Expansion "Worst Crisis Since Cuba"', *The Guardian*, 9 May 1997.
44. V. Zhdannikov, 'Russia Concerned about Possibility of NATO Expansion, published in: Segodnia, 6 January 1994, p. 1', *CDPSP*, vol. XLVI, no. 1 (1994) 18. For similar arguments by Kozyrev, see A. Kozyrev, 'Russian Foreign Minister Warns of Consequences of Eastern Europe Joining NATO', *BBC Summary of World Broadcasts*, 26 August 1993. A. Kozyrev, 'Partnership or Cold Peace?' *Foreign Policy*, no. 99 (Summer 1995) 3–14.
45. Talbott, *The Russia Hand*, p. 136.
46. D. Danilov, 'Perspektivy evropeiskoi bezopasnosti', *Segodnia*, 27 December 1995, p. 4.
47. I. Korotchenko and M. Karpov, 'Bezopasnost' real'nogo rasshireniia NATO na vostok', *Nezavisimaia gazeta*, 7 October 1995. M. Karpov, 'Interview with Vladimir Lukin: My okazalis' v ochen' plokhoi geopoliticheskoi situatsii', *Nezavisimaia gazeta*, 14 March 1995.
48. I. Korotchenko and M. Karpov, 'Rossijskie iadernye rakety budut perenatseleny na Chekhiiu i Pol'shu', *Nezavisimaia gazeta*, 7 October 1995.

49. As the result of an update of the Conference on Security and Cooperation in Europe (CSCE), it changed its name in January 1995 to Organization for Security and Cooperation in Europe (OSCE).
50. 'Programma povysheniia effektivnosti OBSE', *Diplomaticheskii vestnik*, no. 17–18 (September 1994) 13–16.
51. For analyses of Russia's approach towards the C/OSCE, see M. Bowker, *Russian Foreign Policy and the End of the Cold War* (Aldershot: Dartmouth Publishing Company Limited, 1997), p. 218. C. Kennedy-Pipe, 'Russia and the North Atlantic Treaty Organization', in Mark Webber, ed., *Russia and Europe: Conflict or Cooperation?* (Basingstoke: Macmillan Press, 2000), 46–65, p. 53. D. Lynch, 'Russia and the Organization for Security and Cooperation in Europe', in Mark Webber, ed., *Russia and Europe: Conflict or Cooperation* (Basingstoke: Macmillan, 2000), 99–124, p. 112.
52. I. Rodionov, 'Prevent the Appearance of New Division Lines in Europe', *Military News Bulletin (Moscow)*, vol. 5, no. 10 (10 October 1996).
53. 'Primakov Seeks to Invigorate Russia's Role in the Middle East', *Itar–Tass*, 30 October 1996.
54. Ibid.
55. V. Abarinov, 'Moskva i Minsk gotovy otvetit' na rasshirenie al'iansa sozdaniem moshchnoj', *Segodnia*, 15 May 1996.
56. 'Russia and Belarus United in Opposition to NATO Expansion', *BBC Summary of World Broadcast*, 8 March 1997.
57. V. Safronchuk, 'Neposledovatel'naia vostochnaia politika Rossii', *Sovetskaia Rossiia*, 29 March 1997.
58. J. Meek, 'Yeltsin Tells NATO to Keep out of Baltics', *The Guardian*, 15 May 1998 or Y. Primakov, '"Ia chuvstvuiu doverie prezidenta"', *Nezavisimaia gazeta*, 30 December 1997, p. 4. I. Ivanov, 'Interview with Igor Ivanov, published in: Nezavisimaia gazeta, 30 September 1998, pp. 1, 6', *CDPSP*, vol. 50, no. 39 (1998) 10–1 and 20, p. 11.
59. Yeltsin, *Midnight Diaries*, p. 131.
60. Asmus, *Opening NATO's Door*, p. 182.
61. Y. Primakov, *Russian Crossroads – Towards the new Millennium* (NewHaven & London: Yale University Press, 2004), p. 139.
62. Cited in: Asmus, *Opening NATO's Door*, p. 172.
63. Ibid, p. 62.
64. A. Pushkov, 'Eastern Europe – A Time for Gathering Stones, published in: Moskovskie novosti, No. 51, 30 July–6 August 1995, p. 8', *CDPSP*, vol. XLVII, no. 30 (1995) 23–4. For a similar argument by Chairman of the Russian State Duma Seleznev, see G. Seleznev, 'Russian Duma: Defending National Interests', *International Affairs (Moscow)*, vol. 43, no. 3 (1997) 1–12, p. 7.
65. S. Talbott, 'Note To: The Secretary, dated October 17, 1993,' in: Asmus, *Opening NATO's Door*, p. 51.
66. Memo summarized in: Ibid, p. 74.
67. Members of the Russian foreign policy elite argued that article 5 of the 'Treaty of the final settlement with respect to Germany' ruled out the enlargement of NATO eastwards. Furthermore, it is claimed that West German Foreign Minister Hans-Dietrich Genscher declared on 31 January 1990 that '[w]hat NATO must do is state unequivocally that whatever happens in the Warsaw Pact there will be no expansion of NATO territory eastwards, that is to say

closer to the borders of the Soviet Union.' cited in: S. F. Szabo, *The Diplomacy of German Unification* (New York: St. Martin's Press, 1992), p. 58. For Russian analyses of this question, see Primakov, *Russian Crossroads*, pp. 129, 30. A. Pushkov, 'Lidery zapada ne sderzhali obeshchanii', *Nezavisimaia gazeta*, 19 March 1997. Y. Rakhmaninov, 'The Reasons for and Possible Consequences of NATO Expansion', *International Affairs (Moscow)*, vol. 42, no. 4 (1996) 4–15.
68. H. Haftendorn, R. O. Keohane and C. A. Wallander, eds, *Imperfect Unions – Security Institutions over Time and Space* (Oxford: Oxford University Press, 1999), p. 9.
69. D. Averre, 'NATO Expansion and Russian National Interests', *European Security*, vol. 7, no. 1 (Spring 1998) 10–54, p. 20.
70. V. Churkin, 'U Rossii s NATO nikogda ne bylo konfliktov', *Segodnia*, 25 April 1995, p. 9.
71. Talbott, *The Russia Hand*. For similar arguments, see S. Hoffmann, 'US-European Relations: Past and Future', *International Affairs*, vol. 79, no. 5 (2003) 1029–36, p. 1030. A. Forster and W. Wallace, 'What is NATO for?' *Survival*, vol. 43, no. 4 (Winter 2001–2002) 107–22. For theoretical approaches to explain NATO enlargement, see R. W. Rauchhaus, ed., *Explaining NATO Enlargement* (London: Frank Cass, 2001).
72. Asmus, *Opening NATO's Door*, p. 28.
73. 'Rossiia i NATO', *Sovet po vneshnei i oboronnoi politike*, 21 June 1995, available at: http://www.svop.ru/live/materials.asp?m_id=7009&r_id=7044 (accessed: 7 July 2007). T. Parkhalina, 'Stoit li boiat'sia rasshireniia NATO?' *Segodnia*, 28 August 1996.
74. R. Osterkamp, 'Die wirtschaftliche Entwicklung in Russland seit 1991', in Reinhard C. Meier-Walser, et al., eds, *Russland: Kontinuität, Konflikt und Wandel* (München: Hanns Seidel Stiftung, 2002), p. Appendix.
75. Y. Primakov, 'PM Candidate: New Govt Should Focus on Russia's Integrity', *Interfax*, 11 September 1998.
76. 'Kontseptsiia natsional'noi bezopasnosti Rossiiskoi Federatsii – 1997', *Diplomaticheskii vestnik*, vol. 2, no. 2 (1998) 5–18.
77. For such a prescription, seeD. Trenin, 'Russia and the West: Avoiding Complications', *International Affairs (Moscow)*, vol. 42, no. 1 (1996) 30–8.
78. A. Gol'ts, 'NATO – ne sinonim evropeiskoi bezopasnosti', *Krasnaia zvezda*, 27 May 1995. For a similar argument, see V. Markushin, 'Vashington vozomnil sebia mirovym voennym pravitel'stvom?' *Krasnaia zvezda*, 5 September 1996.
79. Interviews with: D. Trenin, *Deputy Director, Programme Co-chair, Senior Associate at Carnegie Moscow Centre*, interviewed in Moscow on 1 June 2005. D. Simes, *President of the Nixon Centre*, interviewed in Washington, D.C. on 20 May 2005. E. Warner, *1993–97 Assistant US Secretary of Defence for Strategy and Requirements; 1997–2000 Assistant Secretary of Defence for International Security Policy and Threat Reduction*, interviewed in Washington, D.C. on 19 May 2005.
80. I. Rodionov, 'What Sort of Defense Does Russia Need?' *Nezavisimoe voennoe obozrenie*, 28 November 1996, cited in: W. D. Jackson, 'Encircled Again: Russia's Military Assesses Threats in a Post-Soviet World', *Political Science Quarterly*, vol. 117, no. 3 (2002) 373–400.
81. V. Gundarov, 'Sbor rukovodiashchego sostava Vooruzhennykh sil', *Krasnaia zvezda*, 13 November 1999.

82. I. D. Sergeev, 'Osnovnie faktori, opredeliaiushchie voenno-tekhnicheskuiu politiku Rossii', *Krasnaia zvezda*, 9 December 1999.
83. B. Yeltsin, 'Yeltsin on Partnership in NATO, published in: Nezavisimaia gazeta, 7 April 1994, p. 1', *CDPSP*, vol. XLVI, no. 14 (1994) pp. 22–3.
84. 'Summary of Conclusion', *NATO Ministerial Communiqués*, 22 June 1994, available at: http://www.nato.int/docu/comm/49–95/c940622a.htm (accessed: 7 July 2007).
85. E. Visens, 'Otnosheniia Rossii s NATO nosiat evoliutsionnyi kharakter', *Segodnia* (22 July 1995) p. 4.
86. 'Speech by Secretary General Javier Solana', *NATO*, 8 July 1997, available at: http://www.nato.int/docu/speech/1997/s970708d.htm (accessed: 7 July 2007).
87. B. Yeltsin, 'Iz poslaniia Prezidenta Rossiiskoi Federatsii Federal'nomu Sobraniiu – 1998', *Diplomaticheskii vestnik*, no. 3 (March 1998) 3–4, p. 3. Yeltsin, *Midnight Diaries*, p. 131.
88. 'Putin – Russia Ready to Expand Relations with NATO', *BBC Summary of World Broadcasts*, 18 February 2000.
89. 'Putin ne vozrazhaet protiv vstupleniia Rossii v NATO', *Kommersant-Daily*, 7 March 2000.
90. V. V. Putin, 'Rossiia–Litva–Vystuplenie V. V. Putina na podpisanii sovmestnogo zaiavleniia', *Diplomaticheskii vestnik*, no. 4 (2001) 61–2, p. 61. V. Fal'kov, 'Putin soglasilsia poekhat v Litvu', *Nezavisimaia gazeta*, 31 March 2001. For similar arguments by Russian Defence Minister Sergei Ivanov, see 'Ministr oborony v Finliandii', *Krasnaia zvezda*, 19 July 2002. 'Baltiiskie zaboty Rossii', *Krasnaia zvezda*, 1 August 2002.
91. S. Gutterman, 'EU, NATO Enlargement Dominate Schroeder's Brief Visit to Russia', *Associated Press*, 2 April 2004.
92. For an evaluation of the work of the Council three years after its creation, see T. Forsberg, 'Russia's Relationship with NATO: A Qualitative Change or Old Wine in New Bottles?' *Journal of Communist Studies and Transition Politics*, vol. 21, no. 3 (September 2005) 332–53.
93. 'A "New Spirit" of Cooperation Between NATO and Russia', *NATO*, 4 December 2003, available at: http://www.nato.int/docu/update/2003/12-december/e1204c.htm (accessed: 7 July 2007).
94. K. Knox, 'Baltics: Tempest Over Minorities Erupts During NATO Assembly', *RFE/RL*, 29 May 2003.
95. V. Mite, 'Baltics: Russia Sensitive to Any NATO Troop Deployment', *RFE/RL*, 3 March 2004.
96. S. Ivanov, 'As NATO Grows, So Do Russia's Worries', *The New York Times*, 7 April 2004. S. L. Myers, 'As NATO Finally Arrives on Its Borders, Russia Grumbles', *The New York Times*, 3 Apr 2004.
97. D. Lynch, *Russia Faces Europe* (Paris: Institute for Security Studies, 2003), p. 34.
98. B. Denisov, 'NATO rasshiraiut radi samosokhraneniia', *Vek*, 6 July 2001.
99. 'The Alliance's Strategic Concept', *NATO Press Release NAC-S(99)65*, 24 April 1999, available at: http://www.nato.int/docu/pr/1999/p99–065e.htm (accessed: 7 July 2007).
100. Averre, 'NATO Expansion', p. 30.
101. M. Light, 'Security Implications of Russia's Foreign Policy for Europe', *European Foreign Affairs Review*, vol. 3, no. 1 (Spring 1998) 53–66, p. 63.

102. V. Zhurkin, *Between the Past and the Future – Russia in the Transatlantic Context*, Russian Academy of Science, Moscow, 2001, cited in: T. Forsberg, 'The EU-Russia Security Partnership: Why the Opportunity was Missed', *European Foreign Affairs Review*, vol. 9, no. 2 (2004) 247–67, p. 268. For similar analyses, see M. Clarke and P. Cornish, 'The European Defence Project and the Prague Summit', *International Affairs*, vol. 78, no. 4 (2002) 777–88, p. 784. For similar arguments, see P. H. Gordon, 'NATO After 11 September', *Survival*, vol. 43, no. 4 (Winter 2001–2002) 89–106. D. Lynch, 'Russia's Strategic Partnership with Europe', *The Washington Quarterly*, vol. 27, no. 2 (Spring 2004) 99–118, p. 100. D. S. Yost, 'The NATO Capabilities Gap and the European Union', *Survival*, vol. 42, no. 4 (Winter 2000–2001) 97–128.
103. A. G. Arbatov, *The Transformation of Russian Military Doctrine: Lessons Learned from Kosovo and Chechnya* (Garmisch-Partenkirchen: Marshall Center, 2000), p. 9.
104. M. Light, J. Löwenhardt and S. White, 'Russian Perspectives on European Security', *European Foreign Affairs Review*, vol. 5, no. 4 (Winter 2000) 489–505, p. 494.
105. For a similar argument, see M. A. Smith, *Russia and NATO since 1991: From Cold War through Cold Peace to Partnership?* (Abingdon: Routledge, 2006), pp. 124 and 7.
106. V. V. Putin, *Ot pervogo litsa: razgovory c Vladimirom Putinym* (Moscow: Vagrius, 2000), p. 160.
107. I. Ivanov, 'Rossiia i strany tsentral'noi i vostochnoi Evropy: novyi etap otnoshenii', *Kommersant-Daily*, 2 July 2003.
108. For a comprehensive analysis of Russia's approach to NATO in this period, see H. Adomeit, 'Inside or Outside? Russia's Policies Towards NATO', *Working Paper*, http://www.swp-berlin.org/de/common/get_document.php?asset_id=3570 (accessed: 7 July 2007).
109. V. V. Putin, 'Interview with Radio Slovensko and Slovakian Television Channel STV', *President of Russia: Official Web Portal*, 22 February 2005, available at: http://www.kremlin.ru/eng/speeches/2005/02/22/2038_type 82916_84445.shtml (accessed: 7 July 2007).
110. Ibid. For similar arguments, see V. V. Putin, 'Transcript of Press Conference with the Russian Foreign Media – 2007', *President of Russia: Official Web Portal*, 1 February 2007, available at: http://www.kremlin.ru/eng/speeches/ 2007/02/01/1309_type82915type82917_117609.shtml (accessed: 7 July 2007). S. Lavrov, 'Democracy, International Governance, and the Future World Order', *Russia in Global Affairs*, vol. 3, no. 1 (January–March 2005) 146–56, p. 151.
111. V. V. Putin, 'Speech and the Following Discussion at the Munich Conference on Security Policy', *President of Russia: Official Web Portal*, 10 February 2007, available at: http://www.kremlin.ru/eng/speeches/2007/02/10/0138_type 82912type82914type82917type84779_118135.shtml (accessed: 7 July 2007).
112. S. Ivanov, 'DM Ivanov Says Russia Dislikes but Tolerates NATO Enlargement', *reproduced in Johnson's Russia List*, no. 39 (10 February 2006).
113. Russia has the right to base its fleet in Sevastopol until 2017 and Moscow made it clear that it would not agree to an annulment of this agreement.
114. S. Stepanenko, 'Guest Workers from NATO, published in: Vremia novostei, 2 June 2006, p. 5', *CDPSP*, vol. 58, no. 23 (2006). Adomeit, 'Inside or Outside?'

174 Notes and References

115. S. Lavrov, 'Ministr inostrannykh del Rossii Sergej Lavrov: Obespechit' konkurentosposobnost' strany v globaliziruiushchemsia mire', *Krasnaia zvesda*, 12 December 2006.
116. I. Plugatar, 'Atlantisty proigryvaiut v Kieve, no torzhestvuiut v Tbilisi,' *Nezavisimoe voennoe obozrenie*, 29 September 2006, cited in: Adomeit, 'Inside or Outside?'
117. V. V. Putin, 'Speech of Russian President Vladimir Putin at the meeting of the Security Council', 28 January 2005, available at: http://www.ln.mid.ru/brp_4.nsf/e78a48070f128a7b43256999005bcbb3/854cb2ebb38d7704c3 256f970049179f?OpenDocument (accessed: 7 July 2007). For similar arguments, see Putin, 'Interview with Radio Slovensko'. S. Lavrov, 'Tezisy Vystupleniia Ministra Inostrannykh del Rossii S.V.Lavrova na vstreche so studentami Fakul'teta mirovoj politiki MGU im. M.V.Lomonosova', 11 December 2006, available at: http://www.mid.ru/brp_4.nsf/sps/C75D6169 BC7444D6C3257241005B6517 (accessed: 7 July 2007).
118. Forsberg, 'Russia's Relationship with NATO', pp. 343–5.
119. S. White, J. Korosteleva and R. Allison, 'NATO: The View from the East', *European Security*, vol. 15, no. 2 (June 2006) 165–90, p. 168.
120. Putin, 'Speech and the Following Discussion at the Munich Conference on Security Policy'.
121. V. V. Putin, 'Annual Address to the Federal Assembly – 2007', *President of Russia: Official Web Portal*, 26 April 2007, available at: http://www.kremlin.ru/eng/speeches/2007/04/26/1209_type70029type82912_125494.shtml (accessed: 7 July 2007).
122. H. Adomeit and A. Bittner, 'Russland und die Raketenabwehr', *SWP-Aktuell*, no. 23 (April 2007).
123. Putin, 'Speech and the Following Discussion at the Munich Conference on Security Policy'. Putin, 'Transcript of Press Conference – 2007'. V. V. Putin, 'Transcript of the Press Conference for Russian and Foreign Media – 2006', *President of Russia: Official Web Portal*, 31 January 2006, available at: http://www.kremlin.ru/eng/speeches/2006/01/31/0953_type82915type829 17_100901.shtml (accessed: 7 July 2007).
124. Putin, 'Speech and the Following Discussion at the Munich Conference on Security Policy'.
125. D. W. Rivera, 'Engagement, Containment, and the International Politics of Eurasia', *Political Science Quarterly*, vol. 118, no. 1 (2003) 81–106, p. 104.
126. Putin, 'Interview with Radio Slovensko'. For a similar statement see 'Putin says Russia may Consider Joining NATO in the Future', *Itar-Tass*, 31 October 2005.
127. V. Baranovskij, 'Russian Views on NATO and the EU', in Anatol Lieven, et al., eds, *Ambivalent Neighbors: The EU, NATO, and the Price of Membership* (Washington, D.C.: Carnegie Endowment for International Peace, 2003), 269–94, pp. 270–1.

Chapter 5: Russia's Responses to the Balkan Crises

1. A. C. Lynch, 'The Realism of Russia's Foreign Policy', *Europe-Asia Studies*, vol. 53, no. 1 (2001) 7–31, pp. 19–21. P. Kubicek, 'Russian Foreign Policy

and the West', *Political Science Quarterly*, vol. 114, no. 4 (1999–2000) 547–68, pp. 567–8. A. Rahr, 'Russlands Interessen auf dem Balkan', *Europäische Sicherheit* (1 July 1999) 43–51. E. Yesson, 'NATO and Russia in Kosovo', *Perspectives (Prague)*, vol. Special Issue (Winter 1999/2000) 11–19, pp. 14–15.
2. Kubicek, 'Russian Foreign Policy and the West', pp. 552–4. For a similar argument, see P. A. Goble, 'Dangerous Liaisons: Moscow, the Former Yugoslavia, and the West', in Richard H. Ullman, ed., *The World and Yugoslavia's Wars* (New York: Council on Foreign Relations, 1996), 182–97, p. 188.
3. V. Kremenjuk, 'The Ideological Legacy in Russia's Foreign Policy', *International Affairs (Moscow)*, vol. 47, no. 3 (2001) 18–26, p. 21.
4. For historical accounts of the origins of the Bosnian conflict, see N. Malcolm, *Bosnia: A Short History* (London: Pan Books, 2002). J. E. Goodby, 'Conflict in Europe: the Case of Yugoslavia', in James E. Goodby, ed., *Regional Conflicts: The Challenge to US–Russian Co-operation* (Oxford: Oxford University Press, 1995), 157–87. M. Bowker, 'The Wars in Yugoslavia: Russia and the International Community', *Europe–Asia Studies*, vol. 50, no. 7 (November 1998) 1245–61. J. M. O. Sharp, 'Dayton Report Card', *International Security*, vol. 22, no. 3 (Winter 1997/98) 101–37.
5. For a comprehensive historical account of the Kosovo problem, see N. Malcolm, *Kosovo: A Short History*, 2nd. ed. (New York: New York University Press, 2002). For a short overview of the conflict's origin, crisis management and its impact on international relations, see A. Schnabel and R. Thakur, eds, *Kosovo and the Challenge of Humanitarian Intervention: Selective Indignation, Collective Action, and International Citizenship* (Tokyo: United Nations University Press, 2000). D. Leurdijk and D. Zandee, *Kosovo: From Crisis to Crisis* (Aldershot: Ashgate Publishing Limited, 2001).
6. The assessment that the Bosnian conflict was only of indirect relevance is supported by former British Foreign Minister Douglas Hurd, see D. Hurd, *The Search for Peace* (London: Warner Books, 1997), p. 89.
7. V. G. Baranovskij, 'Russia's Interests Are Too Important', *International Affairs (Moscow)*, vol. 45, no. 3 (1999) 4–14, p. 7. S. Talbott, *The Russia Hand* (New York: Random House, 2002), p. 77.
8. D. Trenin, 'Russia Rattles Sabers over Kosovo', *Russia Today*, 13 October 1998, cited in: P. K. Baev, 'Russia's Stance Against Secessions: From Chechnya to Kosovo', *International Peacekeeping*, vol. 6, no. 3 (Autumn 1999) 73–94, p. 87.
9. B. Kazantsev, 'Serious Concern over New NATO Strategy', *International Affairs (Moscow)*, vol. 45, no. 2 (1999) 23–8.
10. The Contact Group was created during the Bosnian conflict in 1994 and it was reactivated in 1997 to deal with the conflict in Kosovo. It consisted of six nations: France, Germany, Great Britain, Italy, Russia, and the United States.
11. A. Fedorov, 'New Pragmatism of Russia's Foreign Policy', *International Affairs (Moscow)*, vol. 45, no. 5 (1999) 47–52, p. 49.
12. 'United Nations Security Council Resolution 757', *S/RES/757 (1992)*, 30 May 1992.
13. 'United Nations Security Council Resolution 776', *S/RES/776 (1992)*, 14 September 1992.
14. 'United Nations Security Council Resolution 781', *S/RES/781 (1992)*, 9 October 1992.

15. On the Soviet Union's approach to the Balkan conflicts, see A. Lynch and R. Lukic, 'Russian Foreign Policy and the Wars in the Former Yugoslavia', *RFE/RL Research Report (Munich)*, vol. 2, no. 41 (15 October 1993) 25–32, pp. 27–8.
16. H. Pick and D. Hearst, 'Moscow Breaks Ranks with its Security Council Partners', *The Guardian*, 26 January 1993.
17. D. Williams and E. Robinson, 'Clinton Yields to Europe on Balkans Moves', *The Washington Post*, 18 May 1993, p. A1.
18. M. Albright, *Madam Secretary: A Memoir* (Basingstoke: Macmillan, 2003), pp. 180–1. H.-J. Hoppe, *Russland und der Jugoslawienkonflikt*, vol. 14, Bericht des Bundesinstituts für ostwissenschaftliche und internationale Studien (Köln: Bundesinstitut für ostwissenschaftliche und internationale Studien, 1997), p. 399.
19. 'Press Conference on Yugoslavia Crisis', *Federal Information Systems Corporation*, 24 February 1993. S. Crow, 'Russia Adopts a More Active Policy', *RFE/RL Research Report*, vol. 2, no. 12 (19 March 1993) 1–6.
20. 'Yeltsin Condemns Serb Defiance of Peace Process', *The Financial Times (London)*, 28 April 1993, p. 3.
21. D. Owen, *Balkan Odyssey* (London: Victor Gollancz, 1995), p. 282.
22. 'Allies Forge "More of the Same" Strategy on Bosnia', *Press Association*, 22 May 1993.
23. E. Sciolino, 'U.S. Russia Agree on Strategy Accepting Serbian Gains for Now', *21 May 1993*, 21 May 1993, p. 1.
24. J. Headley, 'Sarajevo, February 1994: The First Russia–NATO Crisis of the post-Cold War Era', *Review of International Studies*, vol. 29 (2003) 209–27, p. 211.
25. A. Kozyrev, 'A. Kozyrev Explains to Parliament Why Russia Joined the Sanctions, published in: Izvestiia, 27 June 1992, p. 1', *CDPSP*, vol. XLIV, no. 26 (1992) 24, p. 24.
26. B. Yeltsin, *Itar–Tass*, 27 April 1993.
27. A. Kozyrev, 'Preobrazhenie ili kafkianskaia metamorfoza demokraticheskaia vneshniaia politika Rossii i ee prioritety', *Nezavisimaia gazeta*, 20 August 1992.
28. Talbott, *The Russia Hand*, p. 74. For a similar warning by Kozyrev, see Talbott, *The Russia Hand*, pp. 73–4 and 76. For a similar argument made by Karaganov, who was at that time an advisers to Yeltsin, see A. Gowers, 'Russia Attacks UN Vote on Serbia', *Financial Times*, 20 April 1993.
29. M. R. Gordon, 'Russia Declines to Support Tighter Sanctions on Serbia', *The New York Times*, 18 April 1993.
30. Y. Ambartsumov, 'Russian Parliament Explains to Minister A. Kozyrev Why There Should Have Been No Hurry to Impose Sanctions Against Serbia, published in: Izvestiia, 29 June 1992', *CDPSP*, vol. XLIV, no. 26 (1992) 25, p. 25.
31. M. Yusin, 'Supreme Soviet Preparing to Review Russian Foreign Policy, published in: Izvestiia, 18 December 1992, p. 4', *CDPSP*, vol. XLIV, no. 51 (1992) 16–17, p. 16.
32. M. Yusin, 'Russian Parliament's Resolution on Yugoslavia Pushes Moscow Towards International Isolation, published in: Izvestiia, 20 February 1993, p. 2', *CDPSP*, vol. XLV, no. 8 (1993) 17–18, p. 17.
33. For example, see M. Yusin, 'Deputies Ambartsumov and Rumyantsev Urge Moscow to Ally Itself With Belgrade, published in: Izvestiia, 11 August 1992, p. 5', *CDPSP*, vol. XLIV, no. 32 (1992) 21, p. 21.

34. A. Kozyrev, 'Russian Foreign Minister Answers Questions, published in: Izvestiia, 18 August 1994', *CDPSP*, vol. XLVI, no. 33 (1994) 27, p. 27.
35. 'Kozyrev Warns Against Repeat of Sarajevo 1914', *BBC Summary of World Broadcasts*, 9 February 1994.
36. UN Security Council Resolutions 819, 824 and 836 of April, Mai and June 1993 designated five UN safe-areas in addition to the one in Srebrenica: Bihac, Gorazde, Sarajevo, Tuzla, and Zepa. 'United Nations Security Council Resolution 819', *S/RES/819 (1993)*, 16 April 1993. 'United Nations Security Council Resolution 824', *S/RES/824 (1993)*, 6 May 1993. 'United Nations Security Council Resolution 836', *S/RES/836 (1993)*, 4 June 1993.
37. P. Zhuravlev, 'Pozitsiia deistviia NATO v Bosnii pugaiut Rossiiu', *Segodnia*, 14 April 1994.
38. S. Sidorov, 'Pozitsiia Rossii iasna', *Krasnaia zvezda*, 19 February 1994.
39. 'Yeltsin Criticizes NATO for Seeking to Exclude Moscow from Regional Conflicts', *BBC Summary of World Broadcasts*, 25 February 1994.
40. 'Churkin, Interview with Churkin on St Petersburg Channel 5 TV', *BBC Summary of World Broadcasts*, 2 March 1994.
41. B. Yeltsin, 'The President of Russia's Speech to the Federal Assembly, published in: Rossiiskaia gazeta, 25 February 1994, pp. 1–2', *CDPSP*, vol. XLVI, no. 8 (1994) 5–8, p. 8.
42. M. Yusin, 'Serby nanosiat zhestokii udar po prestizhu rossiiskoi diplomatii', *Izvestiia* (20 April 1994).
43. Y. Shchedrunova, 'Rossiia gotova k vvedeniiu zhestkikh mer protiv Serbov', *Segodnia*, 28 July 1994.
44. K. Eggert, 'Moscow Comes to Bosnian Serbs' Aid Yet Again, published in: Izvestiia, 3 August 1994, p. 3', *CDPSP*, vol. XLVI, no. 31 (1994) 21, p. 21.
45. For a comprehensive overview of the developments in 1995, see A. Borden and R. Caplan, 'The Former Yugoslavia: The War and the Peace Process', *SIPRI Yearbook 1996* (Oxford: Oxford University Press, 1996), 203–31, pp. 210–24.
46. Y. Shchedrunova, 'NATO stanovitsia tret'ei voiuiushchei storonoi', *Segodnia*, 27 May 1995.
47. 'UN Approves Dispatch of MRRF to Bosnia, Russia Abstains', *Itar–Tass*, 16 June 1995.
48. 'Foreign Ministry Says NATO Airstrikes in Bosnia "Unjustified"', *BBC Summary of World Broadcasts*, 13 July 1995.
49. V. Abarinov, 'Kogda v posrednikakh soglas'ia net', *Segodnia*, 25 July 1995.
50. 'Kozyrev Asks UN Chief to Protect Civilians in Croatia', *Itar–Tass*, 9 August.
51. M. Yusin, 'NATO nachinaet bol'shuiu voinu s bosniiskimi Serbami', *Izvestiia*, 31 August 1995.
52. 'Eto i est' genotsid', *Rossiiskaia gazeta*, 14 September 1995.
53. Bowker, 'The Wars in Yugoslavia', p. 1252.
54. M. Baskin, 'Russia's Double-Edged Diplomacy in the Balkan War', in Geir Flikke, ed., *Russia and International Peacekeeping* (Oslo: NUPI, 1996), 99–112, p. 106. R. Heller, *Russische Interessen im Balkankonflikt: Russland und die internationale Staatenwelt seit 1992* (Hamburg: Lit Verlag, 1998), p. 129.
55. S. Parrish, 'Twisting in the Wind: Russia and the Yugoslav Conflict', *Transition*, vol. 1, no. 20 (3 November 1995) 28–31 and 70, p. 30.
56. M. Dobbs, *Madeleine Albright: A Twentieth-Century Odyssey* (New York: Henry Holt and Company, 1999), p. 363.

178 Notes and References

57. M. Yusin, 'After the Tragedy in Sarajevo, published in: Izvestiia, 8 February 1994, pp. 1, 3', *CDPSP*, vol. XLVI, no. 6 (1994) 6, p. 6.
58. V. Kononenko, 'In Moscow Major Has to Try to Justify West's Impatience in Bosnian Conflict, published in: Izvestiia, 16 February 1994, p. 3', *CDPSP*, vol. XLVI, no. 7 (1994) 32, p. 32.
59. A. Baturin, 'Moscow is Irritated, published in: Izvestiia, 12 April 1994, p. 1', *CDPSP*, vol. XLVI, no. 15 (1994) 5, p. 5.
60. 'Once Again, Russia was not Given Advance Notice, published in: Segodnia 12 April 1994, p. 1', *CDPSP*, vol. XLVI, no. 15 (1994) 5, p. 5.
61. [Emphasis added] Yusin, 'Serby Nanosiat Zhestokij Udar'.
62. M. Yusin, 'Andrei Kozyrev otvergaet ul'timatum Vladimira Zhirinovskogo', *Izvestiia*, 26 January 1994.
63. Interview in Radio Free Europe/Radio Liberty Research Report 3 (15 July 1994), p. 36, cited in: Kubicek, 'Russian Foreign Policy and the West', pp. 551–2.
64. R. Caplan, 'International Diplomacy and the Crisis in Kosovo', *International Affairs*, vol. 74, no. 4 (1998) 745–61. Leurdijk and Zandee, *Kosovo: From Crisis to Crisis*, pp. 21–2.
65. J. R. Smith, '11 Children Among Kosovo Dead', *The Washington Post*, 10 March 1998.
66. A. Dudin, 'Kosovo smotrit na zapad', *Obshchaia gazeta*, 12 March 1998.
67. 'Interview with Foreign Minister Hubert Védrine', *Le Monde*, 11 June 1999. S. Troebst, 'Chronologie einer gescheiterten Prävention', *Osteuropa*, vol. 49, no. 8 (1999) 777–95, p. 785.
68. 'United Nations Security Council Resolution 1160', *S/RES/1160 (1998)*, 31 March 1998.
69. W. Petritsch, K. Kaser and R. Pichler, *Kosovo–Kosova: Mythen, Daten, Fakten* (Klagenfurt: Wieser Verlag, 1999), p. 220.
70. 'Statement on Kosovo', *NATO Press Releases M-NAC-1(98)77*, 11 June 1998, available at: http://www.nato.int/docu/pr/1998/p98–077e.htm (accessed: 7 July 2007).
71. M. O'Connor, 'NATO Jets Patrol Skies Near Serbia in Show of Force', *The New York Times*, 16 June 1998.
72. E. Gujer, 'Russlands ambivalente Haltung auf dem Balkan', *Neue Züricher Zeitung*, 16 June 1998.
73. K. Yelovsky and K. Zhukovsky, 'Yeltsin, Milosevic Confirm Need for Yugoslav Integrity', *Itar-Tass*, 16 June 1998.
74. M. Yusin, 'Ustupki Miloshevicha ne udovletvorili zapad', *Izvestiia*, 18 June 1998.
75. 'United Nations Security Council Resolution 1199', *S/RES/1199 (1998)*, 23 September 1998.
76. P. Münch, 'Warnung ohne Wirkung', *Süddeutsche Zeitung*, 24 September 1998.
77. 'Statement by the Secretary General Following the ACTWARN Decision', *NATO Press Release*, 24 September 1998, available at: http://www.nato.int/docu/pr/1998/p980924e.htm (accessed: 7 July 2007).
78. V. Sycheva, 'Boris El'tsin prizyvaet Slobodan Miloshevicha smirit' gordyniu', *Segodnia*, 6 October 1998.
79. 'United Nations Security Council Resolution 1203', *S/RES/1203 (1998)*, 24 October 1998.
80. D. Lynch, '"Walking the Tightrope": The Kosovo Conflict and Russia in European Security', *European Security*, vol. 8, no. 4 (Winter 1999) 57–83, p. 65.

81. G. Dinmore, 'Villagers Slaughtered in Kosovo "Atrocity"', *The Washington Post*, 17 January 1999.
82. C. Trueheart, 'Talks Extended', *The Washington Post*, 15 February 1999.
83. Leurdijk and Zandee, *Kosovo: From Crisis to Crisis*, p. 35.
84. Lynch, '"Walking the Tightrope"', p. 65. This assessment was also supported in interviews with US decision-makers: J. Bass, *1996–97 NATO Russia Desk Officer in the US State Department; 1998–2001 Special Assistant to the US Deputy Secretary of State and Chief of Staff*, interviewed in Washington, D.C. on 12 May 2005. J. Norris, *1999–2000 Director of Communications for the US Deputy Secretary of State; since 2001 Chief of Staff of the International Crisis Group (Washington office)*, interviewed in Washington, D.C. on 17 May 2005.
85. B. Clinton, 'Statement by the President to the Nation', *White House Office of the Press Secretary*, 24 March 1999, available at: http://www.clintonfoundation.org/legacy/032499-speech-by-president-to-the-nation-on-kosovo.htm (accessed: 7 July 2007).
86. B. Gellman, 'Allies Launch Air Attack On Yugoslav Military Targets', *The Washington Post*, 25 March 1999.
87. P. Kuznetsov, 'Yeltsin Warns of Possible Extreme Russian response', *Itar–Tass*, 25 March 1999.
88. Yesson, 'NATO and Russia in Kosovo', p. 13.
89. 'Security Council Rejects Demand for Cessation of Use of Force Against Federal Republic of Yugoslavia', *United Nations Press Release SC/6659*, 26 March 1999.
90. A. Roberts, 'NATO's "Humanitarian War" over Kosovo', *Survival*, vol. 41, no. 3 (Autumn 1999) 102–23, p. 105.
91. This view, expressed by Putin, was supported in a number of interviews with a number of US foreign policy makers. V. V. Putin, *Ot pervogo litsa: razgovory c Vladimirom Putinym* (Moscow: Vagrius, 2000), p. 157. Bass, *interviewed in Washington, D.C. on 12 May 2005*. J. Dobbins, *1999–2000 Special US Envoy for Bosnia and Kosovo; 2000–01 Assistant Secretary of State for Europe; 2001–02 Representative to the Afghan Opposition*, interviewed in Washington, D.C. on 10 May 2005. M. Medish, *1994–96 Special Assistant to the Assistant Administrator of the US Agency for International Development; 1996 Senior Adviser to the Administrator of UNDP; 1997–2000 Deputy Assistant Secretary of the US Treasury for International Affairs; 2000–01 Special Assistant to the US President and Senior Director on the National Security Council Staff for Russian, Ukrainian and Eurasian Affairs*, interviewed by telephone on 10 August 2005. Norris, *interviewed in Washington, D.C. on 17 May 2005*.
92. Baev, 'Russia's Stance Against Secessions', p. 88.
93. J. M. Goldgeier and M. McFaul, 'A Flawed Pragmatism', *The Moscow Times*, 10 October 1998.
94. M. Webber, ed., *Russia and Europe: Conflict or Cooperation?* (Basingstoke: Macmillan Press, 2000). M. Bowker, *Russian Foreign Policy and the End of the Cold War* (Aldershot: Dartmouth Publishing Company Limited, 1997), p. 242. A. Edemskii, 'Russian Perspectives', in Alex Danchev, et al., eds, *International Perspectives on the Yugoslav Conflict* (Basingstoke: Macmillan Press, 1996), 29–51.
95. Albright, *Madam Secretary: A Memoir*, p. 382.
96. Talbott, *The Russia Hand*, p. 301.

180   Notes and References

97. I. Ivanov, 'Ministra Inostrannykh Del Rossiiskoi Federatsii I.S. Ivanova po itogam vneshnepoliticheskogo 1998 goda', *Diplomaticheskii vestnik*, no. 2 (1999) 3–5, p. 4.
98. Independent International Commission on Kosovo, 'The Kosovo Report', http://www.reliefweb.int/library/documents/thekosovoreport.htm (accessed: 7 July 2007).
99. J. F. Collins, *1990–93 Deputy Chief of Mission and Charge d'affaires at the US Embassy in Moscow; 1993–97 Ambassador-at-large and Special Advisor to the US Secretary of State for the Newly Independent States; 1997 until 2001 Ambassador to the Russian Federation*, interviewed in Washington, D.C. on 11 May 2005. Medish made a similar argument: Medish, *interviewed by phone on 10 August 2005*.
100. Dobbins, *interviewed in Washington, D.C. on 10 May 2005*.
101. Talbott, *The Russia Hand*, p. 299.
102. Petritsch, Kaser and Pichler, *Kosovo – Kosova*, pp. 228–9.
103. A. Gol'ts, 'Kogda zhe russkie pridut?' *Itogi (Moscow)*, 4 May 1999, p. 23.
104. FreeB92 News for Thursday, 30 November 2000 cited in: P. Bonin, 'Die letzten Reserven der eingebildeten Großmacht – Russische Balkanpolitik der 1990er Jahre', *Osteuropa*, vol. 51, no. 4–5 (April–May 2001) 540–53, p. 550.
105. L. Velechov, 'Ot Bagdada do Belgrada', *Itogi (Moscow)* (30 March 1999) 14–18, p. 14.
106. M. Gessen, 'Khronika pikiruiushchei revoliutsii', *Itogi (Moscow)*, 17 October 2000.
107. Goldgeier and McFaul, 'A Flawed Pragmatism'.
108. D. Gornostaev, 'Ivanov razvivaet idei Primakova', *Nezavisimaia gazeta*, 23 September 1998.
109. M. Yusin, 'Why Russia Must Back the Serbs', *The European*, 17 August 1998.
110. 'Interview with Foreign Minster Ivanov', *Izvestiia*, 28 October 1998.
111. Talbott, *The Russia Hand*, p. 300.
112. I. Ivanov, 'Sovmestnaia press-konferentsiia, 25 March 1999', *Diplomaticheskii vestnik*, no. 4 (1999) 11–18.
113. 'The Alliance's Strategic Concept', *NATO Press Release NAC-S(99)65*, 24 April 1999, available at: http://www.nato.int/docu/pr/1999/p99–065e.htm (accessed: 7 July 2007).
114. I. Ivanov, 'Vystuplenie Ministra Inostrannykh Del Rossiiskoi Federatsii I.S. Ivanova na zasedanii Gosudarstvennoi Dumy, 27 March 1999', *Diplomaticheskii vestnik*, no. 4 (1999) 25–8, p. 26.
115. Ivanov, 'Sovmestnaia press-konferentsiia, 25 March 1999'.
116. B. Yeltsin, *Midnight Diaries* (London: Weidenfeld & Nicolson, 2000), p. 256.
117. O. Levitin, 'Inside Moscow's Kosovo Muddle', *Survival*, vol. 42, no. 1 (Spring 2000) 130–40, p. 134.
118. K. Privalov, 'Tupiki i kompromissy aveniu Kleber', *Segodnia*, 17 March 1999.
119. Ivanov, 'Sovmestnaia press-konferentsiia, 25 March 1999'.
120. I. Berezovskaia, 'Konflikt v Kosovo grozit kholodni voinoi', *Izvestiia*, 7 October 1998.
121. Bowker, 'The Wars in Yugoslavia', p. 1254.
122. P. Felgenhauer, 'NATO Crosses Rubicon, published, in: Segodnia, 31 August 1995, p. 1', *CDPSP*, vol. XLVII, no. 35 (1995) 7, p. 7.

123. 'Grachev, Perry Sketch Plan of Russian Involvement in Bosnia', *Itar–Tass*, 8 November 1995.
124. G. Bovt and N. i. Kalashnikova, 'Situatsiia v eks-Iugoslavii', *Kommersant-Daily*, 16 September 1995.
125. I. Ivanov, 'Bosniia: etot mir priduman ne nami', *Moskovskie novosti*, 29 November 1995.
126. R. Holbrooke, *To End a War* (New York: The Modern Library, 1999), p. 209.
127. Ibid., p. 214.
128. Ibid., pp. 209–14.
129. S. Chugayev, 'Duma Votes in Favor of Lifting Sanctions, published in: Izvestiia, 15 April 1995, p. 1', *CDPSP*, vol. XLVII, no. 15 (1995) 24, p. 24. P. Borisov, 'Deputies Meet and Override Nearly all Vetos, published in: Segodnia, 15 August 1995, p. 2', *CDPSP*, vol. XLVII, no. 33 (1995) 22, p. 22. 'Excerpt from State Duma Resolution, published in: Rossiiskaia gazeta, 12 September 1995, p. 1', *CDPSP*, vol. XLVII, no. 37 (1995) 14, p. 14.
130. 'Excerpt from State Duma Resolution', p. 14.
131. A. Jack, 'Chernomyrdin Selected as Peace Envoy', *The Financial Times (London)*, 15 April 1999.
132. Albright, *Madam Secretary: A Memoir*, pp. 416–7.
133. I. H. Daalder and M. E. O'Hanlon, *Winning Ugly: NATO's War to Save Kosovo* (Washington, D.C.: Brookings Institution Press, 2000), pp. 169–71.
134. M. Walker, 'How Deal Was Done in Stalin's Hideaway', *The Guardian (London)*, 5 June 1999.
135. C. Bohlen, 'Accord is Reached on Integrating Russian Troops in Kosovo', *The New York Times*, 19 June 1999.
136. Yeltsin, *Midnight Diaries*, p. 264. G. Dinmore and J. Lloyd, 'Milosevic Agrees to Allow NATO Troops into Kosovo', *The Financial Times (London)*, 31 May 1999.
137. J. Norris, *Collision Course: NATO, Russia, and Kosovo* (Westport: Praeger, 2005), p. 310.
138. 'United Nations Security Council Resolution 1244', *S/RES/1244 (1999)*, 10 June 1999.
139. S. Fischer, 'Schwierige Partnerschaft – Russland und der Westen nach Kosovo und Tschetschenien', in Forschungsstätte der Evangelischen Studiengemeinschaft, ed., *Friedensgutachten 2000* (Münster: Lit Verlag, 2000), 64–73, p. 65.
140. 'IMF Approves Stand-By Credit for Russia', *IMF, Press Release No. 99/35*, 28 July 1998, available at: http://www.imf.org/external/np/sec/pr/1999/pr9935.htm (accessed: 7 July 2007).
141. Talbott, *The Russia Hand*, p. 348.
142. 'Zaiavlenie Narodno-patrioticheskogo soyuza Rossii', *Sovetskaia Rossiia*, 27 March 1999.
143. Fischer, 'Schwierige Partnerschaft', pp. 66–7.
144. K. Khudoley, 'Russia and the European Union: New Opportunities, New Challenges', in Arkady Moshes, ed., *Rethinking the Respective Strategies of Russia and the European Union* (Moscow: Carnegie Endowment for International Peace, 2003), 8–30, p. 10.
145. S. Dardykin, 'Serbov, konechno, zhalko, no eto eshche ne povod gotovit'sia k tret'ei mirovoi voine', *Izvestiia*, 15 September 1995. K. Eggert,

'"Derzhavnaia" vneshniaia politika stoit slishkom dorogo', *Izvestiia*, 16 December 1995.
146. W. K. Clark, *Waging Modern War: Bosnia, Kosovo, and the Future of Combat* (New York: Public Affairs, 2001), p. 390.
147. Yeltsin, *Midnight Diaries*, p. 266.
148. Bonin, 'Die letzten Reserven', pp. 546–7.
149. I. Safronov and G. Sysoev, 'Proderzhat'sia do vosemnadtsatogo', *Kommersant-Daily*, 15 June 1999.
150. [Emphasis added] 'Deputy Foreign Minister Churkin on Bosnian Conflict', *BBC Summary of World Broadcast*, 8 March 1994.

Chapter 6: Russia's Response to the 11 September 2001 Terrorist Attacks

1. A. Grachev, 'Putin's Foreign Policy Choices', in Alex Pravda, ed., *Leading Russia: Putin in Perspective* (Oxford: Oxford University Press, 2005), 255–73, p. 256.
2. D. Trenin, 'Vladimir Putin's Autumn Marathon: Toward the Birth of a Russian Foreign Policy Strategy', November 2001, available at: http://www.carnegie.ru/en/pubs/briefings/48360.htm (accessed: 7 July 2007).
3. S. Talbott, 'Putin's Path: Russian Foreign Policy Since 9/11', *Yale University*, 27 January 2002, available at: http://www.yale.edu/dsj/lectures/01-27-02.htm (accessed: 7 July 2007).
4. For a similar kind of explanation, see A. Stent and L. Shevtsova, 'America, Russia and Europe: A Realignment?' *Survival*, vol. 44, no. 4 (Winter 2002–2003) 121–34.
5. For a similar explanation, see: L. Jonson, *Vladimir Putin and Central Asia: The Shaping of Russian Foreign Policy* (London: I.B. Tauris, 2004), pp. 173–7.
6. J. Starr, *1998–2001 Deputy Assistant Secretary of Defence for Russia, Ukraine and Eurasia Office; 2001–04 Principal Director for Special Operations and Low Intensity Conflict in the Pentagon; since 2004 Senior Advisor for Special Operations and Combating Terrorism*, interviewed in Washington, D.C. on 17 May 2005.
7. J. Dobbins, *1999–2000 Special US Envoy for Bosnia and Kosovo; 2000–01 Assistant Secretary of State for Europe; 2001–02 Representative to the Afghan Opposition*, interviewed in Washington, D.C. on 10 May 2005.
8. A. Pravda, 'Putin's Foreign Policy after 11 September: Radical or Revolutionary?' in Gabriel Gorodetsky, ed., *Russia between East and West: Russian Foreign Policy on the Threshold of the Twenty-first Century* (London: Frank Cass, 2003), 39–57, p. 47.
9. Former Head of the International Military Cooperation Department Ivashov made such a recommendation, see 'Russian General Against Siding with USA in Possible Strikes', *BBC Monitoring Former Soviet Union*, 15 September 2001. For a discussion of this kind of view, see V. Shlapentokh, 'Is the "Greatness Syndrome" Eroding?' *The Washington Quarterly*, vol. 25, no. 1 (Winter 2002) 131–46, pp. 140–1.
10. See Chapter 5 on Russia's response to the Balkan crises for an in-depth analysis of the Russian leadership's approach.
11. S. B. Glasser and P. Baker, 'Putin, Bush Weigh New Unity Against a "Common Foe"', *The Washington Post*, 13 September 2001.

12. 'Russia Cancels Air Force Exercise in Arctic Zone', *Itar-Tass*, 12 September 2001.
13. N. Lenskaya, 'RF FIS Works with Foreign Services to Prevent Terrorist Acts', *Itar-Tass*, 12 September 2001. 'Russian Special Services Working to Aid US Anti-Terrorist Operation', *BBC Monitoring Former Soviet Union*, 12 September 2001.
14. V. V. Putin, 'Zaiavlenie po povodu terroristicheskikh aktov v SshA', *Ofitsial'noe internet-predstavitel'stvo Prezidenta Rossii*, 11 September 2001, available at: http://president.kremlin.ru/text/docs/2001/09/57929.shtml (accessed: 7 July 2007).
15. 'United Nations Security Council Resolution 1373', *S/RES/1373 (2001)*, 28 September 2001.
16. A. G. Arbatov, 'A Russian Note of Caution', *Survival*, vol. 43, no. 4 (Winter 2001) 149–54, p. 152.
17. 'Russia Does Not Plan Any Joint Actions of Retribution', *Itar-Tass*, 14 September 2001.
18. Ibid. 'Tajikistan Not Yet Ready to Offer US Air Space for Possible Riposte', *Agence France Presse*, 14 September 2001.
19. 'Russia Provides Data on Location of Terrorist Training Camps in Afghanistan', *Interfax*, 21 September 2001.
20. V. V. Putin, 'Zaiavlenie Presidenta Rossii', *Ofitsial'noe internet-predstavitel'stvo Prezidenta Rossii*, 24 September 2001, available at: http://president.kremlin.ru/text/appears/2001/09/28639.shtml (accessed: 7 July 2007).
21. B. Woodward, *Bush at War* (London: Pocket Books, 2003), p. 103.
22. K. Ryan, *1998–2000 Regional Director Slavic States, Office of Russian and Eurasia, Office of the Secretary of Defence; 2001–03 US Defence Attaché to Moscow; 2003–05 Deputy Director Strategy, Plans and Policy (G35), Department of Army, Pentagon*, interviewed in Washington, D.C. on 13 May 2005. For a similar assessment, see I. Bremmer, 'The Future of Eurasia', *Security Dialogue*, vol. 34, no. 2 (June 2003) 238–42, p. 239.
23. I. S. Neverov, *Director of the Department of North America; Ministry of Foreign Affairs of the Russian Federation (MID)*, interviewed in Moscow on 9 June 2005. Ryan, interviewed in Washington, D.C. on 13 May 2005.
24. 'U.S.–Russia Working Group on Afghanistan', *U.S. Department of State*, 2 August 2001, available at: http://usembassy.state.gov/islamabad/wwwh00080401.html (accessed: 17 February 2005).
25. 'Joint Statement on Counterterrorism Cooperation', *The White House*, 24 May 2002, available at: http://www.whitehouse.gov/news/releases/2002/05/20020524-5.html (accessed: 7 July 2007). This assessment has been supported in an interview with a Pentagon official: Starr, interviewed in Washington, D.C. on 17 May 2005.
26. N. Dolgopolov, 'Spetssluzhby – tainaia voina razvedki', *Trud*, 20 December 2001.
27. A. Charlton, 'Putin: Future Afghan Government Should Lean on Support of All Ethnic Groups', *Associated Press*, 26 October 2001. I. Korotchenko, 'Lend-liz ot Sergeia Ivanova', *Nezavisimaia gazeta*, 4 October 2001. F. Weir, 'Moscow Denies Rumors that Russia has Gone Beyond Intelligence, Logistic Support', *Christian Science Monitor*, 15 October 2001, p. 13.
28. L. Freedman, 'A New Type of War', in Ken Booth, et al., eds, *Worlds in Collision – Terror and the Future of Global Order* (Basingstoke: Palgrave

Macmillan, 2002), 37–47, p. 43. For a similar assessment, see 'Afghanistan: The Key Lessons', *Jane's Intelligence Review*, vol. 37, no. 1 (January 2002) 20–7, p. 24.
29. T. Liloyan and V. Manvelov, 'Any NATO Operation in CIS Central Asia States Rejected', *Itar–Tass*, 14 September 2001. G. Sysoev, 'Pervaia polosa – America stroit mir', *Kommersant–Daily*, 15 September 2001.
30. I. Ershov, 'Ivanov poka ne vydaet afganskie iavki', *Rossiiskaia gazeta*, 20 September 2001.
31. S. Pifer, *1993–94 Deputy Coordinator for the Newly Independent States in the US State Department; 1994–97 Director, later Senior Director, for Russian, Ukrainian and Eurasian Affairs at the National Security Council; 1998–2000 US Ambassador to Ukraine; 2001–2004 Deputy Assistant Secretary for European and Eurasian Affairs at the US State Department*, interviewed in Washington, D.C. on 19 May 2005. This assessment was supported in other interviews. Ryan, interviewed in Washington, D.C. on 13 May 2005. Starr, interviewed in Washington, D.C. on 17 May 2005.
32. A. Khokhlov, 'Poslednie dni mira . . . Tadzhikistan', *Rossiiskaia gazeta*, 20 September 2001.
33. 'Tajikistan Not Yet Ready'.
34. 'Russians in Tajikistan to Prevent Influx of Afghan Refugees', *BBC Monitoring Former Soviet Union*, 20 September 2001.
35. V. V. Putin, 'National Public Radio Interview and Listener Call-In with Russian President Vladimir Putin', *Federal News Service*, 15 November 2001.
36. Uzbekistan publicly signalled its cooperation with the United States on 17 September and Kyrgyzstan on 19 September 2001, see 'Uzbekistan Says it May Host U.S. Military for Strikes on Afghanistan', *Associated Press*, 17 September 2001. 'Kyrgyzstan Ready to Consider US Request for Help to Attack Afghanistan', *Agence France Presse*, 19 September 2001.
37. D. Burghart, 'In the Tracks of Tamerlane: Central Asia's Path to the Twenty-First Century', *European Security*, vol. 11, no. 3 (Autumn 2002) 1–19, p. 13.
38. Talbott, 'Putin's Path'.
39. '"Seismic Seachange of Historic Proportions" in US–Russia ties', *Agence France Presse*, 3 October 2001. 'Remarks by National Security Adviser Condoleezza Rice at U.S.–Russia Business Council Conference', *Federal News Service*, 4 October 2001. V. V. Putin, 'Wortprotokoll der Rede Wladimir Putins im Deutschen Bundestag', *Deutscher Bundestag*, 25 September 2001, available at: http://www.bundestag.de/geschichte/gastredner/putin/putin_wort.html (accessed: 7 July 2007).
40. Shevtsova argues that this shift was revolutionary, whereas Pravda is more cautious and qualifies the shift as radical. L. Shevtsova, 'Meeting Summary', reproduced in *Johnson's Russia List*, no. 6121 (7 March 2002). Pravda, 'Putin's Foreign Policy'. For an argument similar to Pravda's, see B. Lo, *Vladimir Putin and the Evolution of Russian Foreign Policy* (Oxford: Blackwell Publishing, 2003).
41. GUUAM comprised Georgia, Azerbaijan, Moldova, Ukraine, and Uzbekistan.
42. 'The Foreign Policy Concept of the Russian Federation – 2000', available at: http://www.fas.org/nuke/guide/russia/doctrine/econcept.htm (accessed: 7 July 2007).
43. G. P. Herd and E. Akerman, 'Russian Strategic Realignment and the Post-Cold War Era', *Security Dialogue*, vol. 33, no. 3 (September 2002) 357–72, p. 366.

44. M. Esenov, 'The Anti-Terrorist Campaign and the Regional Security System', *IISS Russian Regional Perspectives,* vol. 1, no. 2 (2004) 26–8, p. 27.
45. A. Lieven, 'The Secret Policemen's Ball: The United States, Russia and the International Order after 11 September', *International Affairs (London),* vol. 78, no. 2 (2002) 245–59, p. 255.
46. R. Dannreuther, 'Can Russia Sustain Its Dominance in Central Asia?' *Security Dialogue,* vol. 32, no. 2 (2001) 245–58, p. 252.
47. V. Panfilova, 'Moskva i Bishkek prodolzhaiut sblizhenie', *Nezavisimaia gazeta,* 28 July 2000, p. 2.
48. The 'Shanghai Five' was created in 1996 and originally consisted of China, Kazakhstan, Kyrgyzstan, Russia, and Tajikistan.
49. 'Central Asia: Insurgency Fears Promote Russian Ties', *Oxford Analytica,* 17 February 2000.
50. P. Baev, 'Turning Counter-Terrorism into Counter-Revolution: Russia Focuses on Kazakhstan and Engages Turkmenistan', *European Security,* vol. 15, no. 1 (March 2006) 3–22.
51. For a historical account of Russia's involvement in Afghanistan post 1992, see M. Griffin, *Reaping the Whirlwind: The Taliban Movement in Afghanistan* (London: Pluto Press, 2001), Chapter 7.
52. Human Rights Watch, 'Afghanistan – Crisis of Impunity: The Role of Pakistan, Russia, and Iran in Fueling the Civil War', vol. 13, no. 3 (July 2001), pp. 40–6.
53. 'United Nations Security Council Resolution 1333', *S/RES/1333 (2000),* 19 December 2000.
54. 'O merakh po vypolneniiu resoliutsii Soveta Bezopasnosti OON 1333 ot 19 dekabria 2000g', *Ukaz N 266,* 6 March 2001.
55. I. Ivanov, 'Glavnoe – chtoby vneshniaia politika ne privodila k raskolu vnutri strany', *Izvestiia,* 10 July 2002.
56. Y. Primakov, 'Is the Russia–U.S. Rapprochement Here to Stay?'*International Affairs (Moscow),* vol. 48, no. 6 (2002) 86–99, p. 87.
57. G. Zyuganov, 'O novom etape natsional'nogo predatel'stva', *Sovetskaia Rossiia,* 18 May 2002.
58. R. O. Keohane, 'The Public Delegitimation of Terrorism and Coalition Politics', in Ken Booth, et al., eds, *Worlds in Collision – Terror and the Future of Global Order* (Basingstoke: Palgrave Macmillan, 2002), 141–51, p. 141.
59. V. G. Baranovsky, 'Russia: A Part of Europe or Apart from Europe?' *International Affairs,* vol. 76, no. 3 (2000) 443–58, pp. 456–7.
60. Putin, 'Zaiavlenie po povodu'. For similar arguments, see Putin, 'Zaiavlenie Presidenta Rossii'. 'Global System Must Confront International Terrorism', *Interfax,* 12 September 2001. Putin, 'Wortprotokoll der Rede Wladimir Putins im Deutschen Bundestag'. For a similar argument by Sergei Ivanov, see S. Ivanov, 'Antiterror – vozmezdie – Ministr Oborony RF Sergei Ivanov otvechaet na voprosy korrespondenta "Truda"', *Trud,* 27 September 2001.
61. I. Golotiuk, 'Vrag naznachen – Rossiia uzhe podobrala tseli dlia amerikanskikh "udarov vozmezdiia"', *Vremia novostei,* 13 September 2001. For a similar argument, see P. K. Baev, 'Counter-terrorism as a Building Block for Putin's regime', in Jakob Hedenskog, et al., eds, *Russia as a Great Power: Dimensions of Security under Putin* (Abingdon: Routledge, 2005), 323–44, p. 323.

62. A. Vershbow, 'Remarks and Q&A with Reporters Outside the U.S. Embassy, Moscow', *Washington File (EPF316 09/12/01)*, 12 September 2001. 'Remarks by National Security Adviser Condoleezza Rice'.
63. Putin, 'Wortprotokoll der Rede Wladimir Putins im Deutschen Bundestag'.
64. 'Putin und Schroeder fuer Entschlossene Bekaempfung des Terrorismus', *DPA*, 25 September 2001.
65. V. V. Putin, 'Zaiavlenie dlia pressy i otvety na voprosy v khode sovmestnoi press-konferentsii s Presidentom Frantsuzkoi Respubliki Zhakom Shirakom', *Ofitsial'noe internet-predstavitel'stvo Prezidenta Rossii*, 15 January 2002, available at: http://www.kremlin.ru/text/appears/2002/01/28774.shtml (accessed: 7 July 2007).
66. New Russian Foreign Minister Lavrov rejected this when he argued that Russia would not negotiate with 'bin Laden's disciples'. S. Lavrov, 'My ne khotim, chtoby amerikantsy poterpeli porazhenie v Irake', *Vremia novostei*, 18 May 2004.
67. R. Burns, 'Rumsfeld Chides Russians for Spreading Missile Technologies', *The Associated Press*, 14 February 2001. For a similar argument, see C. Rice, 'Promoting the National Interest', *Foreign Affairs*, vol. 79, no. 1 (January/February 2000) 45–62, p. 57.
68. See, for example, the first Deputy Chief of General Staff Valery Manilov: 'Rossiia sobliudaet vse dogovorennosti', *Krasnaia zvezda*, 16 February 2001.
69. 'Russia Will Take Part in Disarmament Talks if ABM Treaty Preserved', *Interfax*, 4 February 2001. P. Fel'gengauer, 'Zarubezh'e – Kreml' vnov' daet otpor imperialistam', *Moskovskie novosti*, 13 February 2001.
70. 'Russia FM Reaffirms Commitment to ABM Treaty', *Itar-Tass*, 25 July 2001.
71. 'Joint Statement by US President George W. Bush and President of the Russian Federation Vladimir V. Putin on Upcoming Consultations on Strategic Issues', *The White House*, 22 July 2001, available at: http://www.whitehouse.gov/news/releases/2001/07/20010722-6.html (accessed: 7 July 2007).
72. 'Russia: Moscow Seeks Missile Cuts to Offset Weaker ABM', *Oxford Analytica*, 26 July 2001.
73. 'President Announces Reduction in Nuclear Arsenal', *The White House*, 13 November 2001, available at: http://www.whitehouse.gov/news/releases/2001/11/20011113-3.html (accessed: 7 July 2007).
74. 'President Discusses National Missile Defense', *The White House*, 13 December 2001, available at: http://www.whitehouse.gov/news/releases/2001/12/20011213-4.html (accessed: 7 July 2007).
75. V. V. Putin, 'Zaiavlenie Prezidenta Rossii V. Putina', *Ofitsial'noe internet-predstavitel'stvo Prezidenta Rossii*, 13 December 2001, available at: http://president.kremlin.ru/text/appears/2001/12/28746.shtml (accessed: 7 July 2007). For similar measured reactions by other Russian officials, see G. Sysoev, 'Pervaia Polosa: Raketno-iadernaia potentsiia', *Kommersant-Daily*, 14 December 2001.
76. 'Joint Declaration', *The White House*, 24 May 2002, available at: http://www.whitehouse.gov/news/releases/2002/05/20020524-2.html (accessed: 7 July 2007).
77. 'Putin Accepts Possibility of US Withdrawing from ABM', *Itar–Tass*, 22 September 2001. For a similar comment, see V. V. Putin, 'Interv'iu nemetskoi telekompanii', *Ofitsial'noe internet-predstavitel'stvo Prezidenta Rossii*,

19 September 2001, available at: http://www.kremlin.ru/text/appears/2001/09/28636.shtml (accessed: 7 July 2007).
78. For an in-depth discussion, see Chapter 4 on Russia's approaches towards NATO.
79. A Russian diplomat I interviewed in Moscow in 2005 and who wished to remain anonymous. For a similar argument, see M. A. Smith, *Russia and NATO since 1991: From Cold War through Cold Peace to Partnership?* (Abingdon: Routledge, 2006), p. 95.
80. O. Antonenko, 'Putin's Gamble', *Survival*, vol. 43, no. 4 (Winter 2001–2002) 49–60, p. 49.
81. Primakov, 'Is the Russia-U.S. Rapprochement Here to Stay?' p. 87. For a similar argument, see L. Ivashov, 'V ozhidanii bol'shikh potriasenii v rossii – geopoliticheskii itog 2002 goda neuteshitelen', *Nezavisimaia gazeta*, 20 January 2003.
82. V. Frolov, 'A New Beginning or Just Irrational Exuberance?' *The Moscow Times*, 21 January 2002.
83. For a similar argument, see J. M. Godzimirski, 'Russian National Security Concepts 1997–2000 – A Comparative Analysis', *Security Policy Library no 8* (Oslo: The Norwegian Atlantic Committee, 2000), p. 72.
84. O'Loughlin, Thuathail and Kolossov offer a comprehensive account how the Russian leadership skilfully used rhetoric to emphasize the communality of interests between Russia and the West with the aim to portray Russia as a responsible international actor, see J. O'Loughlin, G. ó. Thuathail, and V. Kolossov, 'A "Risky Westward Turn"? Putin's 9–11 Script and Ordinary Russians', *Europe-Asia Studies*, vol. 56, no. 1 (January 2004) 3–34.
85. V. V. Putin, 'Vystuplenie v Erevanskom gosudarstvennom universitete', *Ofitsial'noe internet-predstavitel'stvo Prezidenta Rossii*, 15 September 2001, available at: http://www.kremlin.ru/text/appears/2001/09/28632.shtml (accessed: 7 July 2007).
86. G. W. Bush, 'Address to a Joint Session of Congress and the American People', *The White House*, 20 September 2001, available at: http://www.whitehouse.gov/news/releases/2001/09/20010920-8.html (accessed: 7 July 2007).
87. Putin, 'Zaiavlenie po povodu'. V. V. Putin, 'Zaiavlenie dlia pressy i otvety na voprosy zhurnalistov na sovmestnoi press-konferentsii s Prezidentom SShA Dzhordzhem Bushem', *Ofitsial'noe internet-predstavitel'stvo Prezidenta SSRossii*, 21 October 2001, available at: http://www.kremlin.ru/text/appears/2001/10/28674.shtml (accessed: 7 July 2007). For a similar argument by Foreign Minister Ivanov, see I. Ivanov, 'Vystuplenie Ministra Inostrannykh Del Rossiiskoi Federatsii I.S. Ivanova v khode obshchepoliticheskoi diskussii na 56-i sessii GA OON 16 noiabria 2001 goda', *Ministerstvo Inostrannykh Del Rossiiskoi Federatsii*, 16 November 2001, available at: http://www.un.org/webcast/ga/56/statements/011116russiaR.htm (accessed: 7 July 2007).
88. V. Solov'ev, 'Generaly ukhodiat v oppozitsiiu Kremliu – Ministr Oborony Sergei Ivavov teriaet kontrol' nad Vooruzhennymi silami, vsia nadezhda na prezidenta', *Nezavisimaia gazeta*, 13 November 2001. 'Sluzhit' Rodine!' *Sovetskaia Rossiia*, 10 November 2001.
89. V. V. Putin, 'Vystuplenie i otvety na voprosy zhurnalistov na sovmestnoi press-konferentsii s presidentom Soedinennykh Shtatov Ameriki Dzhordzhem Bushem', *Ofitsial'noe internet-predstavitel'stvo Prezidenta Rossii*, 13 November

2001, available at: http://www.kremlin.ru/text/appears/2001/11/28698.shtml (accessed: 7 July 2007).
90. A. Kasaev and A. Khanbabian, 'Den' velikogo peredela – ot segodniashego resheniia Vladimira Putina zavisit sud'ba SNG', *Nezavisimaia gazeta*, 20 September 2001.
91. V. V. Putin, 'Vstrecha s shef-korrespondentami moskovskikh biuro vedushchikh amerikanskikh SMI', *Ofitsial'noe internet-predstavitel'stvo Prezidenta Rossii*, 10 November 2001, available at: http://www.kremlin.ru/text/appears/2001/11/28694.shtml (accessed: 7 July 2007). Putin, 'Vystuplenie i otvety na voprosy zhurnalistov na sovmestnoj'.
92. I. Ivanov, 'Vstrecha v redaktsii – Igor Ivanov: my stali myslit' bolee pragmatichno', *Trud*, 23 January 2003.
93. Putin, 'Vstrecha s shef-korrespondentami'. Putin, 'National Public Radio'.
94. V. V. Putin, 'Vystuplenie na vstreche s chlenami komitetov po mezhdunarodnym delam Federal'nogo Sobraniia Rossiiskoi Federatsii', *Ofitsial'noe internet-predstavitel'stvo Prezidenta Rossii*, 22 November 2001, available at: http://www.kremlin.ru/text/appears/2001/11/28713.shtml (accessed: 7 July 2007). V. V. Putin, 'Zaiavlenie i otvety na voprosy zhurnalistov v khode sovmestnoi press-konferentsii po okonchanii besedy s General'nym sekretarem NATO Dzhordzhem Robertsonom', *Ofitsial'noe internet-predstavitel'stvo Prezidenta Rossii*, 3 October 2001, available at: http://www.kremlin.ru/text/appears/2001/10/28651.shtml (accessed: 7 July 2007).
95. Putin, 'Zaiavlenie dlia pressy'. Putin, 'Vstrecha s shef-korrespondentami'. Putin, 'National Public Radio'. Putin, 'Vystuplenie na vstreche s chlenami komitetov po mezhdunarodnym delam'.
96. V. V. Putin, 'Key Tasks of Russian Diplomacy: Statement by RF President V. V. Putin at an Enlarged Conference with the Participation of RF Ambassadors, at the Ministry of Foreign Affairs of Russia', *International Affairs (Moscow)*, vol. 48, no. 4 (2002) 1–7, p. 2.

Chapter 7: Conclusion

1. For summaries and discussions about the implications of the federal reforms, see M. Hyde, 'Putin's Federal Reforms and their Implications for Presidential Power in Russia', *Europe-Asia Studies*, vol. 53, no. 5 (2001) 719–43. T. F. Remington, 'Majorities without Mandates: The Russian Federation Council since 2000', *Europe-Asia Studies*, vol. 55, no. 5 (2003) 667–91. C. Ross, 'Putin's Federal Reforms and the Consolidation of Federalism in Russia: One Step Forward, Two Steps Back!' *Communist and Post-Communist Studies*, vol. 36 (2003) 29–47. M. McFaul, N. Petrov and A. Ryabov, *Between Dictatorship and Democracy* (Washington, D.C.: Brookings Institution, 2004).
2. P. Kennedy, *The Rise and Fall of the Great Powers* (New York: Random House, 1987), p. 514.
3. M. Mandelbaum, ed., *The New Russian Foreign Policy* (New York: Council on Foreign Relations, 1998), p. 4.
4. A. L. Friedberg, *The Weary Titan: Britain and the Experience of Relative Decline, 1885–1905* (Stanford: Stanford University Press, 1988).

5. J. M. Goldgeier and M. McFaul, *Power and Purpose: U.S. Policy Towards Russia after the End of the Cold War* (Washington, D.C.: The Brookings Institution Press, 2003).
 6. Council on Foreign Affairs, *Russia's Wrong Direction: What the United States Can and Should Do* (Independent Task Force Report No. 57, 2006), p. 11.
 7. D. Trenin, 'Russia Leaves the West', *Foreign Affairs*, vol. 85, no. 4 (July/August 2006).
 8. I. B. Neumann, 'Russia as a Great Power', in Jakob Hedenskog, et al., eds, *Russia as a Great Power: Dimensions of Security under Putin* (Abingdon: Routledge, 2005), 13–28, p. 25.
 9. Trenin, 'Russia Leaves the West'. For similar arguments, see C. A. Wallander, 'Global Challenges and Russian Foreign Policy', in Robert Legvold, ed., *Russian Foreign Policy in the Twenty-First Century and the Shadow of the Past* (New York: Columbia University Press, 2007), 445–97, p. 459. Trenin, 'Russia Leaves the West'.
10. Council on Foreign Affairs, *Russia's Wrong Direction*, p. 21.
11. For a seminal study on the role of learning in Soviet foreign policy, see G. W. Breslauer and P. E. Tetlock, eds, *Learning in U.S. and Soviet Foreign Policy* (Boulder, Colo.: Westview Press, 1991).
12. S. W. Garnett, 'Europe's Crossroads: Russia and the West in the New Borderlands', in Michael Mandelbaum, ed., *The New Russian Foreign Policy* (New York: Council on Foreign Relations, 1998), 64–99, p. 69. B. Lo, *Russian Foreign Policy in the Post-Soviet Era: Reality, Illusion and Mythmaking* (Basingstoke: Palgrave Macmillan, 2002), pp. 96, 100. M. Bowker, 'The Wars in Yugoslavia: Russia and the International Community', *Europe-Asia Studies*, vol. 50, no. 7 (November 1998) 1245–61, p. 1258.
13. Neumann, 'Russia as a Great Power', p. 23.
14. Y. Primakov, 'A Minister the Opposition Doesn't Curse, published in: Obshchaia gazeta, No. 37, 19–25 September 1996, p. 4', *CDPSP*, vol. XLVIII, no. 39 (1996) 22–3, p. 22.
15. S. Talbott, *The Russia Hand* (New York: Random House, 2002), p. 84.
16. B. Yeltsin, *Midnight Diaries* (London: Weidenfeld & Nicolson, 2000), pp. 134–5.
17. Quoted in: W. Drozdiak, 'Poland Urges NATO Not to Appease Russia', *The Washington Post*, 17 March 1997. For a similar argument, see H. Kissinger, 'Beware: A Threat Abroad', *Newsweek*, 17 June 1996.
18. W. E. Odom, 'Realism about Russia, originally published in: "The National Interest", no. 65 (Fall 2001)', in Nikolas K. Gvosdev, ed., *Russia in The National Interest* (London: Transactions Publishers, 2004), 209–21, pp. 210 and 218.
19. For a similar argument, see G. W. Breslauer, 'Does Russia Matter Anymore?' *Post-Soviet Affairs*, vol. 20, no. 1 (2004) 38–42, pp. 40–1.
20. For similar attempts with regard to the EU and US foreign policy, see C. Parson, 'Showing Ideas as Causes: The Origins of the European Union', *International Organization*, vol. 56, no. 1 (Winter 2002) 47–84. H. R. Nau, *At Home Abroad: Identity and Power in American Foreign Policy* (Ithaca, N.Y.: Cornell University Press, 2002).
21. On the distinction between offensive and defensive Realism, see section *Realism and foreign policy analysis* in Chapter 2 on the *Framework for Analysis*.
22. Finnemore argues that 'state interests are defined in the context of internationally held norms and understandings about what is good and appropriate.'

190 Notes and References

M. Finnemore, *National Interests in International Society* (Ithaca, N.Y.: Cornell University Press, 1996), pp. 2, 5–6. See also: A. Wendt, *Social Theory of International Politics* (Cambridge: Cambridge University Press, 1999). A. P. Cortell and J. W. Davis, 'Understanding the Domestic Impact of International Norms: A Research Agenda', *International Studies Review*, vol. 2, no. 1 (Spring 2000) 65–87.

23. For such an emphasis, see P. J. Katzenstein, ed., *The Culture of National Security: Norms and Identity in World Politics* (New York: Columbia University Press, 1996).
24. Jackson undertakes such an analysis in her study of Russia's approaches to the conflicts in Moldova-Transdniestria, Georgia-Abkhazia and Tajikistan in the period from 1992 to 1997. N. J. Jackson, *Russian Foreign Policy and the CIS* (London: Routledge, 2003). Jonson analyses various factors shaping Russia's approach to Central Asia. L. Jonson, *Vladimir Putin and Central Asia: The Shaping of Russian Foreign Policy* (London: I.B. Tauris, 2004).
25. For an analysis of Russia's approach to Iran, Iraq and China, see H. Belopolsky, DPhil thesis: *Active Engagement: Russian Strategic Alignment with "Challenger" States (China, Iran, and Iraq), 1992 to 2002* (Oxford, 2004).
26. S. G. Brooks and W. C. Wohlforth, 'Power, Globalization and the End of the Cold War: Reevaluating a Landmark Case for Ideas', *International Security*, vol. 25, no. 3 (Winter 2001/2002) 5–53. For a similar argument, see P. Kowert and J. W. Legro, 'Norms, Identity, and Their Limits: A Theoretical Reprise', in Peter J. Katzenstein, ed., *The Culture of National Security: Norms and Identity in World Politics* (New York: Columbia University Press, 1996), 451–97, p. 469.
27. J. T. Checkel, 'The Constructivist Turn in International Relations Theory', *World Politics*, vol. 50, no. 2 (January 1998) 324–48, pp. 340 and 344. While post-modernist scholars argue that ideas 'matter all the way down', modernist Social Constructivists argue that ideas interrelate with material factors. For a discussion of these schools, see J. G. Ruggie, *Constructing the World Polity – Essays on International Institutionalization* (London: Routledge, 1998). A. Hasenclever, P. Mayer and V. Rittberger, 'Integrating Theories of International Regimes', *Review of International Studies*, vol. 26 (2000) 3–33, pp. 10–1.
28. J. K. Jacobsen, 'Duelling Constructivisms: A Post-Mortem on the Ideas Debate in Mainstream IR/IPE', *Review of International Studies*, vol. 29, no. 1 (January 2003) 39–60, p. 49. J. Fearon and A. Wendt, 'Rationalism v. Constructivism: A Sceptical View', in Walter Carlsnaes, et al., eds, *Handbook of International Relations* (London: SAGE Publications, 2002), 52–72, pp. 57–8. E. Adler, 'Constructivism and International Relations', in Walter Carlsnaes, et al., eds, *Handbook of International Relations* (London: SAGE Publications, 2002), 95–118, p. 95. Parson, 'Showing Ideas as Causes', p. 49.
29. A. Moravcsik, 'Taking Preferences Seriously: A Liberal Theory of International Politics', *International Organization*, vol. 51, no. 4 (Autumn 1997) 513–53. A. Moravcsik, 'Introduction: Integrating International and Domestic Theories of International Bargaining', in Peter B. Evans, et al., eds, *Double-Edged Diplomacy: International Bargaining and Domestic Politics* (Berkeley: University of California Press, 1993), 3–42.
30. J. G. March and J. P. Olsen, 'The Institutional Dynamics of International Political Orders', *International Organization*, vol. 52, no. 4 (Autumn 1998) 943–69, p. 951.

Selected Readings

Chapter 1: Introduction

Realist analyses of Russian foreign policy

Kubicek, Paul, 'Russian Foreign Policy and the West', *Political Science Quarterly*, vol. 114, no. 4, 1999–2000, pp. 547–68.

Lynch, Allen C., 'The Realism of Russia's Foreign Policy', *Europe-Asia Studies*, vol. 53, no. 1, 2001, pp. 7–31.

MacFarlane, Neil, 'Realism and Russian Strategy after the Collapse of the USSR', in Kapstein, E. B. and Mastanduno, M., eds, *Unipolar Politics* (New York: Columbia University Press, 1999), pp. 218–60.

Social Constructivist analyses of Russian foreign policy

Hopf, Ted, *Social Construction of International Politics: Identities & Foreign Policies, Moscow, 1995 and 1999* (Ithaca, N.Y.: Cornell University Press, 2002).

Hopf, Ted, ed., *Understandings of Russian Foreign Policy* (Pennsylvania: Pennsylvania State University Press, 1999).

Legvold, Robert, 'Russia's Unformed Foreign Policy', *Foreign Affairs*, vol. 80, no. 5, Sep/Oct 2001, pp. 62–75.

Legvold, Robert, ed., *Russian Foreign Policy in the Twenty-First Century & The Shadow of the Past* (New York: Columbia University Press, 2007).

Lo, Bobo, *Russian Foreign Policy in the Post-Soviet Era: Reality, Illusion and Mythmaking* (Basingstoke: Palgrave Macmillan, 2002).

Domestic Factors and Russian foreign policy analysis

Dobriansky, Paula J., 'Russian Foreign Policy: Promise or Peril?' *The Washington Quarterly*, vol. 23, no. 1, Winter 2000, pp. 135–44.

Kozhemiakin, Alexander V., 'Democratization and Foreign Policy Change: The Case of the Russian Federation', *Review of International Studies*, vol. 23, no. 1, 1997, pp. 49–74.

Kozhemiakin, Alexander V., *Expanding the Zone of Peace? Democratization and International Security* (Basingstoke: Macmillan Press, 1998).

Malcolm, Neil and Pravda, Alex, 'Democratization and Russian Foreign Policy', *International Affairs*, vol. 72, no. 3, 1996, pp. 537–52.

Malcolm, Neil; Pravda, Alex; Allison, Roy and Light, Margot, *Internal Factors in Russian Foreign Policy* (Oxford: Oxford University Press, 1996).

McFaul, Michael, 'A Precarious Peace – Domestic Politics in the Making of Russian Foreign Policy', *International Security*, vol. 22, no. 3, Winter 1997/98, pp. 5–35.

Chapter 2: Framework for Analysis

On Realism

Legro, Jeffrey W. and Moravcsik, Andrew, 'Is Anybody Still a Realist', *International Security*, vol. 24, no. 2, Fall 1999, pp. 5–55.

Mearsheimer, John J., *The Tragedy of Great Power Politics* (New York: W. W. Norton & Company, 2001).

Morgenthau, Hans Joachim, *Politics Among Nations: The Struggle for Power and Peace*, 5 ed (New York: Knopf, 1949).

Schweller, Randall L., *Deadly Imbalances: Tripolarity and Hitler's Strategy of World Conquest* (Ithaca, N.Y.: Columbia University Press, 1998).

Walt, Stephen M., *The Origins of Alliances* (Ithaca, N.Y.: Cornell University Press, 1987).

Waltz, Kenneth N., *Theory of International Politics* (Reading, Mass.: Addison–Wesley, 1979).

On Social Constructivism

Checkel, Jeffrey T., 'The Constructivist Turn in International Relations Theory', *World Politics*, vol. 50, no. 2, January 1998, pp. 324–48.

Finnemore, Martha and Sikkink, Kathryn, 'Taking Stock: The Constructivist Research Program in International Relations and Comparative Politics', *Annual Review of Political Science*, vol. 4, 2001, pp. 391–416.

Goldstein, Judith and Keohane, Robert O., eds, *Ideas and Foreign Policy: Beliefs, Institutions, and Political Change* (Ithaca, N.Y.: Cornell University Press, 1993).

Ruggie, John G., *Constructing the World Polity – Essays on International Institutionalization* (London: Routledge, 1998).

Wendt, Alexander, *Social Theory of International Politics* (Cambridge: Cambridge University Press, 1999).

Methodology

Eckstein, Harry, 'Case Study and Theory in Political Science', in Greenstein, F. I. and Polsby, N. W., eds, *Handbook of Political Science – Volume 7* (Reading, Mass.: Wesley Publishing Company, 1975), pp. 79–137.

Evera, Stephen van, *Guide to Methods for Students of Political Science* (Ithaca, N.Y.: Cornell University Press, 1997).

George, Alexander L., *Propaganda Analysis: A Study of Inferences Made from Nazi Propaganda in World War II* (Evanston, Ill.: Row, Peterson and Company, 1959).

George, Alexander L. and Bennett, Andrew, *Case Studies and Theory Development in the Social Sciences* (Cambridge, Mass.: MIT Press, 2005).

King, Gary; Keohane, Robert O. and Verba, Sidney, *Designing Social Inquiry: Scientific Inference in Qualitative Research* (Princeton, N.J.: Princeton University Press, 1994).

Lebow, Richard N., 'What's so Different About a Counterfactual?' *World Politics*, vol. 52, no. 4, July 2000, pp. 550–85.

Chapter 3: Evolution of the Russian Leadership's Foreign Policy Thinking

Studies on the evolution of the Russian leadership's foreign policy thinking

Kassianova, Alla, 'Russia: Still Open to the West? Evolution of the State Identity in the Foreign Policy and Security Discourse', *Europe-Asia Studies,* vol. 53, no. 6, 2001, pp. 821–39.

Light, Margot, 'In Search of an Identity: Russian Foreign Policy and the End of Ideology', *Journal of Communist Studies and Transition Politics,* vol. 19, no. 3, September 2003, pp. 42–59.

Tsygankov, Andrei P., 'Vladimir Putin's Vision of Russia as a Normal Great Power', *Post-Soviet Affairs,* vol. 21, no. 2, 2005, pp. 132–58.

Studies on the wider domestic discourse on Russian foreign policy

Adomeit, Hannes, 'Russia as a "Great Power" in World Affairs: Images and Reality', *International Affairs,* vol. 71, no. 1, 1995, pp. 35–68.

Arbatov, Alexei G., 'Russia's Foreign Policy Alternatives', *International Security,* vol. 18, no. 2, Fall 1993, pp. 5–43.

Chafetz, Glenn, 'The Struggle for a National Identity in Post-Soviet Russia', *Political Science Quarterly,* vol. 111, no. 4, Winter 1996–1997, pp. 661–88.

Malcolm, Neil; Pravda, Alex; Allison, Roy and Light, Margot, *Internal Factors in Russian Foreign Policy* (Oxford: Oxford University Press, 1996).

Pravda, Alex, 'The Politics of Foreign Policy', in White, S.; Pravda, A. and Gitelman, Z., eds, *Developments in Russian Politics 4* (Basingstoke: Macmillan Press, 1997), pp. 208–22.

Prizel, Ilya, *National Identity and Foreign Policy: Nationalism and Leadership in Poland, Russia and Ukraine* (Cambridge: Cambridge University Press, 1998).

Tsygankov, Andrei P., 'From International Institutionalism to Revolutionary Expansionism: The Foreign Policy Discourse of Contemporary Russia', *Mershon International Studies Review,* vol. 41, no. 2, November 1997, pp. 247–68.

Core primary sources

Monographs by the Russian leadership

Yeltsin, Boris N., *The View from the Kremlin* (London: HarperCollins, 1994).

Yeltsin, Boris N., *Midnight Diaries* (London: Weidenfeld & Nicolson, 2000).

Putin, Vladimir V., *Ot pervogo litsa: razgovory c Vladimirom Putinym* (Moscow: Vagrius, 2000).

Kozyrev, Andrei, *Preobrazhenie* (Moscow: Mezhdunarodnye otnosheniia, 1994).

Primakov, Yevgenii, *Gody v bol'shoi politike* (Moscow: Sovershenno sekretno, 1999).

Primakov, Yevgenii, *Mir Posle 11 Sentiabria* (Moscow: Mysl', 2002).

Primakov, Yevgenii, *Russian Crossroads – Towards the new Millennium* (NewHaven & London: Yale University Press, 2004).

Primakov, Yevgenii, *Vosem' mesiatsev plius . . .* (Moscow: Mysl', 2001).

Ivanov, Igor, *The New Russian Diplomacy* (Washington, D.C.: Brookings Institute Press, 2002).

Foreign policy concepts and military and security doctrines

'Summary of Draft of Foreign Policy Concept – 1992', *International Affairs (Moscow)*, no. 1, January 1993, pp. 14–6.

'Osnovnye polozheniia voennoi doktriny Rossiiskoi Federatsii – 1993', *Diplomaticheskii vestnik*, no. 23–24, December 1993, pp. 6–16.

'Kontseptsiia vneshnei politiki Rossiiskoi Federatsii – 1993', reprinted in *Vneshniaia politika i bezopasnost' sovremennoi Rossii 1991–2002 (Volume IV)*, Moscow: Rosspen, 2002, pp. 19–50.

'Kontseptsiia natsional'noi bezopasnosti Rossiiskoi Federatsii – 1997', *Diplomaticheskii vestnik*, vol. 2, no. 2, 1998, pp. 5–18.

'The Foreign Policy Concept of the Russian Federation – 2000', available at: http://www.fas.org/nuke/guide/russia/doctrine/econcept.htm (accessed: 7 July 2007).

'Voennaia doktrina Rossiiskoi Federatsii – 2000', *Nezavisimaia gazeta*, 22 April 2000.

'Obzor vneshnej politiki Rossijskoj Federatsii', 27 March 2007, available at: http://www.mid.ru/brp_4.nsf/sps/3647DA97748A106BC32572AB002AC4DD (accessed: 7 July 2007).

Addresses of the Russian President to the Federal Assembly

Yeltsin, Boris N., 'The President of Russia's Speech to the Federal Assembly, published in: Rossiiskaia gazeta, 25 February 1994, pp. 1–2', *CDPSP*, vol. XLVI, no. 8, 1994, pp. 5–8.

Yeltsin, Boris N., 'The Russian Federation President's Message to the Federal Assembly, published in: Rossiiskie vesti, 17 February 1995, pp. 1, 3–7', *CDPSP*, vol. XLVII, no. 7 and 8, 1995, pp. 1–6 (no. 7) and 13–5, 28 (no. 8).

Yeltsin, Boris N., 'Iz poslaniia Prezidenta Rossiiskoi Federatsii Federal'nomu Sobraniiu – 1996', *Diplomaticheskii vestnik*, no. 3, March 1996, p. 3.

Yeltsin, Boris N., 'Vystuplenie Presidenta Rossiiskoi Federatsii Borisa El'tsina pri predstavlenii poslaniia Federal'nomu Sobraniiu RF – 1997', *Rossiiskie vesti*, 11 March 1997.

Yeltsin, Boris N., 'Iz poslaniia Prezidenta Rossiiskoi Federatsii Federal'nomu Sobraniiu – 1998', *Diplomaticheskii vestnik*, no. 3, March 1998, pp. 3–4.

Yeltsin, Boris N., 'Russia at the Turn of a New Era: Annual State of the Nation Address – 1999', *International Affairs (Moscow)*, vol. 45, no. 3, 1999, pp. 1–3.

Putin, Vladimir V., 'Annual Address to the Federal Assembly – 2000', *President of Russia: Official Web Portal*, 8 July 2000, available at: http://kremlin.ru/eng/speeches/2000/07/08/0000_type70029type82912_70658.shtml (accessed: 7 July 2007).

President Putin's addresses from 2001 to 2007 are available at: http://www.kremlin.ru/eng/sdocs/speeches.shtml?stype=70029

Addresses to Russian diplomats

Yeltsin, Boris N., 'What Yeltsin Told Russian Diplomats, published in: Rossiiskie vesti, 29 October 1992', *CDPSP*, vol. XLIV, no. 43, 1992, p. 19.

Yeltsin, Boris N., 'President Yeltsin's Address to Russian Diplomats', *International Affairs (Moscow)*, vol. 44, no. 3, 1998, pp. 1–6.

Primakov, Yevgenii, 'Vstrecha E.M. Primakova s kollektivom MGIMO', *Diplomaticheskii vestnik*, no. 7, July 1996, pp. 64–8.

Putin, Vladimir V., 'Key Tasks of Russian Diplomacy: Statement by RF President V. V. Putin at an Enlarged Conference with the Participation of RF Ambassadors, at the Ministry of Foreign Affairs of Russia', *International Affairs (Moscow)*, vol. 48, no. 4, 2002, pp. 1–7.

Putin, Vladimir V., 'Address at the Plenary Session of the Russian Federation Ambassadors and Permanent Representatives Meeting', *President of Russia: Official Web Portal*, 12 July 2004, available at: http://kremlin.ru/eng/text/speeches/2004/07/12/1323_74425.shtml (accessed: 7 July 2007).

Putin, Vladimir V., 'Speech at Meeting with the Ambassadors and Permanent Representatives of the Russian Federation', *President of Russia: Official Web Portal*, 27 June 2006, available at: http://www.kremlin.ru/eng/speeches/2006/06/27/2040_type82912type82913type82914_107818.shtml (accessed: 7 July 2007).

Chapter 4: Russia's Approaches towards NATO

Adomeit, Hannes, 'Inside or Outside? Russia's Policies Towards NATO', *Working Paper*, available at: http://www.swp-berlin.org/de/common/get_document.php?asset_id=3570 (accessed: 7 July 2007).

Antonenko, Oksana, 'Russia, NATO and European Security after Kosovo', *Survival*, vol. 41, no. 4, Winter 1999–2000, pp. 124–44.

Asmus, Ronald D., *Opening NATO's Door: How the Alliance Remade Itself for a New Era* (New York: Columbia University Press, 2002).

Baranovskij, Vladimir, 'Russian Views on NATO and the EU', in Lieven, A. and Trenin, D., eds, *Ambivalent Neighbors: The EU, NATO, and the Price of Membership* (Washington, D.C.: Carnegie Endowment for International Peace, 2003), pp. 269–94.

Baranovsky, Vladimir G., 'Russia: A Part of Europe or Apart from Europe?' *International Affairs*, vol. 76, no. 3, 2000, pp. 443–58.

Christopher, Warren, *In the Stream of History: Shaping Foreign Policy for a New Era* (Stanford: Stanford University Press, 1998).

Clinton, Bill, *My Life* (New York: Alfred A. Knopf, 2004).

Croft, Stuart, 'Guaranteeing Europe's Security? Enlarging NATO Again', *International Affairs*, vol. 78, no. 1, 2002, pp. 97–114.

Forsberg, Tuomas, 'Russia's Relationship with NATO: A Qualitative Change or Old Wine in New Bottles?' *Journal of Communist Studies and Transition Politics*, vol. 21, no. 3, September 2005, pp. 332–53.

Gardner, Hall, *Dangerous Crossroads* (London: Praeger, 1997).

Goldgeier, James M. and McFaul, Michael, *Power and Purpose: U.S. Policy Towards Russia after the End of the Cold War* (Washington, D.C.: The Brookings Institution Press, 2003).

Kennedy-Pipe, Caroline, 'Russia and the North Atlantic Treaty Organization', in Webber, M., ed., *Russia and Europe: Conflict or Cooperation?* (Basingstoke: Macmillan Press, 2000), pp. 46–65.

Kubicek, Paul, 'Russian Foreign Policy and the West', *Political Science Quarterly*, vol. 114, no. 4, 1999–2000, pp. 547–68.

Light, Margot; Löwenhardt, John and White, Stephen, 'Russian Perspectives on European Security', *European Foreign Affairs Review*, vol. 5, no. 4, Winter 2000, pp. 489–505.

Lynch, Dov, *Russia Faces Europe* (Paris: Institute for Security Studies, 2003).
MacFarlane, Neil, 'NATO in Russia's Relations with the West', *Security Dialogue*, vol. 32, no. 3, September 2001, pp. 281–96.
Smith, Martin A., *Russia and NATO since 1991: From Cold War through Cold Peace to Partnership?* (Abingdon: Routledge, 2006).
Sergounin, Alexander A., 'Russian Domestic Debate on NATO Enlargement: From Phobia to Damage Limitation', *European Security*, vol. 6, no. 4, Winter 1997, pp. 55–71.
Talbott, Strobe, *The Russia Hand* (New York: Random House, 2002).
Yeltsin, Boris N., *Midnight Diaries* (London: Weidenfeld & Nicolson, 2000).

Chapter 5: Russia's Responses to the Balkan Crises (1992–1999)

Albright, Madeleine, *Madam Secretary: A Memoir* (Basingstoke: Macmillan, 2003).
Bowker, Mike, 'The Wars in Yugoslavia: Russia and the International Community', *Europe-Asia Studies*, vol. 50, no. 7, November 1998, pp. 1245–61.
Caplan, Richard, 'International Diplomacy and the Crisis in Kosovo', *International Affairs*, vol. 74, no. 4, 1998, pp. 745–61.
Clark, Wesley K., *Waging Modern War: Bosnia, Kosovo, and the Future of Combat* (New York: Public Affairs, 2001).
Daalder, Ivo H. and O'Hanlon, Michael E., *Winning Ugly: NATO's War to Save Kosovo* (Washington, D.C.: Brookings Institution Press, 2000).
Headley, Jim, 'Sarajevo, February 1994: The First Russia-NATO Crisis of the post-Cold War Era', *Review of International Studies*, vol. 29, 2003, pp. 209–27.
Hurd, Douglas, *The Search for Peace* (London: Warner Books, 1997).
Kremenjuk, V, 'The Ideological Legacy in Russia's Foreign Policy', *International Affairs (Moscow)*, vol. 47, no. 3, 2001, pp. 18–26.
Levitin, Oleg, 'Inside Moscow's Kosovo Muddle', *Survival*, vol. 42, no. 1, Spring 2000, pp. 130–40.
Lynch, Allen C., 'The Realism of Russia's Foreign Policy', *Europe-Asia Studies*, vol. 53, no. 1, 2001, pp. 7–31.
Lynch, Dov, '"Walking the Tightrope": The Kosovo Conflict and Russia in European Security', *European Security*, vol. 8, no. 4, Winter 1999, pp. 57–83.
Malcolm, Noel, *Bosnia: A Short History* (London: Pan Books, 2002).
Malcolm, Noel, *Kosovo: A Short History*, 2nd. ed (New York: New York University Press, 2002).
Norris, John, *Collision Course: NATO, Russia, and Kosovo* (Westport: Praeger, 2005).
Owen, David, *Balkan Odyssey* (London: Victor Gollancz, 1995).
Talbott, Strobe, *The Russia Hand* (New York: Random House, 2002).
Yeltsin, Boris N., *Midnight Diaries* (London: Weidenfeld & Nicolson, 2000).

Chapter 6: Russia's Response to the 11 September 2001 Terrorist Attacks

Antonenko, Oksana, 'Putin's Gamble', *Survival*, vol. 43, no. 4, Winter 2001–2002, pp. 49–60.

Baev, Pavel, 'Putin's Western Choice: Too Good to be True?' *European Security*, vol. 12, no. 1, Spring 2003, pp. 1–16.
Grachev, Andrei, 'Putin's Foreign Policy Choices', in Pravda, A., ed., *Leading Russia: Putin in Perspective* (Oxford: Oxford University Press, 2005), pp. 255–73.
Jonson, Lena, *Vladimir Putin and Central Asia: The Shaping of Russian Foreign Policy* (London: I.B. Tauris, 2004).
Lieven, Anatol, 'The Secret Policemen's Ball: The United States, Russia and the International Order after 11 September', *International Affairs (London)*, vol. 78, no. 2, 2002, pp. 245–59.
O'Loughlin, John; Thuathail, Gearóid ó and Kolossov, Vladimir, 'A "Risky Westward Turn"? Putin's 9–11 Script and Ordinary Russians', *Europe-Asia Studies*, vol. 56, no. 1, January 2004, pp. 3–34.
Pravda, Alex, 'Putin's Foreign Policy after 11 September: Radical or Revolutionary?' in Gorodetsky, G., ed., *Russia between East and West: Russian Foreign Policy on the Threshold of the Twenty-first Century* (London: Frank Cass, 2003), pp. 39–57.
Putin, Vladimir V., 'Zaiavlenie po povodu terroristicheskikh aktov v SshA', *Ofitsial'noe internet-predstavitel'stvo Prezidenta Rossii*, 11 September 2001, available at: http://president.kremlin.ru/text/docs/2001/09/57929.shtml (accessed: 7 July 2007).
Putin, Vladimir V., 'Zaiavlenie Presidenta Rossii', *Ofitsial'noe internet-predstavitel'stvo Prezidenta Rossii*, 24 September 2001, available at: http://president.kremlin.ru/text/appears/2001/09/28639.shtml (accessed: 7 July 2007).
Shevtsova, Lilia, 'Meeting Summary', *reproduced in Johnson's Russia List*, no. 6121, 7 March 2002.
Stent, Angela and Shevtsova, Lilia, 'America, Russia and Europe: A Realignment?' *Survival*, vol. 44, no. 4, Winter 2002–2003, pp. 121–34.
Talbott, Strobe, 'Putin's Path: Russian Foreign Policy Since 9/11', *Yale University*, 27 January 2002, available at: http://www.yale.edu/dsj/lectures/01-27-02.htm (accessed: 7 July 2007).
Trenin, Dmitri, 'Vladimir Putin's Autumn Marathon: Toward the Birth of a Russian Foreign Policy Strategy', November 2001, available at: http://www.carnegie.ru/en/pubs/briefings/48360.htm (accessed: 7 July 2007).
Woodward, Bob, *Bush at War* (London: Pocket Books, 2003).

Index

Bold page numbers refer to figures

ABM treaty, *see* anti-ballistic missile (ABM) treaty
Activation Warning (ACTWARN), 97
ACTWARN, *see* Activation Warning
Albright, Madeleine, 65, 100, 101
al-Qaeda, 113–5, 122–4
anti-ballistic missile (ABM) treaty, 126–8, 131
APEC, *see* Asia-Pacific Economic Cooperation
approaches to explain Russian foreign policy
 Liberal, 5–6, 150–1
 Realist, 2–4, 137, 141–3, 147–51
 Social Constructivist, 4–5, 138–40, 141–3, 147–51
 see also behavioural dimension of Realism, cultural geoeconomic Realism, domestic politics, geopolitical Realism, liberal ideas, pragmatic geoeconomic Realism, Realism, Social Constructivism
Arbatov, Alexei, 73, 115–6
ASEAN, *see* Association of South East Asian Nations
Asia-Pacific Economic Cooperation (APEC), 116
Asmus, Ronald, 60, 64
Association of South East Asian Nations (ASEAN), 126

Baev, Pavel, 100, 122
Baltic states
 NATO enlargement and, *see* NATO enlargement
behavioural dimension of Realism
 Bosnian conflict and, 84–6, 109
 Kosovo conflict and, 84–6, 100–2, 109
 limits of, 7, 147–8

NATO enlargement and, 64–7, 69–70
September 11 terrorist attacks and, 120–9, 132
theory and, 18–20
Bosnian conflict
 Dayton accords and, 95, 106
 embargo and sanctions and, 87, 89, 90, 92, 107
 explaining Russian foreign policy towards, *see also* behavioural dimension of Realism; geopolitical Realism; liberal ideas; Realism; Social Constructivism
 Holbrooke and, 93, 106
 no-fly zone and, 87
 Russia and NATO, 87, 90, 91–4, 105, 106
 Russia and UN, 87, 89–90, 91–3, 107
 Russian domestic politics and, *see* domestic politics
 Russian use of democratic argument during, 104
 Russian use of geopolitical argument during, 104
 Vance Owen Peace Plan, 87
 see also Yeltsin; Kozyrev; Primakov; Ivanov, Igor
 see also Implementation Force; Stabilization Force
Brooks, Stephen, 150
Bush, George W.
 NMD issue and, 76, 126
 September 11 terrorist attacks and, 115, 126, 128, 132
 START and, 126
 withdrawal from ABM treaty sought by, 126–7

CFE, *see* Treaty on Conventional Forces in Europe

Chechnya, 85, 100–1, 114, 119, 124–6, 131–2
Checkel, Jeffrey, 22, 150
Chernomyrdin, Victor, 107
Churkin, Vitaliy, 69, 91–2, 110
Clinton, Bill
 Bosnian conflict and, 93, 106
 Kosovo conflict and, 98–9, 107
 NATO enlargement and, 57–8
Collective Security Treaty (CST), 120–1
Collins, James, 101
Communist Party, 58, 109, 123
Conference on Security and Cooperation in Europe (CSCE), 60, 62–3
Contact Group, 85, 95–6, 97–8, 100–1, 103, 105
CSCE, *see* Conference on Security and Cooperation in Europe
CST, *see* Collective Security Treaty
cultural geoeconomic Realism, 10–11, 31–2, 37–8, 45–6, 48–50
 NATO enlargement and impact of, 74–8, 139–40
Czech Republic
 NATO enlargement and, 59, 63–5, 74

Dayton accords, 95, 105–6
Defence Department, U.S.
 NATO enlargement opposed by, 66–7
de Gaulle, Charles, 3
Dobbins, James, 101
Dobriansky, Paula, 5
domestic politics
 Bosnian conflict and, 89, 94–5, 107, 137, 140
 Kosovo conflict and, 103, 109, 137, 141
 NATO enlargement and, 58–9, 137, 140
 September 11 terrorist attacks and, 141
Duma, *see* domestic politics

Eckstein, Harry, 25
EU, *see* European Union

European Union (EU), 63, 73, 77–8, 107

Fearon, James, 27, 50
Federal Republic of Yugoslavia (FRY), 84–7, 89, 90, 96, 98
Federation Council, 141
Felgenhauer, Pavel, 105
Finnemore, Martha, 24, 149
France
 Bosnian conflict and, 88
 Kosovo conflict and, 96
 NATO enlargement and, 60, 64
 September 11 terrorist attacks and, 125
Friedberg, Aaron, 142
Freedman, Lawrence, 117
FRY, *see* Federal Republic of Yugoslavia

Gazprom, 102
geopolitical Realism, 9–10, 30, 34–5, 41–2, 47–50
 Bosnian conflict and impact of, 90–5, 106, 138
 Kosovo conflict and impact of, 102–4, 138
 NATO enlargement and impact of, 61–70, 138–9
George, Alexander, 25–6
Georgia
 NATO enlargement and, *see* NATO enlargement
Germany
 Bosnian conflict and, 87–8
 NATO enlargement and, 60
Goldgeier, James, 100, 102, 142
Goldstein, Judith, 23
Gorbachev, Mikhail
 New Thinking of, *see* New Thinking
Gorchakov, Alexander, 3, 41
Gourevitch, Peter, 18
Grachev, Pavel, 92
Great Britain
 Bosnian conflict and, 88
 Kosovo conflict and, 96
 NATO enlargement and, 60
Group of Eight (G8), 109
Group of Seven (G7), 64, 69, 109

Holbrooke, Richard
  Bosnian conflict and, 93, 106
  Kosovo conflict and, 97

IFOR, *see* Implementation Force
IMF, *see* International Monetary Fund
Implementation Force (IFOR), in Bosnia, 106
IMU, *see* Islamic Movement of Uzbekistan
International Monetary Fund (IMF), 99, 108
Islamic Movement of Uzbekistan (IMU), 120
Ivanov, Igor
  foreign policy thinking of, 30, 35–7, 41, 42–4
  Kosovo conflict and, 101, 103–4
  NATO enlargement and, 74–5
  September 11 terrorist attacks and, 116–7, 123, 126, 130, 131
Ivanov, Sergei
  NATO enlargement and, 71
  September 11 terrorist attacks and, 117

Jervis, Robert, 20–1

Karadzic, Radovan, 86, 89, 91
Karaganov, Sergei, 72
Kennedy, Paul, 141
Keohane, Robert, 23
KFOR, *see* Kosovo Force
Kissinger, Henry, 147
KLA, *see* Kosovo Liberation Army
Kosovo conflict
  Chechen conflict and, 85, 100, 101
  dash to Pristina in, 110
  embargo and sanctions and, 96–9
  explaining Russian foreign policy towards, *see also* behavioural dimension of Realism; geopolitical Realism; Realism; Social Constructivism
  Holbrooke and, 97
  Rambouillet agreement in, 98, 100, 104
  Russia and NATO, 96–9, 103, 107, 110
  Russia and UN, 96–9, 107, 108
  Russian domestic politics and, *see* domestic politics
  see also Yeltsin; Primakov; Ivanov, Igor; Lavrov
  see also Kosovo Force; Kosovo Liberation Army
Kosovo Force (KFOR), in Kosovo, 108
Kosovo Liberation Army (KLA), 95–8
Kozyrev, Andrei
  Bosnian conflict and, 89, 91–2, 94, 106
  foreign policy thinking of, 29–30, 32–5, 39–42
  NATO enlargement and, 59–61
  Primakov in comparison with, 3, 46
Kubicek, Paul
  Realist explanation of Russian foreign policy, 3–4
  Realist explanation of Russia's approach towards NATO enlargement, 54
  Realist explanation of Russia's response to the Balkan crises, 82

Lavrov, Sergei
  foreign policy thinking of, 31–2, 37, 45
  Kosovo conflict and, 99
  NATO enlargement and, 75
LDPR, *see* Liberal Democratic Party of Russia
Lebow, Richard, 21, 27
Legvold, Robert, 4
Levitin, Oleg, 103–4
Liberal Democratic Party of Russia (LDPR), 58, 94, 109
liberal ideas, 8, 29, 34, 40, 42, 47, 49–50
  Bosnian conflict and impact of, 86–9, 138
  NATO enlargement and impact of, 59–61, 69, 138
Liberal Institutionalism, 3
Lieven, Anatol, 120–1
Light, Margot, 46, 72–3
Lo, Bobo, 4
Lynch, Dov, 44, 97

MacFarlane, Neil 6, 57
Mayorsky, Boris, 104
McFaul, Michael, 5, 100, 102, 142
Midnight Diaries (Yeltsin), 58, 103, 110, 147
Milliken, Jennifer, 25
Milosevic, Slobodan, 91–2, 95–7, 100–5, 108–9
Morgenthau, Hans, 25
multipolarity, 30, 46

NAC, *see* North Atlantic Council
NACC, *see* North Atlantic Cooperation Council
national missile defence, 126
NATO, *see* North Atlantic Treaty Organization
NATO enlargement
  explaining Russian foreign policy towards, *see also* behavioural dimension of Realism; cultural geoeconomic Realism; geopolitical Realism; liberal ideas; pragmatic geoeconomic Realism; Realism; Social Constructivism
  Helsinki summit (1997), 58, 63, 69
  Russia's stance towards Baltic states and, 54, 63–4, 71–2, 75
  Russia's stance towards Georgia and Ukraine and, 54, 75–6, 77–8
  Russian domestic politics and, *see* domestic politics
  Russian use of democratic argument against, 53, 62, 69
  Russian use of geopolitical argument against, 53, 69
  see also Yeltsin; Putin; Kozyrev; Primakov; Ivanov, Igor; Ivanov, Sergei; Lavrov
  see also NATO–Russia Council; NATO–Russia Founding Act; Partnership for Peace; Permanent Joint Council
NATO–Russia Council (NRC), 53–4, 71, 75–7, 127
NATO–Russia Founding Act, 54–5, 57–8, 68–9, 96, 137, 140–1
New Thinking, 3, 4, 8, 47, 86
Nikonov, Viacheslav, 58

NMD, *see* national missile defence
North Atlantic Cooperation Council (NACC), 56, 59, 60
North Atlantic Council (NAC), 57, 94, 97
North Atlantic Treaty Organization (NATO)
  Bosnia conflict and, 87, 90–4, 105–6
  enlargement of, *see* NATO enlargement
  Kosovo conflict and, 96–9, 103, 107, 110
Northern Alliance, 111–7, 122–3
NRC, *see* NATO–Russia Council

Odom, William, 147
Organization on Security and Cooperation (OSCE), 58, 63, 76, 85, 95–8, 101
OSCE, *see* Organization on Security and Cooperation

Partnership for Peace (PfP), 54–9, 65, 68–9, 79, 137
Permanent Joint Council (PJC), 57, 71, 127
PFP, *see* Partnership for Peace
Pifer, Steven, 117
PJC, *see* Permanent Joint Council
Poland
  NATO enlargement and, 59–61, 63, 65, 74
pragmatic geoeconomic Realism, 10, 31, 37, 43–5, 48–50
  NATO enlargement and impact of, 70–4, 139
  September 11 terrorist attacks and, 112, 129–132, 139
Primakov, Yevgeny
  Alexandr Gorchakov in comparison with, 3
  Charles de Gaulle in comparison with, 3
  foreign policy thinking of, 30, 34–5, 41–2
  Kosovo conflict and, 99
  Kozyrev in comparison with, 3, 46

Primakov, Yevgeny (*cont.*)
  NATO enlargement and, 58, 63–4, 67
  September 11 terrorist attacks and, 123, 128
Putin, Vladimir
  ABM issue and, 127–8
  foreign policy thinking of, 30–2, 35–8, 43–6
  NATO enlargement and, 70–1, 74–6, 78
  NMD issue and, 76, 126
  September 11 terrorist attacks and, 115–6, 124–5, 130–2

Realism
  behavioural dimension of Realism, *see* behavioural dimension of Realism
  Bosnian conflict and, 83, 105–7, 109, 137
  explaining Russian foreign policy with external dimension of, 6–7, 12, 137, 141–3
  Kosovo conflict and, 83, 100–2, 107–9, 137
  limits of, 7, 12, 18, 20–2, 143–4
  NATO enlargement and, 55–9, 79, 137
  September 11 terrorist attacks and, 112–9, 132, 137
  theory and, 17–22, 20, 147–51
Realist power-maximizing hypothesis, *see* behavioural dimension of Realism
realpolitik, 3
Rodionov, Igor, 63, 68
Rosecrance, Richard, 19
Ruggie, John, 22
Rumsfeld, Donald, 126
Russia
  ABM issue, *see* Putin
  Asian financial crisis of 1998 and, 67, 84, 108, 145
  CFE and, 54, 62, 76, 140
  IMF loans to, 99, 108
  NMD issue, *see* Putin
  see also Bosnian conflict; Kosovo conflict; NATO enlargement; September 11 terrorist attacks

September 11 terrorist attacks
  explaining Russian foreign policy towards, *see also* behavioural dimension of Realism; pragmatic geoeconomic Realism; Realism; Social Constructivism
  Russian domestic politics and, *see* domestic politics
  see also Putin; Ivanov, Igor; Ivanov, Sergei; Lavrov
  see also al-Qaeda; Nothern Alliance; Taliban
Sergeyev, Igor, 68, 104
SFOR, *see* Stabilization Force
Shanghai Cooperation Organisation (SCO), 121
Sikkink, Kathryn, 24
Social Constructivism
  Bosnian conflict and, 83, 86–9, 109, 138
  explaining Russian foreign policy with, 8–12, 138–140, 141–3
  impact of, 11–12, 143–4
  Kosovo conflict and, 83, 102–4, 109, 138
  NATO enlargement and, 55, 59–79, 138–40
  September 11 terrorist attacks and, 112, 129–132, 139
  theory and, 22–4, **24**, 147–51, **151**
Stabilization Force (SFOR), in Bosnia, 106
START, *see* Strategic Arms Reduction Talks
Strategic Arms Reduction Talks (START), 126
SVR (Foreign Intelligence Service), 116

Talbott, Strobe, 147
  Kosovo conflict and, 101, 107, 109
  NATO enlargement and, 57, 62, 64, 65–6
  September 11 terrorist attacks and, 111–12, 119
Taliban, 113, 115, 122–4
Treaty on Conventional Forces in Europe (CFE), 54, 62, 76, 140
Trenin, Dmitri, 111, 145

Ukraine
  NATO enlargement and, *see* NATO enlargement
UN, *see* United Nations
United Nations (UN)
  Bosnia conflict and, 87, 89, 91–3
  Kosovo conflict and, 96–102, 107–8
  September 11 terrorist attacks and, 113–5, 123
United Nations Protection Force (UNPROFOR), 87
United States-Russia relations
  Bosnia conflict and, 86–8, 93, 105–6
  Kosovo conflict and, 98–9, 102–3
  Marshall Plan as model for, 40
  NATO-enlargement, 57, 64, 66, 72–3, 76
  NMD issue and, 76
  September 11 terrorist attacks and, 111, 115–7, 119
UNPROFOR, *see* United Nations Protection Force

View from the Kremlin, The (Yeltsin), 32–3, 76

Waltz, Kenneth, 19, 25
Wendt, Alexander, 22–3, 149
Wohlforth, William, 150
World Trade Organization (WTO), 143
WTO, *see* World Trade Organization

Yeltsin, Boris
  Bosnia conflict and, 89, 91–2, 94, 105–6
  'cold peace' remark of, 62
  'Cuban missile crisis' analogy of, 62
  foreign policy thinking of, 29–30, 32–5, 40–2
  Kosovo conflict and, 96, 99, 103, 107, 109–10
  memoirs of, *see* Midnight Diaries, The View from the Kremlin
  NATO enlargement and, 57–64, 68–9

Zhirinovsky, Vladimir, *see* Liberal Democratic Party of Russia
Zyuganov, Gennady, 58, 123